LIVING AT THE EDGE OF CHAOS

by

Helene Shulman

Living at the Edge of Chaos

Complex Systems in Culture and Psyche

by

Helene Shulman

DAIMON

Figure 9.1 on p. 151 and Figure 9.2 on p. 150, "Apokalypse IV," 1989 and "Paradies," 1978, are taken from: "Friedrich Dürrenmatt *Schriftsteller und Maler*." Copyright © 1994 Friedrich Dürrenmatt-Stiftung, Zürich, and Diogenes Verlag AG, Zürich.

Figure 11.1 – Tentative framework by K.H. Nuechterlein on page 179: "Developmental Processes in Schizophrenic Disorders: Longitudical Studies of Vulnerability and Stress," in *Schizophrenia Bulletin* Vol. 18, No. 3, p. 392, Figure 2: "A tentative heuristic framework." Reprinted by kind permission of the author.

Figure 11.5 – Kung stick figures on page 196: "Body images of healers," reprinted by permission of the publisher from *Boiling Energy* by R. Katz, Cambridge, MA: Harvard University Press, copyright © 1982 by the President and Fellows of Harvard College.

Figure 12.1 – Lattice tunnel on page 209: Siegel, R.K. 1977. "Hallucinations" by Alan D. Iselin, *Scientific American* 237: 136. Copyright © 1977 by Scientific American, Inc. All rights reserved.

Figure 12.2 – Entoptic Designs on page 211: Lewis-Williams, J.D., Dowson, T.A. 1988. "The signs of the times: Entoptic phenomena in upper paleolithic art." *Current Anthropology* 29: 201-245. Copyright © 1988 University of Chicago Press.

ISBN 3-85630-561-0

"When we live outside ourselves, and by that I mean on external directives only rather than from our internal knowledge and needs, when we live away from those erotic guides from within ourselves, then our lives are limited by external and alien forms, and we conform to the needs of a structure that is not based on human need, let alone an individual's. But when we begin to live from within outward, in touch with the power of the erotic within ourselves, and allowing that power to inform and illuminate our actions upon the world around us, then we begin to be responsible to ourselves in the deepest sense. For as we begin to recognize our deepest feelings, we begin to give up, of necessity, being satisfied with suffering and self-negation, and with the numbness which so often seems like their only alternative in our society. Our acts against oppression become integral with self, motivated and empowered from within."

– Audre Lorde[1]

"Brothers and sisters, there is a drought because of a lack of understanding between us."

– Ali Farka Toure[2]

---

[1] Audre Lorde, *Sister Outsider*, p. 58.
[2] Ali Farka Toure, CD liner notes to "Talking Timbuktu."

Acknowledgments

This book would never have been produced without the encouragement of many mentors, family members, friends, and colleagues. The publisher of Daimon Press, Robert Hinshaw, has been a constant support, giving generously of his time to see the project through to completion. Editor Linda Mehta did an able job of making the manuscript readable. I am grateful to the Susan Bach Foundation for funding portions of my research and its publication. Colleagues and teachers connected with the C.G. Jung Institute in Zürich, Switzerland, read drafts of the manuscript, made suggestions, found relevant articles, or discussed the content with me: Ellynor Barz, Paul Brutsche, Suzanne Gieser, Tula Haukiojo, Ute Jarmer, Annelise Lichtenstein, Janice Maxwell, Cedrus Monte, Eileen Nemeth, Itoku Tsukamoto, Carl Whalen, and Tony Woolfson, as did friends and family members in the United States: Laura Fredrickson, Gertrude Gonzales, Randi Kristensen, Shanna Lorenz, Aaron Lorenz, Anne Mamary, Jaume Marti-Olivello, Peggy Lowry, Bill Meyers, Pam Miller, Gisele Mills, Ellen Salazar, and Stephanie Weinberg. All helped me to think through these ideas, giving me references and useful insights without which I could not have moved forward. My ideas also ripened in discussion with participants in workshops I gave with Effie Brown at Shenoa Retreat and Learning Center in Philo, California and with the students in my psychology and philosophy courses at Sonoma State University. A twenty-year association with La Peña Cultural Center in Berkeley taught me to see the world from multiple perspectives and I am happy to have had the opportunity to learn from *todos los compañeros y compañeras de la lucha*. Each of my clients has taught me some part of this text, and their dreams and mine have been a constant source of inspiration. My orientation toward healing was profoundly influenced by the work of Susan Bach, Aniela Jaffé, and Dora Kalff, all of whom died during the time I researched this project, though they continue to be spirit guides. I am thankful that all of these people have been involved in my work and life; any errors in the book are my own.

Table of Contents

Overview of the Text Diagrams

STAGE 1: FALLING OUT OF CURRENT STRUCTURE, ISOLATION

(not belonging)

CURRENT STRUCTURE OF GROUP

(belonging)

STAGE 2: SOCIAL EXPERIMENTATION

STAGE 3: RITUAL OF REINCORPORATION

HEALER

LIMINAL STATE COMMUNITÁS

Figure 3.1 – Structure / Liminal Space

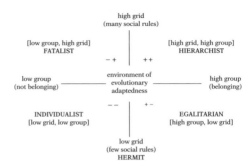

high grid
(many social rules)

[low group, high grid]
FATALIST

[high grid, high group]
HIERARCHIST

low group
(not belonging)

environment of evolutionary adaptedness

high group
(belonging)

INDIVIDUALIST
[low grid, low group]

EGALITARIAN
[high group, low grid]

low grid
(few social rules)
HERMIT

Figure 4.1 – Grid / Group

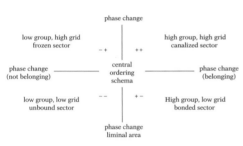

phase change

low group, high grid
frozen sector

high group, high grid
canalized sector

phase change
(not belonging)

central ordering schema

phase change
(belonging)

low group, low grid
unbound sector

High group, low grid
bonded sector

phase change
liminal area

Figure 6.1 – Bonded / Unbound

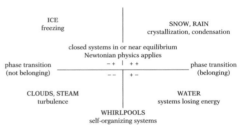

ICE
freezing

SNOW, RAIN
crystallization, condensation

closed systems in or near equilibrium
Newtonian physics applies

phase transition
(not belonging)

phase transition
(belonging)

CLOUDS, STEAM
turbulence

WATER
systems losing energy

WHIRLPOOLS
self-organizing systems

Figure 7.1 – Phase transitions

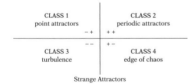

CLASS 1
point attractors

CLASS 2
periodic attractors

CLASS 3
turbulence

CLASS 4
edge of chaos

Strange Attractors

Figure 7.4 – Wolfram's rules

Thunder (Jen)
Lightning (Li)

The Lake (Dui)
The Creative (Yang)

Tao

Receptive (Yin)
Mountain (Gen)

Wind (Sun)
Water (Kan)

Figure 8.1 – Tao

Shadow

Ego

Self

Collective
unconscious

Anima
Animus

Figure 8.2 – Psychic self-organization

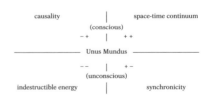

causality

space-time continuum

(conscious)

Unus Mundus

(unconscious)

indestructible energy

synchronicity

Figure 8.3 – Unus Mundus

List of Illustrations

Introduction

Power must be analyzed as something which circulates, or rather as something which only functions in the form of a chain. It is never localized here or there, never in anybody's hands, never appropriated as a commodity or piece of wealth. Power is employed and exercised through a net-like organization. And not only do individuals circulate between its threads; they are always in the position of simultaneously undergoing and exercising this power. They are not only its inert and consenting target; they are always also the elements of its articulation. In other words, individuals are the vehicles of power, not its points of application. ... One needs to investigate historically, and beginning from the lowest level, how mechanisms of power have been able to function.[3]   – Michel Foucault

This book developed out of the experience of moving back and forth between worlds, both literally and symbolically. For several years, I spent part of my time teaching philosophy and psychology at Sonoma State University in California and part of my time studying psychoanalysis and seeing clients in connection with a training program at the C.G. Jung Institute in Zürich, Switzerland. I also returned to the United States during this time to work intensively with schizophrenic patients in a mental hospital. Throughout the same period, I maintained a long-term involvement with human rights movements in Latin America and the United States. Traveling in connection with this work over the years, I met liberation theologists, revolutionaries, and neighborhood organizers; and I sometimes found myself in communities with a shared the belief that their healers could communicate with ancestors, encounter spirits, or turn themselves into animals or birds to serve as guides. If, as I shall claim in these pages, there is an autonomous human need to integrate disparate experience, my work on this manuscript is concrete evidence of its existence.

At the Jung Institute in Zürich, I attended lectures by psychotherapists and medical doctors from various countries discussing experiences with psycho-

[3] Michel Foucault, "Two Lectures," in Gordon, Colin, ed. *Power/Knowledge*.

logical healing that were off the map of the known world in terms of what is considered "normal" subject matter in most university psychology departments in the United States. Meanwhile, in many American bookstores, books about what is called psychology in Zürich or healing in Latin America were being shelved in the "Occult" section. In my own work with clients in Zürich and at the mental hospital, I began to experience phenomena connected with dreams and creativity that were inexplicable in terms of the canon of contemporary Western philosophy. As a result, I became particularly interested in the subject of synchronicity which is central to Jungian thought, and which, until recently, had no basis in either Western science or philosophy. Synchronicity is the experience of meaningful connections in space and time which cannot be explained causally. Precognitive dreams, divination, parapsychology, out-of-body experiences, shape-shifting, spontaneous healing, spiritual awakening, unexplained coincidence, and many other phenomena which have been held to be "supernatural" or "unreal" by modern science are based in the phenomenon of synchronicity.

As I traveled back and forth across the Atlantic during these years, several parts of my own psyche carried on a cultural war. There was that part of me which had been trained in Western philosophy and science and was logical and rational. From another perspective, I could see very well that the ecological and cultural disasters of the modern world clearly indicated an irrational shadow side to this way of thinking. My own experience of the irrational in dreams and synchronicities also demanded a place in theory. To make matters more complicated, both the academic world and the Jungian community were involved in profound inner conflicts over the direction and meaning of their disciplines. At the mental hospital where I worked, and where this book begins, the cultural war I had encountered in my own experience was enacted around me in a reflecting parallel world. In trying to rethink and heal its ruptures, I have also been knitting together my own. A new paradigm was surely needed to integrate these diverse worlds.

Until recently, most academic psychologists and philosophers in the West assumed that the "normal person" is an autonomous, self-determining, self-sufficient adult with a controlling "mind" at the center. Child development is often theorized as a series of universal fixed stages leading to the development of critical thinking, and failure to achieve a certain type of abstract, logical thinking has been presented as evidence of moral and cultural inferiority or mental illness. Mostly outside of these discourses, however, a chorus of contemporary writers have suggested that this conception is far from universal or desirable, and, in fact, is part of the invisible cultural baggage of modern urban life. It may belong more to men than to women, more to developed than developing countries, more to those in power than to those oppressed by power. A new wave of critique from feminists, people-of-color, ecologists, cultural theorists, and political activists has challenged this view of personal identity, making a place for alternative views by digging up the soil for new growth.

In the psychology of C.G. Jung, which has not been generally accepted in the academic milieu, each human individual is considered an embodied psyche, a many-layered, lived world. The embodied psyche is known within an organized field of conscious awareness, a subset of the larger whole called "ego," where there is only limited voluntary control of the rest of the embodied psyche. The ego opens toward the world through its work, intentionality, and perceptual and cognitive experience, toward community or "collective consciousness" through language, habitat, custom, and values, and toward its originating matrix of bodily life in fatigue, moods, feelings, symbols, dreams, and creativity. Psychoanalytic theory refers to this matrix as the "unconscious," and assumes that one can learn about the relationship of a particular ego to its matrix by analyzing various dream series, fantasy images, and expressive artistic productions of the individual involved. Jung also claimed that one could discern behind the outpouring of images from the unconscious a kind of self-organizing, meaning-creating function he called the "Self," which attempts to integrate and synthesize personal experience.

As a result of the emergent quality of ego consciousness in this Jungian view of the "person," authentically knowing oneself, the world, and the "other" become related problematics to be approached again and again without closure and with humility. Both the "inner" and "outer" world happen to the ego, arising within the embodied psyche as self-organized systems largely outside the ego's awareness of the process. People in different cultures and classes experience, name, and understand various aspects of the process in different ways. Every theory and schematic image arises from a particular psyche in a particular place, and shows as much about its origin as its destination.

Though classification systems are "constructed" or "projected" models in this approach, they are not entirely consciously invented. We need to avoid two extremes in theory on this topic: one, typical of modern science, which sees the world spread out before an impartial observer waiting to be discovered, and the other, typical of some literary theories, which sees each individual world as an invented personal narrative. The lived situation of the embodied psyche is far more complex and ambiguous, with bodily experience, human community, objects, ideas, memories, metaphors, images, symbols, language, and values appearing spontaneously from an unconscious matrix we can know little about because it is more complex and dense than the ego which attempts to know it. The historical development of all of these elements in personal experience forms a kind of lens or focusing device which organizes the background of our thoughts into a slowly evolving reality-binding paradigm that provides a somewhat reliable interface with the environment. Within this paradigm, consciousness of self, other, and world are involved in "mutual arising," to borrow a term from Buddhist philosophy. Conscious ideas can then feed back into the paradigm and alter its evolution, but they do not control its evolution. We can wish we felt powerful or were interested in something, but quite often we cannot force the issue. Philosopher Daniel Dennett has put the problem this way:

> I envisage the mind to work rather like the Reagan presidency – lots of sub-agencies and coalitions and competitive functionaries working simultaneously to create the *illusion* that one Boss agent is in control.[4]

It is all of these agencies and functionaries that we need to take into account in understanding the human psyche. If the embodied psyche involves multiple agencies, what we need to explain is not how its unity can fall apart, but rather how it can be maintained. This has been called the binding problem in information theory. In a constantly changing physical, economic, and social world, the psyche must perform a continual activity of reintegration in order for the ego to think of the world and the self as unified and historically continuous entities. Where there are social structures of domination and control, public activities of reintegration become difficult. Health, for both a community and the individuals in it, means that a binding process is going on successfully and mysteriously. People seek out mental health practitioners when the process begins to fail. Two or more psyches then enter a dialogue of which only a small part can be conscious. Mental health practitioners need to know something about the unconscious as well as the environmental background of integration in order to support the process. We need to avoid the reification of the practitioner's diagnostic system, and at the same time, avoid attributing to the patient an idealized authenticity of personal voice not shared by the practitioner. Both partners enter the dialogue with evolving symbolic modeling systems in a constantly changing social environment; both have an ongoing capacity to rethink their lives.

A health practitioner who attempts to deal with human suffering, whether medical doctor, shaman, priest, therapist, or folk healer, begins the work of healing in a specific cultural and social setting, embedded in personal history and experience. In order to diagnose or categorize the symptoms of patients, practitioners must have theoretical assumptions on the basis of which they can sort differences. According to medical anthropologist Arthur Kleinman:

> Disease … is what the practitioner creates in the recasting of illness in terms of theories of disorder. Disease is what the practitioners have been trained to

---

[4] Dennett, D., in Coveney, P. and Highfield, R., *Frontiers of Complexity*, p. 320.

see through the theoretical lens of their particular form of practice. That is to say, the practitioner reconfigures the patient and family's illness problems as narrow technical issues, disease problems.[5]

Every theory emerges from a frame of reference that defines which elements to include and which to exclude in making a diagnosis. We have to decide what is to be diagnosed and what signs to take as indicators. Such decisions are the first principles of any discipline, and unconscious cultural assumptions necessarily seep into them. First principles are value decisions that can never be judged according to any principle of truth or falsity, but rather according to how well the resultant classification system helps us to understand regularities, think about research, or predict behavior.

The operating procedure at most mental hospitals is that the diagnosis is made by a psychiatrist through an interview or series of interviews with the patient, perhaps assisted by a battery of psychological tests given by a staff psychologist, and a short discussion in a team meeting on the patient's ward. In most hospitals, the doctor's training, cultural point of view, attitude, and classification system are taken as a literal and unquestioned given. The cultural biases and subjectivity of the staff are not assumed to have importance. The patient is viewed as an object to be studied by neutral observers. This is what Kleinman refers to as reconfiguring illness as narrow technical issues.

I want to diagnose the illness and healing I saw at the mental hospital where I worked by including and excluding different elements than those in the current medical model being used there; and I want to analyze the functioning of the medical model by including and excluding different elements than those used currently in the Western academic world. For the most part, the academic world in the United States is organized according to disciplines, or schools within disciplines, which attempt to reduce theoretical questions to separate and mostly non-overlapping fields of research. Medical education, for example, focuses primarily on the physical body of the individual. Although many important discoveries result from these choices, there has been an unfortunate side effect over time. Western academic thought is now divided into separate disciplines with competing and contradictory findings. In many cases, this has resulted in either a chaos of relativism or a retreat into disciplinary closure, with too little attempt to cross disciplinary boundaries in order to form a coherent picture.

A corrective is needed in the form of an intercultural and interdisciplinary exploration of human consciousness, illness, and healing, searching out both general patterns and exceptional states from various perspectives. The goals of this exploration must include cultural reflexivity, because alternative cultures and disciplines add things up in different ways.

---

[5] Kleinman, A., *Illness Narratives*, p. 5.

Reflexivity is the attempt to locate the effects of the observer in the activity of observation. It means thinking critically about one's own cultural biases while speaking a particular language and using current classifying systems. Accepting the limitations of all cultural perspectives relativizes every cultural location. Every human view is partial. Reflexivity requires that we struggle with the changing background of our social, physical, and ideological embeddedness and try to make the projections or constructions of our personal and social history more conscious. Cultural and theoretical differences are viewed as dialogic from the perspective of reflexivity. Many plausible and useful formulations can frame the same set of variables, yielding alternative perspectives. The differences between them can then be negotiated through dialogue only to some level of agreement. None have a direct access to fact unmediated by culture. Each allows us to know some things, and prevents us from knowing others. This type of reflexivity, which always considers knowing as an interactive process between subject and object, observer and observed, has been called constructivist or postmodern thought, although I am not at all sure it is a recent invention. I believe it is the central idea both in Jung's notion of "individuation," and in the experience of "enlightenment" sought after in some schools of Buddhist meditation, which involve protracted efforts of reflexivity.

In these pages, I do not want to frame my diagnosis of mental illness as a narrow technical issue but as a broad, interdisciplinary exploration, using both a series of reflexive questions and the application of classification systems, both a hermeneutic and a descriptive approach. I am particularly interested in connecting recent cultural studies and cultural anthropology with new work in mathematics and computer science called complexity theory. Computer programs which enact evolution have modeled new ways of understanding how life forms are organized. Biologists have suggested that biological life evolves "at the edge of chaos" where change and conservation of form reach a delicate balance in each ecosystem. Those organisms which survive find ways to maintain this balance. They are self-organized "complex adaptive systems." Linking cultural studies with evolutionary science involves deconstructing environments of knowing at the same time that we study what is known within them. Obviously, this new paradigm for postmodern psychology will include a much more complex analysis than the current diagnostic system.

As a result of this analysis, I also want to question the uses to which the entire project of diagnosis has been applied in the Western mental hospital setting. It is not the case that every healing system begins the encounter between patient and practitioner with an attempt at diagnosis. Particularly in dealing with the type of discomfort labeled "mental illness" in most modern Western medical systems, it is not at all clear that the patient is best served by being told in which fixed category the practitioner places him or her. If the experience of the patient is one of disorientation or loss of meaning, then the problem for that patient is to reclaim his or her own capacity to find meaning and orientation, to balance at a psychological edge of chaos between too much change and too little. Being told that a condition is already understood by experts who know more about it than the patient does, or worse, that it has been judged incurable, will not facilitate the patient's sense of integrity and empowerment.

The kinds of suffering that have been labeled "mental illness" can be more complex than the ones we know as "physical illness." There seem to be multiple conditions in which they originate. The symptoms through which they are identified are often found in people who are supposedly "normal." Their course can rarely be predicted with accuracy, and there are many cases of spontaneous healing. Furthermore, there is strong disagreement among psychiatrists and psychologists of different schools over types of therapy that can be effective for each diagnosis. When we add to these problems within Western medical disciplines the immense variety of diagnostic systems, healing practices, and outcomes that have been studied in other cultures, it seems to me that we arrive at a postmodern situation where diagnostic categories for mental illnesses must be seen as relative, culturally constructed, and only locally useful shorthand conventions. There is no one overarching theory against which different diagnostic systems could be measured, though there are many interesting ways we can look at similarity and difference among them.

Jungian psychology traditionally avoids diagnosis as part of therapy, though practitioners study both non-Western healing practice and Western psychiatric diagnosis and are aware of how they might be applied. Jung stated the problem with diagnosis in 1945:

> It is generally assumed in medical circles that the examination of the patient should lead to the diagnosis of his illness, so far as this is possible at all, and that with the establishment of the diagnosis an important decision has been arrived at as regards prognosis and therapy. Psychotherapy forms a startling exception to this rule: the diagnosis is a highly irrelevant affair since, apart from affixing a more or less lucky label to a neurotic condition, nothing is gained by it, least of all as regards prognosis and therapy. In flagrant contrast to the rest of medicine, where a diagnosis is often, as it were, logically followed by a specific therapy and a more or less certain prognosis, the diagnosis of any particular psychoneurosis means, at most, that some form of psychotherapy is indicated. As to the prognosis, this is in the highest degree independent of the diagnosis.[6]

6 Jung, C.G., *The Practice of Psychotherapy*, Vol. 16, p. 86

Western psychiatric care is based on the notion of diagnosis which distances the practitioner from the patient. The psychiatrist becomes the knowing subject who classifies; the patient becomes the passive object of classification. Yet, there is good evidence that the experience of psychological healing is promoted exactly by the empathetic sharing of the more distressing elements of the human condition. Unfortunately, one of the most distressing elements for all biological organisms is the constant transformation in our inner and outer environments that prevents us from ever arriving at a permanent and unchanging understanding of our situation. We all have to suffer ambiguity in our day-to-day encounters. Health for biological life forms might be defined by their capacity to continue to reorganize and reproduce order as "autopoietic systems," or self-organizing unities, according to biologists Humberto Maturana and Francisco Varela.[7] If we diminish the capacity of mentally ill people to do this by refusing to accompany them in their efforts, or by doing it for them with a diagnostic system, we may be taking away their ability to heal themselves. In the act of diagnosis, the practitioner privileges his or her complex autopoietic point of view, while simplifying that of the patient. This is a power relationship, masking a political system that determines whose voice is important. These dynamics become more questionable when we take into account the fact that most psychiatrists in the United States and Europe have been men, while most patients with serious mental illnesses are women, many of whom are uneducated and from impoverished families.

Diagnosis in psychological relationships, if seen as a purely "objective" activity, allows the practitioner to retreat to a point of observation supposedly not compromised by cultural assumptions or subjective bias. It edits out the complexity of the personal encounter between therapist and patient. On the other hand, when viewed as a model, each diagnostic system is a schema that captures some regular features of experience and can help us in our quest to understand the many diverse ways in which our world has been constructed. According to Jung,

> All knowledge is the result of imposing some kind of order upon the reactions of the psychic system as they flow into our consciousness. ... It is not a question of *asserting* anything, but of constructing a *model* which opens up a promising and useful field of inquiry. A model does not assert that something *is* so, it simply illustrates a particular mode of observation.[8]

In my analysis of what is problematic in mental illness and healing, it will not be assumed that phenomena to be studied are primarily in the brains or

---

[7] Maturana, H.R., Varela, F.J. "Autopoieses and Cognition: The Realization of the Living," *Boston Studies in the Philosophy of Science*, Vol. 42.

[8] Jung, C.G., *The Structure and Dynamics of the Psyche*, Vol. 8, p. 171, 184.

subjective experiences of the patients or the medical staff. Instead, there will be a focus on how the entire environment – including geography, economics, social conventions, culture, history, perceptual and cognitive structures, and personal experience – creates organized systems of affiliation and information exchange that each individual, whether patient or staff member, has to negotiate. Information systems can have different ecostructures. If there are many linkages, news can be passed rapidly among many individuals. If information is hierarchically managed, the spread of information can be uneven and slow. Some people can be "in the loop" and others not. Through complexity theory, we now know that different informational ecostructures can produce surprisingly different self-organized effects.

In the following pages, the situation in a contemporary American mental hospital is analyzed by interweaving current models from several disciplines that give some insight into the dynamics that occurred there. Chapters 1 and 2 focus on two case studies of schizophrenic patients in dialogue with the hospital system. These patients are people I met in the hospital, but their personal histories have been somewhat disguised in order to protect their privacy and that of their families and caretakers.

Chapter 3 begins with the results of a World Health Organization study completed during the 1980's on the incidence and outcome of schizophrenia in ten countries. The study produced some startling results with regards to the difference in treatment outcomes in industrialized and nonindustrialized countries. Affiliation and information flow in various healing environments in the United States, Europe, Africa, and Latin American is explored along with some of the theories of anthropologist Victor Turner, which could help us to understand which elements might be important.

Chapter 4 begins a more general analysis of the social environment of various healing methods based on recent cultural anthropology, which has applied systems theory to ethnographic data. The dynamics observed by this theory will be compared with those recorded by several Jungian psychologists.

In Chapter 5, anthropological material discussed in the previous section is used to understand the social environment in which the current psychiatric diagnostic manual, DSM-IV,[9] was produced. Here some of the questionable assumptions grounding the social production of the diagnostic system are analyzed. Doubts that have been raised by practitioners within the mental health system about its goals, objectivity, and usefulness are presented.

This leads to a more general discussion in Chapter 6 of how human beings develop neurologically so that any models at all of the environment can be made. The dynamics of social environments and information processing are

[9] American Psychiatric Association: The Revised Diagnostic and Statistical Manual of Mental Disorders (DSM-IV) 1994.

compared to the activities of the immune system and neurological networks, showing that these must be based on nested, hierarchical, and emergent structures of organization. A series of philosophical and psychological problems are explored concerning the relativity and reliability of the interface between models and the worlds they attempt to know.

Chapter 7 provides a brief overview of the development of the new paradigm in complexity theory that is being applied to psychological and biological development. The theory is based on the work of computer scientists using parallel rather than serial computer processing to simulate evolutionary learning and adaptation. They have discovered various systems grammars that apply when nodes in any information system connect to pass on information. In some situations, self-organizing systems arise in which order develops spontaneously without an outside cause. The stage is set to show that the dynamics that have been examined in previous chapters can be defined within complexity theory, suggesting that this is a fruitful new way to consider psychological issues.

In Chapters 8 and 9, new work in the field of complexity theory is compared with various philosophical and psychological attempts to understand human consciousness, symbol systems, and healing experiences. Complexity theory gives a grounding in natural science for regularities that have been noted by both Jungian psychology and many other healing systems that have traditionally been rejected by Western medical practitioners. Through the lens of complexity theory, the experience of synchronicity can be viewed as an autonomous and unconscious speed-up in information processing which brings a system to an "edge of chaos," where self-organized systems mutate at a very rapid rate. Under the right conditions, this can produce a heightened experience of meaningful connectedness as well as a symbolic integration of models which function to promote a sense of well-being and wholeness. In Chapter 10, these ideas are connected with psychological and anthropological research on possession states and other altered states of consciousness.

In Chapter 11, complexity theory is applied to a consideration of mental illness. Using the material developed so far, the many different diseases listed in the DSM-IV are modeled as variations of affiliation and information-processing strategy. It is suggested that these strategies move unconsciously across thresholds in painful environments resulting in emergent qualities of experience. A threshold of experience at the edge of chaos in terms of ego permeability and brain physiology is connected with schizophreniform episodes as well as with religious ritual, healing, divination, and mystical states.

Chapters 12 and 13 take up the question of health and expanded states of consciousness in a postmodern context. With examples from my own practice and from other analysts, cases of healing by people who are no longer part of traditional cultures are discussed. Analyzing images produced by schizophrenic patients, normal laboratory subjects, Jungian analysands and individuals in cultural groups which experience healing trance, characteristic patterns are illustrated which can be used as an index for a psychological state "at the edge of chaos." By exploring creativity reflexively, a spiritual pilgrimage can develop out of states of alienation or "loss of soul" toward experiences of meaningfulness. Finally, psychological healing, creativity, synchronicity, and the spontaneous end states of Buddhist meditation practices are compared in terms of complexity theory.

In the Conclusion, spontaneity is looked at from an evolutionary perspective as a marker of the possibility of an emergent psychological state at the edge of chaos. A cultural "restoration ecology"[10] that seeks to "garden" our personal and social affiliation systems could be undertaken now that we can begin to conceptualize their differences, instability, and constant evolution. Whatever we do from an ego perspective has consequences for surrounding information systems even when we are not aware of them, whether our actions involve withdrawal, control, negotiation or resistance. In many environments, we need to recreate rituals of inclusion and expression for lost portions of our psyches, excluded members of our communities, objectified subjects of discourse, and all other ecosystems which have been classified as marginal through information systems currently in use. Otherwise, if too much is repressed with too much energy, parts of the system can lose energy and go dead or else go over into a state of anarchic chaos. There is evidence in the dying economies and polluted environments of small towns in the northeastern part of the United States and the unemployment, discontent, and violence in big cities that such a scenario is already underway here. The widespread use of alcohol, tranquilizers, anti-depressive medication, and street drugs suggests that there is a problem in regulating inner economies as well. As individuals and as a culture, we need to learn how to hear the voices of "otherness" which have been silenced or have not yet spoken and reintegrate them creatively in an ongoing project of information-sharing and dialogue. To reduce these issues to separate "technical problems" of medical practitioners, academics, engineers, city planners, or police overlooks the important personal, philosophical, and political work of restoration in which all members of the community need to participate in order for it to succeed.

[10] Wilson, A., *The Culture of Nature: North American Landscape From Disney to the Exxon Valdez.*

1. A Call in the Forest

The same mental structures which render identity, definition, the outlines of the body, a relationship with a large social order and even the very meaning of existence are also meant to provide protection from anarchy, chaos, and an inhospitable wilderness.[11] – Susan Griffin

Several years ago, I lived for six months in a Canadian wilderness area near a small lake surrounded by forest. Because the area was on an island, it took almost a day to get there from the nearest town. First, one had to travel by boat over a stretch of ocean, and then climb up a rugged trail to the top of a mountain where the lake was hidden. I loved the walk to the cabin where I lived with friends and family that year. There was always a sense of leaving behind the known and entering another world that was primordial and mysterious, a past that had entered the present as my personal Eden, though in fact it had been inhabited for centuries.

Two loons lived on the lake every summer. When they heard us approach along the trail, the male sounded a long, haunting call that echoed through the woods. Loons are very protective of their lake territories. When other loons appear at the lake and hear the call, they dive and then leave the area. In this way, loons establish boundaries that are rarely violated by other members of their own species. The song carried two or three miles away from the lake, and whenever I heard it, I felt as if my heart stopped for a moment. The sound was like a voice of the forest itself; it communicated a sense of something old and indigenous announcing its strength. In fact, the loons are descendants of an ancestral species *(Colymboides minutus)* that is believed to have lived in these forests for forty-five million years.

I was fascinated with the loons, so whenever it was warm enough, I swam out into the lake near their nesting area for a visit. If I got too close, the male would dance across the water to distract my attention. I dutifully followed

---

[11] Griffin, S., *The Eros of Everyday Life*, p. 46.

where he led, and in time, he seemed to accept that I meant him no harm. Swimming behind him at what he seemed to feel was a safe distance, I practiced imitating his calls in the hope that he would accept me as a sociable neighbor. I spent many hours observing which song went with which situation.

During the summer when they are busy with nesting, the loons almost never leave the lake. Their feet are positioned far back, so they are very clumsy walkers. Water is their natural habitat, and they spend ninety-eight percent of their lives in or on it. They can fly long distances, but can only get into the air if they have a wide stretch of open water to take off from. Their diving abilities are phenomenal; they can stay submerged for three to five minutes and swim underwater for six to eight hundred meters.

Sadly, the forest in which my loon neighbors lived is year by year being ripped apart by logging and development. Each time I go back, more roads are cut through the area. Fortunes are made by selling the coveted board-feet (or cunits) of lumber the trees now represent. The silt from the clear-cuts washes down into streams, and they become clogged. The levels of the lakes go down; some become muddy swamps. Eventually, people arrive on the new roads to build large insulated homes. Then the loons retreat to more remote areas. Other species fill the remaining woods with their sounds, but the call of the loon is missing. What was once forest has become a developed area, contiguous with the rest of the known urban environment. There are electric lights, indoor plumbing, frozen foods, and television. Human life is more comfortable, but the sense of mystery that first called me to the island is almost gone.

I had not heard the call of the loon for many years when I entered the state mental hospital where I had come to learn more about schizophrenia and to do art therapy with hospital patients. Not in my wildest imagination would I have expected to hear the call of a loon at the hospital, but unmistakably, there it was, perfectly rendered. I heard it at odd times, coming from different parts of the hospital.

At first I was lost in the turning, twisting corridors that always seemed to double back on themselves, but soon I was able to find my way around and explore. I began to track the loon. One day, I saw Edward Coe[12] standing at the fence in the small courtyard between the lunchroom and main hospital. As he gazed out at the trees on the hills in the distance, I heard him make his loon call. I stopped to watch, fascinated. Here was someone who had once been as close to the loons as I, who also must have lived in the wilderness, watching loons for hours. He, too, had learned their language and had not

---

[12] Edward Coe is an invented name. Many details of personal history have also been altered in order to protect the identity of patients discussed.

been able to forget it. I wondered what mystery the call might represent to him and why it was the primary form of language he was now using.

I had seen Edward often in the courtyard at lunchtime feeding sparrows with bread crumbs. When he wasn't there, I passed him sometimes in the corridors where he walked very fast much of the day, conversing with himself. He behaved like one of the hospital maintenance workers being called out on an emergency. I never saw him talking with anyone on the staff, but occasionally he was with a small group of patients smoking in the garden. I began to sit near him for a few minutes each time I saw him feeding the birds. I had experience in approaching loons; perhaps since we shared "common friends," we could communicate as well.

Little by little, we began to talk in human language, first about loons, and then about people. Edward was from a Native American tribal group that several hundred years earlier had as its territory a vast region of the state we lived in. The region had been the northern part of Mexico until 150 years ago. Like the forests of the loons that were so impressive to both of us, Edward's ancestral territory had been invaded and developed by outsiders. His people had been conquered, and now many lived in cities or in trailers or cabins on the border between the city and the territory from which they had been displaced. The group had been scattered, and much tribal ritual lost. Edward's parents had both died when he was a child. He was raised in a series of foster homes that were heavy on abuse and light on affection. In time, he ran away and lived on his own. He was often unemployed and lived with terrible economic hardships. During the Sixties, he experimented with drugs and was briefly married. When his ex-wife had an abortion, he had his first psychotic episode at the age of twenty-four.

Since that time, Edward had cycled between mental hospital stays, where he was instructed in taking medication, and time on the streets, where he was told not to take "drugs." People had turned out to be rather disappointing on the whole. They were irrational and inconsistent, and he never knew if he could trust them. When I sat and talked with him, I found him intelligent and sensitive. He had a depth of feeling and a sense that something "more" existed beyond what society offered. A loon cannot live well away from water, because it evolved around forest lakes. The ability to dive deeply is useless on land, and webbed feet make walking difficult. The "loon in Edward" (and undoubtedly the "loon in me") needed a social world with the equivalent of a water habitat, but his was now extinct. He knew he needed something, but he didn't know where to find it. There was nowhere to retreat to, except inside. It is my interpretation that he had given up looking for what he needed in his modern urban environment. He would stand behind the chain-link fence of the mental hospital calling like a loon for a lost territory in which he could feel safe and whole. Somewhere along the line, Edward had begun to limit his communication to birds: "They don't hurt each other and they care for their young."

I had decided to approach my work in the hospital as much as possible with "beginner's mind." Concretely, that amounted to getting to know the patients in their hospital context as people before I read about them as "cases." That way, I would have two points of view to compare. The people I encountered were invariably far more complicated and many-sided than their case histories would indicate. To fit Edward into the diagnosis "schizo-phrenic," or worse, to think of him as "a schizophrenic," I would have to cut away all my interactions with him that might yield other descriptions. In order to be diagnosed as a schizophrenic according to the DSM-IV,[13] the patient must be socially and occupationally dysfunctional and exhibit two or more of the following five symptoms for at least six months: (1) delusions, 2) hallucinations, (3) disorganized speech, (4) disorganized behavior, (5) flattening of emotion or alogia.

But what about the time in between these exhibited symptoms? What if different situations elicited completely different responses? When I sat feed-ing sparrows with Edward, he was often quite socially functional, at least as much as I or any of my friends were, and none of the five symptoms were observable.

Contemporary psychological anthropology has begun to question the notion that human beings have a fixed personality structure. It may be that "identity" is more an issue of boundary than core; that is, one is called upon to represent and define one's personality in certain kinds of social interac-tions. It is much more of an issue at a job interview, for example, than when on a hike with old friends. Anthropologists Geoffrey White and Catherine Lutz have attempted to synthesize this point of view in their recent book, *New Directions in Psychological Anthropology.* They write: "Ethnic, gender, or class identities and symbolizations are most evident at their peripheries, where contact with others evoke articulations and dramatizations of the self."[14] In their view, we should see "identity as emergent, culturally con-structed, and context dependent ... " Edward's diagnosis was based on a police report and an intake interview by a psychiatrist in a large mental hospital. I wonder how comfortable he felt there, and what he felt free to disclose. What kind of symptom is a loon call?

To diagnose, you have to make a decision about what is important and what is not, in order to limit the signs you will need to consider. There are conventions in a mental hospital that help the staff to do this. The DSM-IV provides us with prototypical models of mental illness. Each diagnosis is

[13] American Psychiatric Association, *Diagnostic and Statistical Manual of Mental Disorders-IV*, p. 285.
[14] Schwartz, T., White, G.M., & Lutz, C.A., eds., *New Directions in Psychological Anthropology*, p. 3.

intended to be discrete and distinguishable from others, and the goal of the intake staff is to find which diagnosis fits the new patient. But I was an outsider, and I wanted to think through for myself where to locate the problem, or malfunction, that the diagnosis attempts to pinpoint. It was exactly this question of what signs and symptoms to consider that troubled me. So in my own exploration, I allowed myself to frame the situation differently, in order to explore other possibilities of meaning.

I could not easily rule out environmental factors in Edward's illness. I wanted to consider, for example, the chain-link fence behind which he sounded his loon call. This fence had a social meaning that lay in defining those on one side as normal and those on the other side as abnormal. When the hospital was first built many years ago, it was in an isolated rural area, and there was no fence. Then there was an equation of normal/center and mentally ill/margin. Staff and patients alike remembered the time without the fence as the golden age of the hospital. In those days, patients were allowed to go on hikes and field trips, and the staff did not have to work indoors all day. As time passed, urban development spread almost to the door of the hospital. Then mental patients took their walks a few hundred feet from the backyards of wealthy, conservative homeowners. Occasionally they escaped, and there were even police and neighborhood chases through the yards. The local residents were frightened and outraged; they campaigned for the closing of the hospital or, at minimum, installation of a ten-foot chain-link fence with barbed-wire on the top.

The part of the hospital that is fenced-in looks like a prison or concentration camp. Instead of being pushed out to a margin, the patients are now being held in isolation zones within the city limits. So there are at least three primary vectors of motion in this story. The wilderness is invaded by Europeans, pushing first Native Americans, then the loons and other animals, then forest, then any marginal, maladapted "others" off the land. On the other side, there is a retreat to the north of birds, of animals, of conquered peoples, of old growth forest, of the marginal, of the powerless. As the conquest of territory is completed, "others" are then contained in safety zones. This is a system of vectors that has produced vast changes in the American landscape.

When there is no more marginal wilderness to retreat to and the landscape is frozen in a network of road and building construction, only isolated islands of free space remain as protected areas. State parks and recreation areas, for example, are policed and serviced. Like the "pacification zones" in the Vietnam war, the homelands in South Africa, and the reservations for remaining Native American tribal groups, the enclosed areas are held within a sociopolitical system under the theme of control and domination. Edward Coe's schizophrenia has also been placed in an isolation zone both physically and symbolically. He has a chronic disease in which isolated symptoms lead to social segregation. It is part of an evolutionary process in which older technologies and rituals are being replaced by, some would say, a "brave new world" which is not necessarily better. When Edward stands at the fence that separates the tiny territory he has been reduced to from the mainstream culture of power and privilege, his loon call truly expresses lost worlds and dying values.

It is not that I am against custodial care. I have visited and heard about some fine clinics. There are times in most people's lives when it is wonderful to be taken care of. Almost everyone has occasional days when everything is just too much. Schizophrenia itself is a kind of "time out" from daily life, and one truly needs protection and support during an acute episode of psychosis. The question for me is, under what sign, through what schema of relations is the protection managed? Every system of custodial care is constructed symbolically as well as physically. The personal cost of care must not be so high that we trade our self-respect for it.

I see the structure and function of the hospital, and its illness and healing categories, as an information flow constrained by an inherent ordering principle or schema. Every ordering principle combines some elements and separates others. Decisions have to be made about where to cut. The fence is a cut, and so is Edward's bird call. It is the patterns that will interest us. The hospital, the fence surrounding it, the diagnosis, and the care given within are all related to the paradigm in which mental illness is understood in American society.

I spent almost every break and lunch hour at the hospital reading about schizophrenia in the medical library journals. For over a hundred years, until recently, the primary thrust of research on schizophrenia was the search for a "local cause," a discrete and unique abnormality that inevitably led to the disease. Medical doctors analyzed millimeters of tissue under microscopes for a small lesion in the brain or a genetic difference that could be shown to be present in all cases. Object relations psychologists observed family interactions in order to find the unique traits of the "schizophrenogenic mother." The effort was intended to isolate the data, count or weigh small interactions, eliminate difference, and locate commonalities. This approach has been spectacularly successful in some scientific areas, producing the technological revolution that allowed the development of modern industry. In medicine, it produced penicillin, polio vaccine, and insulin.

By extension of this model, it was hoped one could find a primary cause of schizophrenia that could be eliminated with a "magic bullet," like the neuroleptic medications that are routinely used on all schizophrenic patients in American mental hospitals today. While these have been successful in reducing the florid delusions and hallucinations of an acute psychotic episode, they do not seem to affect the long term negative symptoms of schizophrenia, which represent a shrinking back from life and engagement. Psychiatrist Albert Scheflen argued in his 1981 book, *Levels of Schizophrenia:* "Classical neurology has not found the lesion or disorder in schizophrenia in spite of six generations of research. Classical psychologies have for four generations been unable to come up with a generally accepted formulation, nor have social theorists. When we consider the enormity of the problem of schizophrenia, we must face the fact that our classical paradigms have suffered a serious failure."[15] After many years of working in mental hospitals, Scheflen wondered whether schizophrenia was even being treated. "In my view the classical triad of hospitalization, drugs, and family reaffiliation will usually ameliorate the psychosis but sustain the schizophrenic condition."[16]

In the late 1970's, Scheflen was connected with philosopher Gregory Bateson and many other psychiatrists in trying to work out how new developments in systems theory might allow consciousness, schizophrenia, and healing to be understood differently. Bateson expressed some of his ideas in *Mind and Nature*,[17] published in 1979. Unfortunately, both men died of lung cancer before a burst of new developments in systems theory in the late 1980's. Georgetown University psychiatrist Murray Bowen was a colleague of both authors, and wrote in the introduction to Scheflen's book that, as a thinker, Scheflen was "far ahead of his time." Bowen believes that both were reaching for a new paradigm for thinking about schizophrenia which would link biology, sociology, and schizophrenia with general systems theory. "It can require 50 to 200 years for a new paradigm to be woven into the accepted fabric of society," he wrote. "Until the new paradigm is accepted, science tends to focus on phenomenological segments of the problem. ... Psychiatry has had a conceptual enigma with schizophrenia. Some 40 years ago it was conceptualized as having a psychological cause with a psychological theory designed to fit the biological model. The fit was inaccurate and the therapy based on the theory not very effective."[18] In Bowen's view, the difficulty was partly that schizophrenia was defined "by a biological, or medical, or cause and effect model."[19]

In my consideration of environmental factors in healing, I am also reaching toward a new paradigm that will link mental illness with culture, systems theory, and evolutionary biology. My work is a part of this dialogue that Bowen thinks might take two hundred years. In contrast with the local cause approach, my encounter with schizophrenia set off a chain of ecological reflections reaching back forty-five million years. I am unable to imagine

---

[15] Scheflen, A.E., *Levels of Schizophrenia*, p. 105.
[16] Ibid., p. 159.
[17] Bateson, G., *Mind and Nature*.
[18] Scheflen, *Levels of Schizophrenia*, p. viii.
[19] Ibid., p. viii.

locating the problem of Edward Coe's symptoms solely in his body or in his personal life without considering how they fit into the entire ecosystem of which he is a part. The human ecosystem includes not only the physical environment, but also social relationships and internal representations, the schemata through which various people try to model and respond to their interactions with the world. My response and that of the medical researchers, the hospital psychiatric staff, the chain-link fence, and the neighboring city, are all a part of a system connected with culture, representations, and information exchange, and must be part of any theory of health and illness. In this I am influenced by contemporary psychological anthropology as well as critical theory. According to anthropologist Nancy Scheper-Hughes,

> Critical theories differ radically in their epistemology from positivist theories derived from the natural sciences. All theories in the "natural" sciences presuppose an "objective" structure of reality knowable by minds that are likewise understood as sharing a uniform cognitive structure. Critical theories assert the subjectivity of knowable phenomena and propose "reflection" as a valid category and method of discovery. ... Medicine falsely objectifies patients and their afflictions by reducing them to reified biomedical diagnostic categories. The objectivity of science and of medicine is always a phantom objectivity, a mask that conceals more than it reveals.[20]

Jung wrote that all psychology is a "subjective confession"; but if it were only personal history that influenced one's ideas, there would be as many psychologies and scientific theories as there are individuals. Clearly there are not that many, but there are several primary paradigms, each a unique way of focusing a set of problems. I am wedded to an environmental paradigm, but many of the psychiatrists in the hospital thought in terms of local causes. Each seeing Edward from within a system of assumptions, we were impressed by different aspects of his behavior and evoked from him different responses. These paradigmatic models are so basic to the way we approach the world that they are like eyes or ears, focusing devices without which there would be no sorting of information into patterns that could be understood. Our paradigms define for us what is important, what are data to be considered, where the problem is, and what would constitute a solution. We each assumed we knew what a "person" is, how "emotion" is felt, what "knowing" means. The paradigms were "reality-binding" models rather than consciously thought-through ideas. That is, they allowed and contained our thinking, but were rarely an object of thought. Contemporary cognitive psychologists have called these reality-binding models "schemata" and psychological anthropologists have referred to them as "indigenous psychol-

---

[20] Scheper-Hughes, N., "Hungry bodies, medicine, and the state," in: Schwartz, T., White, G.M., & Lutz, C.A., eds., *New Directions in Psychological Anthropology*, p. 229.

ogy." In postmodern psychology, we also have to consider how these models are created, become embedded in a culture, and dissolve. They are an important part of the environment. To understand this aspect of the environment, we have to learn how to watch ourselves watching others.

Like everyone else who uses language, Edward, too, had a primary reality-binding model. The members of his peer group were birds, and his primary allegiance was to them rather than people. If none of our basic paradigms could be proved "true," what was the difference between Edward's and ours? In the psychiatric literature, a delusion is defined as an odd belief not generally shared by members of one's own culture. In earlier times, the definition was undoubtedly just "an odd belief," but with the development of cross-cultural psychology, we now know that many beliefs that would be considered odd in our culture, are widespread in others, and vice versa. By this definition then, though I find the medical local cause paradigm odd, it is not delusional, because it is widely shared. Edward's ideas are delusional because he is alone, except for my appreciation of his symbols. The connectionist paradigm could land me in either camp, depending on how widely shared it is and how odd people find it. Is the primary difference between the medical model, Edward's model, and my model their adaptiveness in terms of how successful we can be in influencing and surviving our social and physical environment? If so, there is a general pressure toward social conformity, because it is much easier to get along with others when you share their basic beliefs. We know now that in many cultures it is a shared belief that people can turn into birds or animals, encounter spirits of ancestors, or time and space travel in out-of-body experiences. If Edward were to live in one of these cultures and not an American city, perhaps it would be easier for him to adapt and integrate.

Recent literature in philosophy of science has stressed the fact that scientific paradigms, and in fact, all models and metaphors about reality, have to be considered as schemata with which we organize and test experience. If they are dissonant with experience, we can say they are wrong, but if they are not contradicted by experience, this doesn't mean they are "right" in any sense. It only means it makes sense to go on using them. The difference between scientific models, and other types of models in this view, is that ideally, scientific models are open to testing, and suggest many fruitful possibilities for testing (although this has been questioned). Religious and cultural models, by contrast, do not yield testing situations, and in fact, defend against testing. At the same time they may function to create meaning in cultural experience and allow a successful encounter with the social environment. It may be that what we call science sometimes functions more like a religious or cultural myth, rejecting information inconsistent with current theories.

In some of the academic postpositivist reflection of the last ten years, no particular cultural paradigm is assumed to be privileged. University of Chicago anthropologist Richard Shweder has summed up this thinking as follows:

> The postulation of our own internal mental constructs as external forces lending intelligibility to the data of the senses seems to be a central and indispensable feature not only of imaginary, fanciful, hallucinatory, and delusional thinking but of scientific thought as well.[21]

Jung was concerned about this issue as early as the 1920's when positivism was in its heyday:

> It seems to me that the error of every *Weltanschauung* so far has been that it claims to be an objectively valid truth, and ultimately a kind of scientific evidence of this truth. This would lead to the insufferable conclusion that, for instance, the same God must help the Germans, the French, the English, the Turks, and the heathen – in short, everybody against everybody else. Our modern consciousness with its broader grasp of world events has recoiled in horror from such a monstrosity, only to put in its place various philosophical substitutes. But these in turn laid claims to being objectively valid truths. That discredited them, and so we arrive at the differentiated fragmentation of consciousness with its highly undesirable consequences ... There have been numerous attempts in our time to put the clock back and indulge in a *Weltanschauung* of the old style – to wit, theosophy, or, as it is more palatably called, anthroposophy. But if we do not want to develop backwards, a new *Weltanschauung* will have to abandon the superstition of its objective validity and admit that it is only a picture which we paint to please our minds, and not a magical name with which we can conjure up real things. A *Weltanschauung* is made not for the world, but for ourselves. If we do not fashion for ourselves a picture of the world, we do not see ourselves either, who are the faithful reflections of that world. Only when mirrored in our picture of the world can we see ourselves in the round. Only in our creative acts do we step forth into the light and see ourselves whole and complete. Never shall we put any face in the world other than our own, and we have to do this precisely in order to find ourselves. For higher than science or art as an end in itself stands man, the creator of his instruments.[22]

The word, *Weltanschauung*, remains untranslated in the above quote because translators believed there was no equivalent word in English. The essay quoted was first translated into English in 1928. Perhaps at that time, without the rich experience of cross-cultural encounter in the post World War II era, English speakers were not yet thinking about cultural relativity.

---

[21] Shweder, R.A., *Thinking Through Cultures: Expeditions in Cultural Psychology*, p. 60.
[22] Jung, C.G., *The Structure and Dynamics of the Psyche*, p. 378.

Today, academicians, politicians, and business people regularly discuss this problem, and we talk about *Weltanschauung* as paradigms through which different cultural groups organize their world. Since the publication of Thomas Kuhn's groundbreaking work, *The Structure of Scientific Revolutions*[23], in 1962, we know that paradigms also have an evolutionary history. There are periods when most people in a certain culture group have a homogeneous reality-binding paradigm. During the early Middle Ages, for example, most people in Europe believed the earth was flat. When people began to promulgate dissonant information, the first response was to burn the messenger rather than hear the message. In traditional India, the caste system determined virtually every aspect of one's life from birth to death. Today, many young Anglo-Indians being raised in England do battle against it culturally as old-fashioned and backward, often scandalizing older adults. Ideas appear to evolve the way species evolve.

When we look at the history of biological evolution, we can see that there are long periods of stability when many species find stable ecological environments in which to survive. These are punctuated by periods of rapid change when many species become extinct and many new ones develop all at once. At the end of the Permian era, seventy-five percent of amphibia and fifty percent of reptiles vanished. At the end of the Cretaceous era, twenty-five percent of animal families perished. At the same time, new species burgeoned. During the same Cretaceous era that produced a catastrophe of extinctions, flowering plants seized the field from conifers, and mammals from dinosaurs.

It is now believed[24] that cultural history may follow the same pattern. When we look back, we can see that certain stable cultural ensembles – the Roman Empire, the French Monarchy, the Ming Dynasty, the Toltecs, the Soviet Union – dominated various ecosystems and then rapidly fell apart. Long periods of relative stability are punctuated by periods of rapid change, leading to many small extinctions and occasional large ones. We may be in such a period now. There is ample evidence of catastrophic cultural change as regional languages, old customs and rituals, and traditional ways of thinking fall from use with new generations of youth, as they come under the onslaught of television, the music industry, and fashion trends from metropolitan areas. Economic change and imperial conquest have set in motion huge migrations of populations and information across borders. The last hundred years have seen the most massive alteration of technological and material infrastructure in human history. Paradigms are dying all around us in the effort to manage waves of social and economic change. The pattern of extinctions that can be seen in biological and cultural history can also be

[23] Kuhn, Thomas S., *The Structure of Scientific Revolutions*.
[24] See, for example, Lewin, R., *Complexity*.

observed in scientific development and the evolution of social and psychological theories.

Thus, when Edward, the psychiatrists, and I form our schemata about the world through reality-binding paradigms, we are doing it on a theoretical landscape that could be described in terms of extinctions and punctuated equilibria. The doctor's "local cause" paradigm is the old dominant species that has controlled a part of our ecostructure for a long time. The mental hospital is the environmental niche where its adaptation is most complete. For me, the mental hospital is a foreign culture whose ground rules I am trying to understand. I am a visitor in this world and the connectionist paradigm I bring is that of a newcomer competing for space. The world of Edward's tribal culture, unlike many others, is an almost extinct paradigm we learn about like that of dinosaurs, from bones and material artifacts. Edward himself has developed a personal reality-binding model that allows him to survive, but doesn't seem destined for broad popular applications.

In my view, schizophrenia and other forms of mental illness are one way the psyche speaks. The binding paradigms through which we classify it are another. When we speak, we model our world, partly through conscious intention and partly through our unconscious use of cultural schemata. Speaking is a dialogue with the environment that grows and changes as the environment grows and changes. Some ways of speaking dominate personal and social fields for a long time and then suddenly become extinct. When we respond creatively to our environment with speech, gestures, song, and symbols, we organize it into meaningful patterns which help us to situate ourselves comfortably and negotiate with others as long as we share a common language. It is the evolution of this "speaking" that we need to understand.

The connectionist paradigm places local events in the context of affiliative and information sharing networks that are constantly changing. What has been uncovered by the theory is a set of grammatical rules operative in a wide array of networks, irrespective of their local content. The theory has been used to understand economic markets, traffic problems, immune system activity, avalanche patterns, archeological data, and neurological networks, yielding many new insights about how relational systems function. It predicts conditions for rates of extinction, complexity catastrophes, phase changes, and chaotic behavior, which have suggestive and interesting implications if applied to a consideration of mental illness and healing in social contexts. Connectionist theory asks us to notice systems of relationship and patterns of interaction linked with the transmitting of information in networks. It is more concerned with roads, channels, traffic, dams, and fences than with end states or individual locations. Some types of connected environments characteristically cause "freezing" and others "melting."

Through reading, conversations, and pictures, these ideas have infused into my way of thinking, though there are technical aspects of the theory for which I don't have the mathematical background. Nevertheless, as a psychologist, I find complexity theory fascinating and cannot stop thinking about what it might imply about my work and my clients.

When Edward stands at the fence near the dense grid of an American city, his repetitive loon call is a "frozen" behavior in a "frozen" landscape. There are problematic signs and symptoms in the city where he became ill, as well as with Edward. The city has a skyrocketing unemployment rate with the fishing and forest industries failing; a serious problem with drugs, gangs, and violent crime; and an enormous and chaotic population of homeless people and runaway youths living on the streets. The city itself is in a state where only one percent of the old-growth forest remains. The hills, which were richly wooded in the past, are barren slash and stumps. Where once many connected, growing, life systems were exchanging their energies so that all could flourish, there is now a dead and frozen wasteland. Many rivers are polluted and the fish no longer spawn in them. The community is also divided into class and racial neighborhoods with antagonistic, oppressive, and sometimes violent relationships. The Ku Klux Klan is active, and still burns crosses in front of homes to threaten unwanted inhabitants. Where and how healing rituals could change this situation is the crucial question for our times. We need an environmental healing that includes the community, the economy, the forest, the rivers, the hospital, and Edward. I am not able to imagine each of these separate problems in isolation, because they connect in my internal schema. This is a part of my own personal environmental healing of the ruptured schemata I have inherited from an education which separated culture, science, and psyche.

As a psychotherapist, I also need to understand how the ideas of healing I bring to my analytical hours might fit into this dynamic. It seems natural to me to understand the psyche in relationship to culture, environment, and biology. The depths of the psyche are embedded in history and reach back into the primordial and mysterious forest that was the origin of human life. If Jungian psychologists want to assert the existence of a self-organizing center in the psyche, we need to be able to explain how and where it developed in the evolutionary past.

When the psyche speaks, it is like the call of a loon from a lake. The psyche is a report of strength and integrity, a declaration of territoriality and order. It is old and indigenous as well as up-to-the moment. The problem of schizophrenia develops when the psyche stops speaking, when, as for Edward Coe, the ancestral voice becomes mute and there is silence in the forest.

2. Inner Voices, Outer Silence

When people say that knowledge is "universally true," we must understand that it is like railroads, which are found everywhere in the world but only to a limited extent. To shift to claiming that locomotives can move beyond their narrow and expensive rails is another matter. Yet magicians try to dazzle us with "universal laws" which they claim to be valid even in the gaps between the networks.[25]

– Bruno Latour

I met Gina Bertoli[26] on the R ward, designated for those hospital inmates not expected eventually to make their way through the rehabilitation unit back to the outer world. Except for the blaring television set, the day room of the R ward was almost always silent when it was not time for medications or meals. There were many people on the ward who almost never spoke, sitting much of the day bent over in chairs, eyes facing knees. I say almost, because odd things can happen. One day, such a woman sat bolt upright next to me, looked me in the eye and said, "It's the fault of my second grade teacher. She said I couldn't learn to read and then I never did." Then she returned to her posture and I never heard her speak again. I frequently saw this strange conjunction of perceptive analytical capabilities embedded in the schizophrenic person side by side with highly unconventional behavior.

Gina was brought to me by a ward psychologist for art therapy because she did not fit the profile of the typical R ward patient at all. Although she was 33, she looked like a college student. She was small, slight, dark-haired, and quite charming. We hit it off right away and began to spend an hour each day in the consultation room on the ward. I brought art supplies with me that she used whenever she felt like it, but often we just talked. That she could hold a long conversation was itself unusual on the R ward. Beyond that, I experienced her as intelligent, funny, and engaging as she gradually told me about the events of her life that had led to the current situation. Not surprisingly,

---

[25] Latour, B., *The Pasteurization of France*, p. 226.
[26] Not her real name. Many personal details have also been altered to protect her identity.

she felt trapped, depressed, and bored in the hospital, where her only meaningful activity was to play classical music for an hour each day on the out-of-
tune dayroom piano. As a result, she was very happy to have a visitor.

I learned she had been raised on a farm in the Midwest by her parents and
grandparents along with seven brothers and sisters. She had loved the farm
animals and the rural environment, but felt constrained by her strict Catholic
upbringing. Her parents fought frequently, and her mother, she thought, was
mean and cold. Nevertheless, she did well in school and was able to leave the
state to go to a university in a large city. There she studied humanities and
fell in love with a fellow student named Frank. She lived with him for several
years, visiting his family on school vacations. Frank's mother didn't really
approve of Gina as a marriage partner for him because she wouldn't help him
socially. She put pressure on him to break up with Gina rather than become
engaged. In her senior year, Frank jilted her, which she experienced as a
crushing blow. During that year, her father died as well, leaving her family in
difficult financial straits. After his death, she "no longer felt safe." She
dropped out of school and became a waitress, gradually losing her way.
When she was 23, she began to see a psychologist, who told her she was
schizophrenic and gave her drugs. In Gina's view, this was a "lazy" diagnosis,
made by a man who didn't want to take the time to understand her real
problems. Afterward, she returned home to the Midwest and married an
older Swedish hired hand from a nearby farm. She felt progressively unable
to keep up with her social environment because of a lack of energy. She
began to take amphetamines as an "upper," which would allow her to
socialize with her husband's friends, who drank a lot. In time, she became
addicted, and her family sent her to a recovery clinic. The story became
unclear after that.

The sensitive woman I met in the consulting room for an hour each day
bore no resemblance at all to the "monster" I found in her case report when
I finally got around to reading it. Here was a dangerous psychotic patient
with poor impulse control feared by the staff, though at the time I met her
she weighed under one hundred pounds. Reported were frequent bursts of
anger and aggression with unprovoked attacks on staff and other patients,
which included scratching and hair-pulling. They said she had broken into
the nursing station several times to steal coffee and sometimes tried to take
medications from other patients. Every five to seven days, the staff found it
necessary to place her in seclusion and restraints for several hours. The
report from practically every day shift said: "Patient delusional and agitated."

The goal of the medical staff in this case was to teach Gina the management of psychotic episodes and impulse control. This would then allow her
to be placed in a group home somewhere in a small town nearby. This is the
current aim of the state health plan, because there has been so much

criticism of the treatment of patients in mental hospitals. The medical staff considered Gina a "chronic member of the state hospital system," which meant that it wasn't anticipated she could ever return to normal life. Given the "local cause" orientation of medical psychiatry, her treatment therefore consisted of the search for the right combination of medications that might change the central nervous system abnormality held to be responsible for Gina's disease.

I have seen neuroleptic medications produce near miracles in the new psychotic patients who came into the intake ward regularly each week. Sometimes within two or three days, patients who had been screaming and out of control on entry could talk quietly about precipitating conditions and long term plans. These medications don't work on all patients, however, and Gina was not one of the success stories. Over the previous ten years of engagement with the mental health system, Gina had been tried out on Stelazine, Navane, Clozaril, valproic acid, lithium, Ativan, Benadryl, and Depakote. They had caused permanent neurological damage in the form of tardive dyskinesia, a tremor like that in Parkinson's disease, but everyone agreed they hadn't helped her or changed her behavior. A few years before I met her, Gina had also been given "a trial of ECT therapy," that is, over a dozen shock treatments, usually reserved these days for patients who are severely depressed. They were held to produce only a temporary improvement, after which the "patient returned to baseline."

Gina was therefore a very inconvenient patient on ward R, and nobody liked her much. The doctor spoke to her once or twice a week for a few minutes to see how she was responding to the current medication trials. The nurses monitored her vital signs and made sure she took her medications, but spent most of their time attending to administrative duties. Her social worker, whom she had once accused of sexual harassment, told me, I thought vindictively, that she would "never get out of there." He refused to speak with her. As he was in charge of her rehabilitation, he exercised considerable control.

The daily living schedule was enforced by a group of low-paid, often overworked aides, who in some cases cared a lot about their wards. Most had little educational experience with mental illness. When they were hired from the community, they were given state-mandated training in safety procedures, which stressed the unpredictability of mental patients and the need for protective measures in dealing with them. Shortly after I left the hospital, a patient was accidentally killed by a group of aides implementing these procedures. Understandably, what the aides liked most were cooperative, docile patients; what they liked least was unpredictability. They didn't like Gina at all. As a result, she had the lowest level of "privileges" in the behavior modification program and was never allowed to leave the ward to go to the lunchroom or recreation area.

The ward was constructed so that the day room could be overseen from a glass-walled nursing station at one end. All the bedrooms and consulting rooms also had glass windows facing onto the corridors for easy observation. The aides tended to make forays into the patient areas to carry out their duties and then retreat to the safety of the glass-walled "safety zone" as soon as they could. Often when patients tried to engage them in conversation, they were rushing back to this observation post and didn't want to stop. As soon as they finished their duties, they could return to the staff room behind the observation area where they could drink coffee and relax with other aides. The patients tended to cluster around the glass wall looking back at the staff, because there wasn't much else of interest to do on the ward except go to the smoking room for a cigarette. Thus, the relationship between the staff and the patients was enacted through a metaphor, both physical and social, of distancing, observing, and recording. Accepted as a visiting psychologist, I was allowed to move freely on both sides of the glass wall as a "participant observer." I was trying to understand a code that wasn't my own, in a "caste system" with a grammar of behavior rules, rather like an anthropologist studying another culture. I was doing ethnography, as well as a Jungian analysis of the hospital rather than the patients.

Once a week, the "treatment team" of each ward met to consider various patients. The team was made up of the ward psychiatrist, a psychologist, a social worker, an occupational therapist, and one or more nurses. I was allowed to attend whenever I wished and usually visited more than one each week because I found them fascinating. Here one could watch the process of analysis that went into diagnosis and treatment. The task was to come up with a written treatment plan for each patient and to review its application. The hospital that I was in had set up a committee to computerize this activity. The idea was to have a program that would give the operator a set of choices about each patient: delusions, yes or no; depression, yes or no; and so on. Then the computer would print out a treatment plan, saving many hours of treatment team discussion.

The most interesting part of the meeting was when various patients were brought in for five-minute interviews by the staff. Often I had met the patients myself outside the team meeting and had my own sense of how they were, so I could watch how they adapted to the team context. There they might be driven to their wit's end and begin screaming at the doctor, be on best behavior as on an employment interview, or be lost and confused about the purpose of the meeting. The patient was usually questioned by the psychologist or the psychiatrist. The most notable psychiatrist was a comical man whose basic orientation was toward common sense adjustment to the conventional world. It seemed to me he had a heartfelt wish for these patients to be normal and was truly mystified at their "refusal." He would roll his eyes at the staff when patients didn't appear to understand him. Pushed beyond his limits, he would look at them with exasperation and explain things as if they were naughty children. "Why don't you comb your hair and wear shoes? You don't look nice like that." or "Why do you think you are pregnant when you have had a hysterectomy?" or "Why do you take drugs when you know they aren't good for you?" After these encounters, the staff had to produce a written statement. There seemed to be a few dozen basic building blocks that were used as formulae under the headings of "goals" or "methods." We could apply "milieu therapy," which seemed to mean leaving them to their own devices on the ward, or the psychiatrist could "adjust medications." Our short term goals could be "symptom management" or "behavior modification." The long term goal might be "return to the community" or "living in a group home format." Given the simplicity of the options, it seemed logical that a computer could replace our activity.

It was a mystery to me at first, why Gina, who was so intelligent, behaved in such a way as to lose all her privileges. At the time, I was assuming that it was obvious anyone would want to leave the hospital, and her goal must be to get out. In the rehabilitation ward where I spent one afternoon a week, I had been impressed with the ability of schizophrenic patients to adapt and use the state hospital system. For example, I got to know a young Mexican immigrant, Juan Sanchez[27], who was on the point of being released. As I sat with him and his friends one day, he told me the story of his involuntary committal. His family were terribly poor farm workers and had moved around a lot while he was a child. He fell further behind in school and soon refused to go. The school medical doctor had examined him and during the examination had implanted a black metal box in his brain. Though the box had not been picked up in x-rays, he knew this was a trick of the medical staff who wished to control him. Ever since that time, the box sent him messages whenever he watched television telling him things about himself. When the family brought him to a psychiatrist for a consultation, he was committed to the state mental hospital. Here was a case of paranoid schizophrenia that the medications hadn't helped. Why, then, was he being released? "Because," Juan explained, "everyone knows the doctors here are only concerned with delusions, or other very specific symptoms, so you have to be careful when you talk with them never to admit to delusions. After a few weeks, they will send you home." The medications he had been given were, in his view, part of the plot to make him compliant, and he planned to stop taking them as soon as he left.

Because the diagnostic procedures in the hospital were based on observed symptoms, when there were no symptoms to observe the disease was consid-

---

[27] Name changed.

ered to be in remission due to successful drug therapy. Juan had "beat the system," and perhaps this in itself was evidence he was recovering. One of the symptoms of schizophrenia is supposed to be the loss of social adaptation, but Juan had understood the rules of his social environment all too well.

Another patient in the hospital, Nana Ajanaku[28], was a well-educated woman who was an African immigrant with many problems in the outside world relating to housing and employment. She had been committed after she conceived the idea that her television set, when it was turned off, broadcast Congressional hearings in which she was awarded a certain property in a nearby city because of her special status. She started to spend all her time on the porch of this house, ringing the doorbell and telling the people who lived inside they were evicted because she wanted her house back. Naturally, they called the police who then brought her to the hospital. After many drug trials, she continued to sit calmly in the dayroom discussing her return to the new home. She appeared normal in every way except for this grandiose delusion. I cannot forget the scene where the agitated treatment team psychiatrist threw up his hands as she patiently explained to him over and over again in her even, cultured voice, that of course she would go back to the house if released. Congress had given it to her. I suspected that she needed the respite of the time in the hospital, and that she could have easily followed Juan Sanchez's strategy if she really wanted to leave. Her delusion, in fact, was proving useful in maintaining her presence in a safe, protected environment. I am not suggesting it was a conscious plan, but I believe from her behavior that she knew well enough the difference between conventional reality and private delusion. She never discussed her delusions except in the treatment team meetings.

It seemed, then, that at least some schizophrenic patients, in certain phases of the illness, had delusions that they could recognize as different from reality and had a choice about how to enact them in their social worlds. The delusions seemed to have the same status as alcohol and drug addictions, or even destructive love affairs: you could know they were considered bad for you and, unable to give them up, could learn to hide them socially while indulging in private vice. Or, alternatively, you could chose to share them in specific situations. The problem did not seem to be so much the loss of outer adaptedness, as a loss of inner reality testing.

I wondered if Gina could make these distinctions and discussed with her what I had observed in the rehabilitation ward. The aides on her ward were afraid of her delusions, but I was actually quite interested in them. I suggested that she sort them, revealing them during our visits, and the rest of the time behaving in the conventional way the staff wished. That way, she could

[28] Name changed.

work her way up through the privilege levels and make her hospital stay more bearable.

Almost overnight, Gina's behavior altered dramatically on the ward. The staff log entries started to say, "Patient cooperative and helpful on this shift." or "Patient quiet and agreeable." Her privilege levels went up. Within a week she could visit the store, cafeteria, and hairdresser. She looked better and more alert because there was more social stimulation in her day. In the recreation area, several male patients were soon courting her attention. It was considered a kind of miracle cure, and the medical staff huddled for a new evaluation as the observed symptoms were now different. My status rose on the ward. But I believed nothing at all had really changed, and that there was the possibility of a profound gulf just below the surface.

While Gina told me her story and worked on drawings over many hours in the consulting room, I looked for signs of her illness. I often thought it must all be a mistake. She seemed much more "normal" and related than many of the hospital staff that were caring for her. In time, I began to see some clues. At one end there was "problem A," a slight lack of detail in her life history stories. We could go back to Frank, his family, and college days; but eventually we landed in a kind of fog where beginnings and endings became indistinct. She remembered, but the memories didn't have a complete grip on the past. Of course, everyone forgets what happened ten years ago, and we all construct a "myth" about our history, selecting some events as important and others as unimportant in a process that is only partly conscious. But for most people, once the myth is complete, we commit to it as reality-binding. We treat it as a kind of inner photograph of real events as known through the lens of our personal point of view. In Gina, the lens didn't quite focus. Her inner photographs were blurred, so she couldn't tell parts of her story.

A blurring of boundaries occurred in another area as well, "problem B," that had to do with metaphor. Her descriptions were full of the imaginative tropes used by creative people everywhere, but sometimes I lost the line between the "as-if" quality and reality. For example, she told me her mother filled her with "spooky ideas." I understood this to mean that her mother was superstitious, and spoke to her children of bad luck, sin, and punishment by a supernatural being. I don't think this is uncommon and I accepted it as a literal description of her experience. Another day, she told me a certain nurse gave her "the red feeling" on the back of her neck. I tried to watch what my own reactions were to the same nurse and discovered that her critical, cold, and suspicious demeanor made me slightly anxious. So perhaps Gina was reporting a somatic reaction to the nurse's treatment of her. Yet sometimes, these metaphors seemed to slip to another level entirely. For example, she told me she had felt a dark sadness within her all her life, and felt she was haunted by Beelzebub, the wife of Methuselah. Because Methuselah is the "oldest man," Beelzebub could be the oldest woman, or perhaps the shadow side of Methuselah. I suppose in Jungian psychology we could translate this to mean she felt something ancient and archetypal was at work in her. I couldn't be sure whether this was a bizarre delusion of thought control, or an imaginative as-if fantasy. Here problem A and problem B met and interacted. One can't distinguish the line between fantasy and reality with an inner soft-focus lens. Because of Gina's incomplete memory grip on her experience, I couldn't find a way to formulate a question that would help sort this out. When I tried, we encountered fog. Occasionally, we moved up to a level of definite delusional material, where Beelzebub came out of her stomach as a green man, her mother turned into a crow and followed her, controlling her psyche, and inner voices in conversation told her what to do or say. These notions seem clearly to fall in the category of bizarre delusions, which warrant a diagnosis of paranoid schizophrenia.

In our daily work together, Gina was gentle, open, and friendly. She was always happy to see me come through the door and usually was waiting for me. I tried to be supportive without pushing her in any way, waiting for her to indicate what we could do with each hour. She had a good imagination so that reflections about her life and art work representing her experience symbolically interpenetrated. She loved doing it and soon proved very expressive. A series of family portraits and scenes from childhood brought back a flood of emotional memories. A self portrait in red had a tear-shaped hole at the heart labeled "anxiety." A horse grazed near an old dead tree with a tear-shaped knot at heart level and "phantom" green branches that had sprouted new leaves.

One day she wanted to work in clay and decided to make one of the trees she had been drawing from her memories of the family farm. She rolled out green and brown clay flat and shaped it into the form of a two-dimensional "pancake" tree. Then she made a yellow island and tried to stand her tree on it. I watched in fascination and horror as the tree flopped over again and again because it didn't have the strength to stand up. Though I tried to hide it, I was frustrated to the nth degree watching her. I needed the tree to stand up, but Gina was philosophical about the affair. She thought maybe it was all right if the tree lay down on the island. I proposed to give her another piece of clay to build up the trunk of the tree. She used it to build a wall of clay on the outside of the island, between her and me. She wondered if the colors of clay she had chosen might be the colors of the national flag of Sweden, her former husband's home country.

As we discussed what all this might mean, it became clear, I believe, to both of us, that Gina and I had different agendas regarding her illness and that mine had to change. I had unconsciously hoped her illness was a temporary mistake of some kind and wanted to be able to imagine her someday healthy and free. I needed her and the tree to stand up, but I didn't know how that might happen. I couldn't then, and still cannot, bear the thought that she will spend her entire life in a place like ward R. For Gina, on the other hand, her schizophrenia had been something like a solution for insoluble problems. "I am not finished with my schizophrenia yet," she told me, "or it is not finished with me." Essentially, she wanted to remain in the hospital because she did not feel strong enough in her current state to cope with the outside world, and especially, her family of origin. If I could not go along with the program, I would have to be walled off. She knew that I was concerned about her and that I was worried about the tree that couldn't stand up by itself. Occasionally, she reassured me. "Don't worry," she said, "one day I will be able to make a good tree." I realized from this discussion I needed to face the unthinkable and that in doing so, I could perhaps make a space for the unthinkable gulf I felt in Gina's psyche.

A few days later, in a particularly moving session, which she declared to be the best we had spent, she quietly drew a small yellow circle, surrounded by bands of green, blue, and violet. The circle, she said, was something like the host in church. The green surrounding it was nature, and the blue, peace. The final purple band was God. She imagined that this host could transform her, if she could find a way to swallow it. We thought it looked like an egg or seed; perhaps it was the seed from which a strong standing tree could grow. She decided to draw in the earth and sky and a green grass nest for the seed to grow in, working in hushed and focused silence. Afterward, we took the picture to her room and taped it to the wall next to her bed so she could remember it.

This session led to a discussion of a number of religious themes. If there was a God, she wondered, why had he given her this illness? Perhaps her concern with Beelzebub and Methuselah was an attempt to find a wider framework in which to think about a life in which good and evil mixed freely. She thought schizophrenia was like not having the center the host represented, and that when you had this disease you were forced to try to steal other people's center. The picture of the host was a numinous image in our work for many days, its simple mandala form functioning as a Jungian Self image; but I was also aware of Jung's many references to the idea that no one needs an image of unity more than someone who is fragmented and dissociated.

After we had worked this way for a number of weeks, Gina seemed to become more thoughtful and even a little depressed. This sometimes happens in the course of the healing processes set off by analysis. In outpatient practice, clients often decide to take some time off work during this period to enter into a kind of meditative discernment for some weeks or months. They sleep and dream more and try to express what they are feeling in creative projects. I usually advise them to go with the process, while paying attention to the need for a healthy diet and adequate exercise. The issues of feeling comfortable and protected are also important in such transitions. Often in this time they cook special favorite childhood foods or become closer to certain friends or relatives who accompany their process. They may buy or make special "healing symbols" – a picture, candle, sculpture, plant, bowl, or religious artifact – which, like Winnicott's "transitional objects," seem to be comforting and holding during painful moments. Gina did not have any of these possibilities open to her. If she attempted to step out of the strict program of the ward regime, it was viewed as seriously aberrant behavior and punished. One day she felt too tired and depressed to get out of bed at the wake-up call. When the aides came and attempted to drag her out, she pushed them away. Soon, a Major Incident was happening, and Gina was again restrained and secluded. During this time, an older relative to whom she had been very close died without a wished-for good-bye phone conversation, contributing to the stress and sadness of her inner life.

One day when I came into the ward, she was in confrontation with the nurses. The medications station was open, and Gina was across the room, eyeing it like an angry bull. Clearly she was agitated and feeling desperate. I asked her what she needed and she said she had to have caffeine or amphetamines. She seemed to feel she was falling into a hole and did not have the energy to prevent it without the drugs which were forbidden. We went into the consulting room, and I asked her to show me what she was feeling by drawing it. She filled a paper with chaotic and angry red, blue, and black scribbles. They covered everything and went off the edge, leaving no space in her world for anything else. Then I asked if we could not think of a way to contain them, the way we were now contained in the consulting room. She drew a blue circle, and filled the circle with red, blue and black, but it did not go over the edge, leaving space on the paper for something else. This interested her and she decided to draw a tree to the left of the angry circle. All of this activity took about twenty minutes. When she was finished, she noticed she was quite calm and the terrible feeling was gone. She drew a bluebird by the side of the tree. We had taken a detour from another Major Incident.

The problem, we decided in our discussion, was not having a container for her feelings. The amphetamines were a symbol for a physical container, but the art therapy and our discussion provided other symbols for containment. When the feelings had a container, there was room for an observing ego, which, like the tree, could stand outside and maintain an independent point of view. In this hour, I felt that I had watched a war between what I have been calling problem A and problem B. Monstrous feelings from the inner world had overwhelmed her. Flooded by their intensity, a kind of fog seemed to take over her attention, so that she was in the grip of archaic impulses. When she had a symbolic model to channel the feelings, emotion and impulses could pour into the model, leaving her free as the "modeler," a creative center separate from the momentary experience.

I appeared to be functioning as a kind of bridge for this modeling because I treated her problem as symbolic rather than literal. When she asked for drugs on the ward, the nurses assumed she literally wanted the drugs and set up a massive and often angry defensive system to keep her physically separated from them. When she asked me for drugs, I saw "drugs" as schema that she was using to try to organize her chaotic experience. In my view, "drugs" was a name for what Jung called a complex, a network of emotionally-toned contents that attempted to contain and model her inner world. In this case, the schema was part of a maladaptive paradigm. By treating it as a symbol, we could imagine it differently and create a climate for change. There was also a factor of emotional relatedness, one could even say love. The fact that Gina and I had an intense personal relationship probably added a weight to the schema we developed together. On her own, she was held by the habitual complex. With my supportive mirroring, new schema could sometimes begin to outweigh the old.

Because I have an evolutionary perspective, I believe that models can grow and evolve. Human beings, as the outcome of millions of years of natural selection, have developed to be able to respond adaptively to environmental change through a broad range of creative strategies. The survivors of this evolutionary process had ever greater neural and brain capacity, which is related to the ability to create more complex models. My appearance on ward R was an environmental change for Gina, and it seemed to be triggering the trying out of new schemata.

By rejecting her models as literal, delusional, unimportant, or forbidden, the medical staff appeared to me to be preventing change. In their paradigm, her behavior was so deviant and unconventional it needed to be sedated, restrained, secluded, and locked up like the medications, the nursing station, and the hospital itself. Because the aides had been taught to think of schizophrenics as dangerous and unpredictable, they were afraid of Gina, and when people are afraid they are defensive and cold. Then, relationships take place, not under a schema of love or guidance, but under one of control. A few years earlier, this would have been enacted through the metaphor of white uniforms for the hospital staff, indicating the intention to isolate and sterilize. No one actually thought schizophrenia was caused by bacterial infection, but there was a transfer of schemata from the laboratory to the mental hospital setting. Gina entered the hospital during the post-60's era, so the staff wore street clothes. They were distinguished from the patients by badges resembling those worn at nuclear reactors indicating who had the clearance to enter zones of potential radioactivity. In this model, the patients could be considered dangerously contaminated, and it was important to prevent a possible chain reaction. What was new and unpredictable was treacherous.

I have no way of knowing whether it was some factor in the outer situation, our work, or an endogenous development in her psyche that moved Gina into a new phase. When I came into the hospital one Monday, a different Gina was waiting for me, the one I had always known must be there. She seemed to have entered a deep uncharted forest filled with fascinating, strange, and unpredictable phantasms. She recognized me and was happy to see me and spend an hour in the consulting room. But she was so busily occupied in exploring the forest that she only had a few moments to come out and talk. She would begin a theme in conversation, only to be distracted by an inner drama that would stop her in mid-sentence.

Gina didn't seem surprised or panicked by this turn of events. It was familiar territory she had been visiting for years. Thinking about it later, I tried to imagine the landscape. It seemed to me that normally functioning people have worked up an ego structure like a big city with many communications networks – roads, electrical lines, phone, and computer hookups. Gina, by contrast seemed to be living in a small village near a wilderness area. Some communications pathways were installed, but if you walked through the village for a while in any direction, you would soon come to the edge of a forest without roads or human cultivation. At this margin, the lack of fixed communications infrastructure – problem A – left open the possibility of an encounter with an archaic "other" in the wilderness – problem B. The symbols that could form channels for her monstrous feelings were like trails cut through the wilderness. She didn't seem to know how to create new trails, and she didn't have as many roads as other people.

Of course, every city has a margin, but in large cities, one could live for a long time without ever encountering it. If one lives in a highly developed and civilized landscape, where cities run into each other, the wilderness could be reduced to fenced-in parks and never become known. The goal of medical and modern urban technology seemed to me to involve constructing this second kind of landscape. My preference was for some of each, with the capacity to make new trails when necessary.

As I continued to sit with Gina while she floated through her inner world, she tried to share it with me. Sometimes she reported the news: "Nancy has come back from Italy where they were having a civil war. I thought she was lost in hell, but she has come back." She had the instinct to want to organize some of the material by sorting and discussing it, and a counter instinct to suppress it. Often there were inner debates between competing voices that I was kept apprised of. "Janice, can I speak to Helene about my secrets?" She would be silent for a while, and then shrug her shoulders apologetically: "Holly says no."

Little by little, I began to make out the outlines of what I took to be fragmented experiences of the past or a "pathogenic secret." There were frequent attempts to draw "St. Francis of Assisi," a head with purple or green eyes who always looked frighteningly demonic. With each attempt I would get bits of a story that couldn't be spoken. He was connected thematically with Dr. Marconi, the resident medical doctor at the hospital, who, I later learned, gave Gina a gynecological exam each year. Sometimes she said his name over and over, in apparent anguish. Once she snatched a drawing of St. Frances from the table and crumpled it up, saying "This isn't St. Francis of Assisi!" Another time, "I'm tired of being angry and sad. I won't help him masturbate anymore," or "I was furious when he locked me in the barn," or "I think Carlo hurt Nancy. Is that a delusion? I think he burned her." After several completed pictures of St. Francis, she announced, "I think he's burning in hell."

Every few days, she attempted to draw a kind of ladder or stairway in pale pinks and blues which I associate with early childhood experience. Each time it appeared, it was a little longer and more solid. Meanwhile, her ability to take some control over the material by organizing fantasy excursions gradually grew. We could explore together. A typical example:

> "Let's go on a trip to Africa."
> I: OK, what shall we do?
> She: I have a heavy load to carry. I don't know if I can make it.
> I: Perhaps I could help you carry it.
> She: Wouldn't it hurt you?
> I: I don't think so. I'm quite strong and used to hiking.
> She: It is a beautiful landscape.
> I: What do you see?
> She: There are giraffes and other wonderful animals.
> I: Can we go further?
> She: It might be dangerous. A snake could eat you, or a rhino could stick his horn in your horse.
> I: What would happen then?
> She: [long silence] Dr. Marconi [silence] I have a heavy load.

I had read Dr. John Perry's reports of work with psychotic patients at Agnew State Hospital in San Francisco. He had recorded the delusional material in many cases of first-episode psychosis in which he believed the psyche of the patients was autonomously enacting a kind of ritual healing strategy. The delusions took a characteristic course as the patients returned to health. He claimed that if the patients were protected, supported, and understood during this process, a spontaneous rebuilding of personality structure could take place. Through many different mythologies similar to typical narratives of shaman's journeys, Perry's patients imagined a world fragmented and torn apart, then separated into opposites, and finally, reunited and reborn in a new era of harmony. Usually, this process completed itself in six to twelve weeks. Most of his patients were never rehospitalized, unlike the vast majority of schizophrenics in America. So I was not surprised when Gina began to spontaneously produce a set of similar images.

It began one day when she came in and reported a dream: "I caused the end of the world, but now there was a new hope for harmony." Over a period of several weeks, I heard the story of a world war. There were two teams and two different principles. In America, John Kennedy was a hero, and if you knew things about him that would ruin his reputation, you weren't allowed to tell because it would weaken the war effort. Then the FBI would send people to watch you and tap your phone and listen to your thoughts to make sure you never told what you knew. Gina had been raised in America but she knew things about Kennedy's dark past in Ireland. The FBI had probed her and spoken to her about extortion. She had cousins still living in Ireland who would be put in danger. On the other side were the Russians and the KGB. The Soviet Union was a place where questions were asked and people wanted to know the truth. Gina wondered if I had visited the Soviet Union and how close Switzerland, where she knew I had lived, was to Russia. Switzerland is a neutral country in world wars, a safe place that harbors refugees and Jungian analysts. She wanted to know if she could come to visit Switzerland. Near the end of this time, she reported another dream: "I married my lover from the Soviet Union." It seemed to me from this material that some kind of internal war had been sapping her energy for years.

I cannot say what might have happened if I had been able to work with Gina in another kind of institutional setting for a longer period of time. Given the environment in ward R, it seemed her process could not be supported, protected, and understood. I believe that the conditions for healing did not exist where we were. I also don't know if there were enough energy resources in her inner "village" to begin the construction of new roads in the uncharted territories. Her schemata – the war between Russia and America – seemed to be going through a spontaneous evolution; but I didn't know if she could observe it and make something of it. The schemata seemed to function apart from the binding paradigms of her ego world, and I didn't know where the point of contact could be.

I dreamed at this time that she came to my house and put all of the furniture out in the yard. The dream image captured my felt sense of her psychic process. In the "village" part of her personality, thoughts, feelings, and fantasies appeared to be "housed" in an observing point of view through a reality-binding paradigm. The schemata concerning Russia and America seemed to be an attempt to organize and house the furniture out in the yard. The schemata were evolving outside the container of voluntary thinking processes. I suspected that the only interaction between the Russia-America schemata and the "village" of her organized ego function occurred in our hours together.

By the time I was ready to leave the hospital, Gina was once again back in her inner village and could reflect on the situation. "It's too bad," she said, "you are not going to stay in the hospital for several years. If we could have met together for a long time, I think it would have worked." The fact that she believed she, and our work together, had a healing potential would certainly have been a strong factor in any possible transformation of her situation. On the other hand, in American mental hospitals, schizophrenia is considered to have a very poor prognosis when symptoms have developed over a long period as they had in Gina's case.

I think I saw some small changes over the time we worked together. Perhaps the most important for me was that Gina started to treat other patients on the ward the way she was being treated by me. She became interested in them and started to listen, to feel their suffering, to try to comfort. I would like to think our time together provided an experience of relatedness she was able to use to make her life more bearable. I hope I didn't make it any worse, but it almost doesn't seem possible. I still often think about Gina, because there is much unfinished in our encounter and joint reflection. We have listened together in an ancient wilderness. It is not the kind of experience you forget, and there are still sounds I am trying to hear.

There was a wonderful minister in the hospital, an older man who, after retiring from a successful career and raising a family, had felt a calling to religious work. His ministry was in the hospital where he attempted to help when he could. I arranged a meeting between him and Gina, and he agreed to go on seeing her after I left. In the hour we all spent together, Father Thomas suggested prayer. We held hands while he spoke about God's grace and capacity to comfort. His quiet strength and calming words provided some structure for our parting. When he was finished, he asked Gina if she wanted to say a prayer. After a long silence, she offered, "Please make children safe, everywhere in the world."

3. Evolving Speech

We are all *chiasmatic borderlands, liminal areas where new shapes, new kinds of action and responsibility, are gestating in the world.*[29]

– Donna Haraway

If Gina and Edward had developed schizophrenia in Africa, Latin America, or India, rather than in the United States or Europe, their chances of healing might have been ten or twelve times greater. Cross-cultural anthropological and medical research during the last twenty years has yielded some rather surprising results. Though about one percent of the population develops symptoms of schizophrenia sometime in life in every culture studied, the course and outcome of the illness varies dramatically. The World Health Organization (WHO) has sponsored several ongoing studies of schizophrenia that have shown that environment has a profound effect on the course of this illness. For example, in one report, five years after onset, sixty-six percent of the schizophrenic patients studied in Nigeria and India were asymptomatic. In the same study, only five percent of those in Denmark and Russia were asymptomatic, and sixty percent were still in active phases of psychosis.[30]

The first WHO study was begun in 1968, when the International Pilot Study of Schizophrenia, or IPSS, located 1202 patients in nine countries. An internationally trained psychiatric staff attempted to ensure common standards of interview and selection. They discovered that the syndromes labeled schizophrenia in the DSM could be found in all populations at about the same rate. They were very surprised to find, however, that "the two year follow up data revealed that patients with an initial diagnosis of schizophrenia had a considerably better course and outcome in developing countries than in developed countries. This remained true whether clinical outcome,

---

[29] Haraway, D., "The Promise of Monsters: A Regenerative Politics for Inappropriate/d Others," in: Grossberg, L., Nelson, C., Treichler, P.A., eds., *Cultural Studies*, p. 314.

[30] Leff, J., Sartorius, N., Jablensky, A., Korten, A., & Ernberg, G., "The international pilot study of schizophrenia: Five year follow-up findings," *Psychological Medicine*, 1992, 22:131-145.

social outcome, or a combination of the two was considered."[31] Not only did schizophrenia have a better outcome, but so, in fact, did many other mental illnesses.

> It is noteworthy that patients in the IPSS sample with diagnoses other than schizophrenia also had better clinical and social outcomes in developing than developed countries. Therefore it is possible that the social and cultural factors responsible for a good outcome operate across diagnostic boundaries.[32]

Researchers speculated in the discussion of their results that there must be something in the cultural attitude toward mental illness in the developing countries that promoted healing.

> In terms of clinical outcome, measured by symptomatic status at the time of follow-up, time spent in a psychotic episode, and pattern of course, schizophrenic patients from Agra (India) and Ibadan (Nigeria) did conspicuously better than from the six other centers. An exceptionally good social outcome also characterized these patients, and additionally, the patients from Cali (Columbia). This resulted despite the fact that Cali had double the proportion of patients with the worst pattern of course as those in Agra or Ibadan. This may be explained by a much greater tolerance and acceptance of symptomatic schizophrenic patients in Cali than there is in developed countries. Supportive evidence for this is provided by a survey of public attitudes to the mentally ill in Cali (Leon and Micklin, 1971) and by a study of relatives' attitudes to schizophrenic patients in Mexican-American families (Jenkins, et al.1986).[33]

It seems that the schemata of the people surrounding schizophrenics could have a healing effect. Could they also have something to do with the development of the illness in the first place? This would imply that the locus of mental illness and healing was in the schemata rather than in the brain.

A follow-up study on schizophrenia was begun by WHO in 1975. A total of 1379 schizophrenic patients in twelve centers in ten countries were contacted beginning in 1978. The patients were followed for two years to determine the course and outcome of their illness. In this research, schizophrenia was found to occur in all the cultures studied in the same patterns of age and gender onset, leading the researchers to conclude that the same disorder had been identified in different cultures. The new study attempted to follow only patients who were making their first lifetime contact with a mental health system. One of the criticisms of the earlier study was that there was no way to tell whether the statistics from the developing countries had been skewed by admitting more first-contact patients, who would therefore be more likely to go into remission than chronic schizophrenics. The new research design

---

[31] Ibid., p. 132.
[32] Ibid., p. 145.
[33] Ibid., p. 142.

controlled this factor and was able to find very similar patients in all the centers used for the study. As a result, it was more able to study what its designers called a "natural history" of schizophrenia, not already contaminated by years of contact with the attitudes and definitions of the medical model. This area has been poorly explored during nearly a century of research on schizophrenia. The authors assessed the state of current understanding:

> Few clinical studies have been based on representative samples of cases in early stages of the illness, before its symptoms and course have been modified by treatment and, very likely, by social attitudes. This has hampered research on the natural history of schizophrenia, which continues to be viewed by many as a process invariably leading to some degree of deterioration and disablement.[34]

In fact, the studies showed the opposite. In some developing countries, two-thirds of the patients who become ill and were diagnosed as schizophrenics, were in full remission after two years.[35] They were able to return to their social environments with no impairment of functioning.

The outcome of the second study was the same as the first. It was summed up as follows:

> The Outcome study replicated in a clear, and possibly conclusive way the major finding of the IPSS, that of the existence of consistent and marked differences in the prognosis of schizophrenia between the centers in developed countries and the centers in developing countries. On five out of six of the measures and dimensions of two-year course and outcome which have been used in the analyses reported here (pattern of course, proportion of the follow up period in complete remission, proportion of the time during which the patient was on anti-psychotic medication, proportion of the follow-up period spent in psychiatric hospital, and proportion of the follow-up during which the social functioning of the patient was unimpaired), patients in the developing countries show a more favorable evolution than their counterparts in the developed countries (the only dimension showing no difference was the percentage of the follow-up period spent in psychotic episodes). As demonstrated by the multivariate statistical analysis, these differences between patients in the two types of setting cannot be explained by other variables, and remain highly significant when such possible influences are controlled for. It can now be said with a fair amount of confidence that they are not the result of differing sample composition in the two groups of centers, in the sense of a selection bias in favor of more pre-inclusion chronicity in the developed countries and

---

[34] Jablensky, A., Sartorius, N., Ernberg, G., Anker, M., Korten, A., Cooper, J.E., Day, R., & Bertelsen, A., "Schizophrenia: Manifestations, incidence, and course in different countries," *Psychological Medicine, Monograph Supplement 20, 1992*, p. 80.
[35] Ibid., p. 2.

more recent onsets in the developing countries. In this study, the average length of the illness prior to inclusion into the study did not differ significantly between the developing and the developed cultures. ... Having excluded for lack of support by the data described in this report, the explanation of the observed difference between the prognosis of schizophrenia in developing and developed countries as an artefact, a strong case can be made for a real pervasive influence of a powerful factor which can be referred to as "culture."[36]

More than half of the schizophrenics in the study from the developing countries were never hospitalized. Only about sixteen percent were on antipsychotic medication for most of the follow-up period. The strongest indicators of good prognosis seemed to be related to how much of a social network the patient had. It did not seem to matter if it was made up of family members, close friends, or casual friends. Of the factors studied, what was most important in a good outcome was social inclusion, meaning some social network rather than isolation. The results of this study are summarized in Table 1.[37]

	Course and outcome category	Developing countries	Developed countries
1	Remitting course with full remission (1+3+5)	62.7	36.8
	Continuous or episodic psychotic illness, without full remission (2+4+6+7)	35.7	60.9
2	In psychotic episodes 1-5% of FU period	18.4	18 7
	In psychotic episodes 76-100% of FU period	15.1	20.2
3	Incomplete remission 0% of FU period	24.1	572.
	In complete remission 76-100% of FU period	38.3	22.3
4	No antipsychotic medication throughout FU	5.9	2.5
	On antipsychotic medication 76-100% of FU period	15.9	60.8
5	Never hospitalized	55.5	8.1
	Hospitalized for 76-100 % of FU period	0.3	2.3
6	Impaired social functioning throughout FU	15 7	41.6
	Unimpaired social functioning for 76-100% of FU period	42.9	31.6

Table 1 – WHO study summary
Percentage of patients in the developing countries and in the developed countries falling into selected categories of course and outcome variables

[36] Ibid., p. 89.
[37] *Psychological Medicine, Monograph Supplement 20, 1992.* "Schizophrenia: Manifestations, incidence, and course in different cultures," by A. Jablensky et. al., p. 64, Table 4.10. Reprinted with the permission of Cambridge University Press.

Mental illness and healing are apparently understood very differently in different cultures. Accounts of ritual healing events in the developing world abound in anthropological literature. Various hypotheses have been advanced to account for their results. It is clear that each culture must attempt to make sense of illness through local cultural schemata, but these definitional models vary widely. The illness that psychiatrists diagnose as schizophrenia has been seen variously as possession by ancestral spirits, a punishment for the omission of religious duties, an invasion by witchcraft, an outcome of powerlessness and economic oppression, or the result of a biological abnormality. Each paradigm brings with it a complex network of social expectations and emotional responses. What is so interesting here is that the modern scientific paradigm that denies the existence of spirits has been less successful in treatment of schizophrenia than those cultures that include such schemata.

Although there is no way to know exactly what type of healing environments worked on the individuals in the WHO research, many studies show characteristic scenarios and attitudes in the developing world. It seems to be the case that people now often combine personal and traditional ritual with visits to modern medical clinics. In any case, indigenous attitudes toward mental illness in each culture provide the backdrop against which it is understood. In an environmental reflection, these schemata seem important. Although it is impossible to explore the rich ethnographic material available on healing in any detail here, nevertheless one may be able to see the outlines of general differences in attitude toward mental illness and healing between industrialized and developing countries by looking at a some examples.

A group of anthropologists working with the *Grupo de Registro y Comunicacion Audiovisual* of Temuco Chile, produced a videotape on traditional Mapuche healing ritual in 1988 called *Vida Entre Dos Mundos*, or "Life Between Two Worlds."[38] The Mapuche are an indigenous tribal group in southern Chile never conquered by the Spanish. The videotape documents the illness and healing in 1987 of a young man named José Arnoldo D. from a village near Temuco. The story has many elements unique to Mapuche culture, but one can also analyze the general character of the human environment created.

José was raised near an indigenous community by a *Mapuche* father and mother from a local non-*Mapuche* farm family. He went to a nearby village to find work as a young adult. There he encountered the racism of the dominant Spanish-speaking culture and worked at a low-paid, low-status construction job. In time, he stopped functioning socially and was brought to the village hospital. His doctor explains on the tape that the young man

---

[38] Oyarce, A.M., *Vida Entre Dos Mundos*.

was first brought to the hospital in January, 1987, and then treated on an outpatient basis. He was given vitamin B injections, aspirin, and valium. According to the patient, he was told he was lazy and sent home. José's condition continued to deteriorate, and a month later the family brought him to the regional mental hospital in Temuco. An interview with his psychiatrist, wearing a white coat, is shown on the tape. The patient was admitted to the hospital with auditory and visual hallucinations and "poor reality judgment" and a diagnosis of schizophreniform psychosis. He was released a month later with a ten-day follow-up appointment that he did not keep.

Then the tape presents an interview with his mother, who has not accepted the psychiatric diagnosis. She took her son from the hospital to the respected healer of their home village, a *Machi*. Traditionally, in *Mapuche* culture, it is women who play this role, and the inherited mythology seems to focus primarily on a moon Goddess. The *Machi* is shown in her home, where the young man has been installed in preparation for healing ceremonies that will be organized in the village. The *Machi* then diagnoses the illness as *huelefan quelonco*, which she understands as "a deviation of purpose or distorted thought." It is a dangerous illness she says, caused by a damaging environment which José must henceforth avoid. The *Machi* explains it is a problem of *biches*. This could be translated as insect pests or as unwanted, irritating intrusions, schemata, or problems. It is impossible to know exactly what level of metaphor she intends.

The patient remains at her home during an extended period of assessment and healing, living with her family, participating in their daily life, and drinking herbal preparations. According to the *Machi*, the illness causes a lot of work as she gradually, step by step, brings the patient back to the memory of his homeland and his home. She says, "He has to be shown 'light.' He has to be taken in someone's arms. He has to be appreciated."

But the human aspect of the treatment is only the beginning. For a real healing, a divine intercession is needed. Healing can occur only by the grace of the gods. Prayer and ritual are crucial in calling ancestral spirits for help. *Machis* are believed to have the capacity to enter into a trance, a *cohimin*, during which they gain healing energies from the spirit world if the gods agree and the ritual is done in the right way by the whole community.

Then the ceremony is presented, a *Machitun*, which has never been filmed before and goes on for several days and nights. The whole village is involved, perhaps 60 people. There is a great deal of movement, singing, and dancing connected with a story of a cosmic battle. The illness is contextualized within a cultural myth and given meaning and orientation through its narrative. In the center, the machi stands part way up a tree, a sacred ladder in the center of a sacred altar, and enters a trance state which brings her close to the world of the supernatural. She prays, "You made me *Machi*. I have planted my

twelve trees on an altar. I have my drum. ... Mother in the midst of the blue
sky, Father in the midst of the blue sky ... we pray on our knees for this sick
young man ... To have a good tomorrow, this child who has suffered so much
will be refreshed, he whom you have created." José sits wrapped in a blanket
below the tree. He has been given herbal tea and he is sweating. Psychic
"warriors" enter and leave, calling back the soul of the sufferer: "Return to be
with your people, José Arnoldo! Return to your family!" Finally it is over, and
everyone is revitalized. A big meal is prepared, and José is unwrapped and
fed. Every man, woman, and child in the village goes to him individually,
shaking his hand and welcoming him back to the community. The ritual has
worked. Afterward José smiles and can talk about his experience in a way
considered normal in his group.

In a very similar community healing atmosphere, Psychiatrist Vera Bührmann from South Africa reports on her participation in healing practices
among the Xhosa and Pedi in her country.[39] Those who are ill, and those who
wish to receive training present themselves to traditional healers. Community rituals are organized that include singing, clapping, drumming, and
dancing over several days and nights. Ancestors are considered to be drawn
into the healing effort by these activities. Possession states occur in which the
ancestor and the spirit of the healer contend for space and power so that they
can make an accommodation. The ill participate, drink herbal medicines,
and sweat in the center of community activity. In the case of the Pedi, a series
of rituals and periods of instruction take place over twelve to eighteen
months. Afterward, the ill may become healers themselves, as they have
demonstrated the capability to bridge the space between ancestors and
community.

Psychiatrist K. Koranteng lectured on related healing rituals among the
Akan of Ghana at the Jung Institute, Zürich, in 1990. Dr. Korentang is a
European-trained psychiatrist who returned to his home country after his
education to study with traditional healers in the countryside. Although
chronic schizophrenia exists at the same rate in urban areas of Ghana as in
Europe, he found it was almost unknown in rural villages where people were
still treated with traditional ritual. He described for us one case in which a
young woman had promised to marry a certain man, who went away for
several years to find work in the city. During his absence, she had married
another. When the first man returned, she suffered a psychotic break. The
family brought her to the compound of a traditional healer, where she was
housed and fed for several weeks while the healer studied the problem. Then
the whole family and all the affected parties were called together for a healing
ritual. The problem was interpreted as one of breaking taboos that offended

[39] Bührmann, M.V., "Psyche and soma: Therapeutic considerations," in: Saayman, G., ed.,
Modern South Africa in Search of a Soul.

ancestors. There was a struggle going on between the requirements of ancestral spirits and the needs of the living. An accommodation, involving sacrifice and prayer, needed to be found through which these conflicting demands could be harmonized. Once this solution was achieved and enacted in ritual, the woman could return to normal. Then she was able to go back to her home village and take up her life anew.

Most contemporary American anthropologists would be more interested in the differences among these cultural situations, the unique local formulations which do not translate into other schemata with equivalence.[40] In a recent work entitled, *Spirits in Culture, History, and Mind*, Robert I. Levy et al stated their concerns.

> Many contemporary scholars argue for confining the treatment of these phenomena to particular communities. They often dismiss the transcultural usefulness of terms like "spirits" and "possession," finding in them various dangers: the imposition of our own biased values and conceptions; the meaning destroying intellectual game of searching for essentialistic and reductionistic explanations; and the submerging of local cultural inventions into abstract schema.[41]

While I respect these important considerations, I think there are also features of healing rituals that can be studied comparatively, particularly those that are large-scale such as the comparison of how many people are involved in the healing activity, how they connect and interact, and for how long. In doing so, we need to be clear that the models through which we make comparisons are not foundational or universal, but simply one lens through which we can frame similarities and differences from a certain perspective. Anthropologist Michael Lambek suggests that local phenomena in different cultures are "incommensurable" but not "incomparable":

> Incommensurability is distinguished from both incompatibility (logical contradiction) and incomparability. The incommensurability argument claims neither that there is an overarching framework in terms of which the key terms could be measured against each other point by point, nor that each is encased in a radically different framework such that comparison between them is impossible. Rather than rule out comparison, it implies that the forms of comparison and interpretation will be multiple. The incommensurability of key concepts is analogous to that of distinct art styles.[42]

As examples of discourse or performance, rituals of healing are messages which separate or connect many or few individuals. They can create novel

---

[40] See, for example, Geertz, C., *Local Knowledge*.
[41] Levy, R.I., Mageo, J.M., and Howard, A., "Gods, Spirits, and History: A Theoretical Perspective," in Mageo, J.M. and Howard, A., *Spirits in Culture, History, and Mind*, p. 20.
[42] Ibid., p. 20.

lines of communication, undermine habitual practices, or set up barriers of exclusion from information-sharing. They can produce comforting and meaning-creating experiences for participants which can then be interpreted variously in many different cultural contexts.

Anthropologist Victor Turner attempted to describe a formal structure of healing rituals.[43] Turner, following the work of von Gennup, has noted that many rituals have a characteristic form. In stage 1, a problem develops in the normal ongoing structural organization of the group. Something no longer fits. The problem is then noted and isolated for special treatment. In stage 2, a special environment is created in the isolated area, called a liminal or marginal space. Here the rules of the normal structure are relaxed, and many experimental and creative possibilities are allowed and encouraged. As a result, people relate less through formal social roles and more through spontaneous expression, sometimes creating a temporary intimate and loving environment that Turner has called *communitás*. One thinks here of *Fastnacht, Mardi Gras,* and Carnival as Western social enactments of *communitás* in liminal space. In this stage, the old order is symbolically overturned. Those high in the social status system – the king, the president, the pope – can be mocked, and those low in the system – the clown, the beggar, the fool – can be enthroned. There is often a symbolic contest or battle between groups, bands, crews, dance teams, or parade floats that is resolved by the crowning of a new king who brings a new reign of harmony. Finally, in stage 3, the renewed participants are reintegrated into the formal social structure, which has been shaken up and reorganized a bit so that there is more "breathing space" and more community acceptance for new ideas. Sometimes, stage 3 is not or cannot be completed, and then there is schism and break up of the previous whole. We could diagram these stages as follows in Figure 3.1.

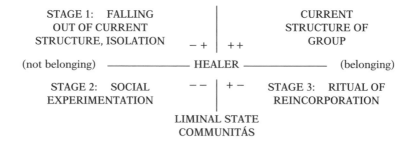

Figure 3.1 – Structure / Liminal Space

---

[43] Turner, V., *The Ritual Process.*

It seems that the rituals for healing schizophrenia that I have described above generally follow this pattern. The patients have each become dysfunctional in their traditional cultures and no longer fit in stage 1. They are removed from home and maintained in the safe environment of the healer, who engages creatively, personally, and emotionally with the inner world of the schizophrenic in stage 2. Hopefully, this produces a liminal state in which a context is provided for the illness, usually in the imagery of a war between worlds or contending powers. The patient and the healer symbolize the illness ritually. That is, they not only speak about the illness, but also engage in some kind of bodily or creative representation of it. The problem may be imagined as the intrusion of something unwanted that has to be exorcised through healing acts. When the patient is considered ready, a ritual of integration takes place in which a war for the soul of the patient may be enacted and completed by the whole group. The renewed patient is then welcomed back to the recreated community with a new status in stage 3. A crucial part of the story is the presence of a charismatic healer. In most cases where this type of healing takes place, the healer is someone who has had a special calling, often in the form of a personal illness followed by a long period of training and preparation. No one in the community believes "just anyone" could manage the ritual. A charismatic healer is a local phenomenon, involving a unique person in a unique community at a unique time in its history.

In many cases as well, the atmosphere of healing is extraordinary, religious, numinous, emotional, and gripping for the participants. It takes place within a rich context of myth and symbol, which hold the most treasured and sacred values of the culture involved. These representations are combined with exhausting physical activities which lead to heightened experiences of feeling and connectedness with the group. The central symbols, Turner noted, seem to be multi-layered. They connect expected social roles with body experience at what he called the oretic or bodily pole, and with religious values at the normative or ideological pole. For example, among the Ndembu where he did field work, the *mudyi* tree is the location of many healing rituals as well as the ritual of first menstruation for women. Its sap represents breast milk, lactation, breasts, and nubility. At first menses, a woman is isolated and buried under leaves at the foot of the tree in the forest away from the village. The tree is then *ifwilu*, the "place of dying" where the child dies and the woman arises. It is also "where the ancestress slept" and "the place where our tribe began." This center of transformation is the creative womb of Ndembu culture, which is a matriarchy. The initiate is attended by a group of women elders. There she fasts, creating an intense bodily experience of isolation and a weak and vulnerable mental state in which social contact is highly impressive. The ritual itself includes drumming, dancing, and singing during which there is a kind of battle of the sexes in which the women lampoon and deride the men. Later they all join together to recreate tribal harmony. Then the woman is instructed by the women of her village in the new knowledge she will need to manage her fertility, sexuality, and childbirth. The tree eventually comes to represent the immortality of the clan, its culture, and ritual itself.[44]

Turner hypothesized that the rituals are effective exactly because a powerful bodily experience is connected through symbol and ritual with social values and religious feeling. The fact that symbols carry many overlaid schemata which combine the oretic and normative poles of meaning is what gives them their power. He wondered in a late article written just before he died, whether these symbols and rituals might be affecting neurological networks in the brain by linking up the older limbic, paleomammalian, or emotion-organizing portions of the brain with newer neocortical layers which underpin intentionality.[45] He thought the oretic or bodily pole of symbols activated in ritual might engage the limbic system, which is closer to control by involuntary systems. The normative pole might connect more with the neocortex, which allows voluntary control over impulse and habit. Human beings might naturally tend toward dissociation between emotional impulses and voluntary control. We all have the potential to stand before a desired but forbidden object with an angel on one shoulder and a devil on the other. Central symbols would be each society's way of encoding the relationship between emotional impulse and voluntary control. Through education, conditioning, and ritual, many different cultural choices might be made about conflict, repression, or cooperation affecting semi-autonomous neurological networks. Because we are intentional beings, and to some degree have voluntary capabilities, we are always in dialogue with the our own desires and the collective consciousness of our home culture. We oscillate all our lives between unconscious acceptance and identification with the values of our companions, and other states of dis-identification and alienation that can lead to despair or creative reordering. Turner suggested that we humans have a potential for inner conflict because our world is mediated by semi-autonomous neurological networks which it is the function of culture and religion to integrate.[46]

Interestingly, it is exactly this link between the limbic system and the neocortex that is thought to be disturbed in schizophrenics.[47] Specifically, it has been theorized that the problem of schizophrenia can be modeled as a failure of the capacity for creating internal representations of environmental

[44] Ibid.
[45] Turner, V., *Body, Brain, and Culture*.
[46] Ibid.
[47] For example, in Scheflen, A., *Levels of Schizophrenia*, p. 141.

context. The world without an integrating context appears as a fragmented set of experiences in conflict with each other. The world then operates according to a rule of chance, without rhyme or reason. Ritual, according to Turner, may function to imprint or encode a harmonious, integrated, and loving relationship, not only between members of the social group, but also within the physiological structure of each individual. Perhaps we could think of schizophrenia, originally described as a schism between thought and emotion, as an environmental illness in which people suffer from a lack of integrative rituals, powerful unifying symbols, and a healing community of elders. Occasionally, even in cultural groups with adequate rituals, there must be cases where the ritual fails to "take" and needs to be repeated. There may be individuals with particular vulnerabilities who need special treatment in every society.

Aspects of the healing rituals described by Turner and other anthropologists have sometimes been reproduced in the Western world in connection with the treatment of mental illness. There are a number of interesting case reports in Jungian literature about the successful healing of schizophrenia. Jungian analyst Dr. C.T. Frey has lectured at the Jung Institute in Zürich about various patients who were treated for many years at the Klinik am Zürichberg.[48] During these years, various patients painted hundreds of pictures that gradually moved from chaotic to ordered forms. The pictures, which were done in the art room of the clinic, were respectfully shared in many analytic hours. An understanding and healing environment was provided for the process in the clinic community. Eventually, several patients were able to leave the clinic and return home to live independently and work. Other such cases are written up by Dr. Heinrich Fierz and Dr. C. A. Meier who also worked at the Klinik.[49]

The healing process at the Klinik has certain similarities with the pattern noted in Turner's work and in the *Mapuche* ritual. The patients were removed from home and had an intense period of contact with a charismatic healer, in this case, a Jungian analyst who had undergone a long period of personal analysis and training. The healing took place in a context where numinous religious and cultural symbols were expected, valued, and interpreted as part of the healing process. Although there was probably less fasting, dancing, or singing than in the tribal examples above, the atmosphere would have been one of intense emotional relatedness between the analyst, other caregivers, and patient. The clinic environment, during its first years, was set up in an open and communal way, with the patients working in groups on gardening

---

[48] Frey, C.T., in a lecture presented at the Jung Institute in Zürich, Switzerland in November of 1992.

[49] Meier, C.A., *Healing Dream and Ritual*, and Fierz, H.K, *Jungian Psychiatry*.

and creative projects as they wished. The entire staff was expected to participate in the healing process.

When we compare both the Jungian and the traditional healing contexts
with the ones in which I found Gina and Edward, some structural differences
leap out. Gina and Edward are being treated through isolation, pacification,
and behavior modification in an attempt to symbolically and physically
"freeze out" the symptoms. This is done partly through neuroleptic medications, which attempt to bind or inhibit excess chemicals in the brain. They
are also isolated from mainstream society until they learn to conform their
behavior to its rules. They are trapped at the beginning of stage 1 in our
diagram. In the healing rituals in the developing world, the patients are being
treated in a heated, emotional, and richly symbolic communal "bath," a kind
of collective "melting" and reforming of structure. They move from stage 2
through a group liminal space to rituals of reincorporation in stage 3. Could
this freezing and melting metaphor help us to understand something about
the environmental factors involved in causing, maintaining, and healing
schizophrenia? There is something frozen, as well, in Western thinking about
personality structure. The DSM[50] assumes that when someone "has" a mental illness, a fixed structure is in place. In the case of schizophrenia, it is
assumed to be chronic and possibly permanent. Many other cultures see
human personality as much more fluid and context-dependent. Anthropologist Clifford Geertz writes that "The Western conception of the person as a
bounded, unique, more or less integrated motivational and cognitive universe, a dynamic center of awareness, emotion, judgement, and action organized into a distinctive whole and set contrastively both against other such
wholes and against its social and natural background, is, however incorrigi-
ble it may seem to us, a rather peculiar idea within the context of the world's
cultures."[51] Yet, it is this bounded whole that is at the center of Western
psychiatric definitions of "normal." Perhaps these cultural schemata are a
clue to differences in outcome.

---

[50] American Psychiatric Association, *Diagnostic and Statistical Manual of Mental Disorders*.
[51] Geertz, C., "From the native's point of view," in: Shweder, R.A. & Le Vine, R.A., eds., *Culture Theory*, p. 126.

4. Patterns in Culture

But whether studying other communities, our communities or any other social phenomenon, it is important to see phenomenon in nature, society, and even in academia, not in its isolation but in its dynamic connections with other phenomena. It is important to remember that social and intellectual processes, even academic disciplines, act and react to each other not against a spatial and temporal ground of stillness but of constant struggle, of movement, and change, even in human thought. In a situation of flux, the effective use of the delicate skills of navigating our way through may well depend on whether we are swimming against or with the currents of change or for that matter whether we are clear in what direction we are swimming, towards or away from the sea of our connections with our common humanity. Local knowledge is not an island unto itself; it is part of the main, part of the sea. Its limits lie in the boundless universality of our creative potentiality as human beings.[52] – Ngugi Wa Thiong'o

If, as the WHO report suggests, something in culture is important in healing schizophrenia, how could we understand this factor? Different subcultures in Europe, Africa, Asia, or the Americas vary greatly in social relations, language, religion, and custom. Is there a useful way these subcultures could be categorized or classified? Anthropologists Mary Douglas has defined two dimensions of information-sharing in social environments that will help to name and understand some characteristics to be considered.[53] Social worlds can be ranked according to "grid" requirements. The grid of a social environment is the network of obligations and customary rituals that constrain individual behavior and communication. In a high-grid subculture, almost every action is considered in reference to the expectations of others. Information is very carefully controlled and hoarded. A "stiff upper lip" is valued over expressive freedom. In a low-grid subculture, one is more liberated to be as eccentric as desired without fear of social censure or conse-

---

[52] Ngugi, wa Thiong'o, *Moving the Center: The Struggle For Cultural Freedoms*, p. 28-29.
[53] First developed by Douglas, M., *Natural Symbols*.

quences. Experimentation and information-sharing can speed up rapidly. In Jungian terms, the persona is at a premium in high-grid environments, while much less important or even devalued in low-grid ones. Of course, human beings are able to foil the expectations of those around them, but there is always a subtle pressure to conform. Each subculture tends to reproduce itself if things are going as expected. Usually, it takes a series of failures or surprises in expected outcomes before people rethink their moral and social codes. Then they can try to change or reconstruct their participation in surrounding subcultures, depending on available resources. Some people may be in a better position to change than others.

Another dimension that cuts across grid is called "group." In high-group subcultures, people feel bonded and connected in identity to all the others, as to a clan, tribal, or kinship environment. In low-group subcultures, people feel alienated and separate from others. These two dimensions yield 4 possible information sharing combinations if superimposed on each other, which have been named, FATALIST, HIERARCHIST, INDIVIDUALIST, and EGALITARIAN. A fifth position in this work is reserved for the HERMIT, the outsider who does not identify with any subculture but sees the connection between socially constructed identity and the informational environment. Each of these positions will be described below. Here, I am adapting a system developed by Michael Thompson, Richard Ellis, and Aaron Wildovsky, in their recent book, *Cultural Theory*.[54]

We could imaginatively graph the information-sharing strategies of any large or small subculture within a society, or any tribal group in the schema shown in Figure 4.1.

The particular names for these dimensions are not important, but the pattern is. Extensive work has been done in cultural anthropology over the last twenty years, exploring how subcultures in each of these sectors are different from the others. Of course, many groups cluster near the middle of the graph, where "environment of evolutionary adaptedness" is written and there it is the difference and uniqueness of each that is most notable. In big cities, there are probably many pockets of each sector mixed together in a chaotic brew.

The idea has been advanced that our makeup as biological organisms is the result, not of the conditions we are in today, but of conditions in the past. Natural selection took place over millions of years in what has been called the "environment of evolutionary adaptedness," or EEA.[55] During several hundred million years, primates and then hominids lived in small kinship bands of probably not more than sixty adults. These must have had some

[54] Thompson, M., Ellis, R., & Wildavsky, A., *Cultural Theory*.
[55] Tooby, J., & Cosmides, L., "The past explains the present," in: *Ethology and Sociobiology* 1990, 11:375-424.

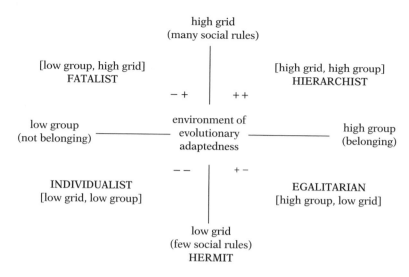

Figure 4.1 – Grid / Group

range of group identity and grid expectations near the middle of our diagram. Natural selection would have favored those individuals who could survive in this type of personally related setting. It has only been in the last five thousand years that large scale civilizations developed, and only in the last five hundred that the huge urban environments of the modern state evolved. Large, rapidly changing urban settings have a much higher incidence of mental illness than either rural or stable urban environments. These new social settings may be placing human beings under stress in characteristic ways, depending on whether group or grid is exaggerated in one direction or another. It is in cases of the extremes that the theory can be most fruitful.[56]

In addition, this research implies that the same person may exhibit very different behavior, and feel very different needs, depending on the type of informational environment he or she is placed in, though each individual can, to some degree, contest conventions creatively and transform the environment. Conscious or unconscious choices about clothing, hair fashions, household furnishings, body posture, facial expression, and life-style send many symbolic social messages to other people whether or not this is intended. Mary Douglas claims in *Natural Symbols* that these messages can indicate cultural patterns.[57] For example, she argues that people in low-grid environments tend to have longer hair than those in high-grid environments within the same society, symbolizing the relaxation of order. On the high-

---

[56] This is not a part of the original grid/group theory.
[57] Douglas, M., *Natural Symbols*.

grid side of American society, for example, could be the crew cuts in the U.S. Marine Corps, the conservative dress of Senators, the short hair of business women. On the low-grid side, there are Rastafarians with dreadlocks, hippies with long hair, and movie stars with flamboyant styles. People may value what appears "natural" and unprocessed on the low-grid side, like natural foods, country gardens, herbal medicine, and wilderness areas. On the high-grid side, people may value what appears skillfully processed – stylish clothing, elegant furnishings, fashionable restaurants, formal settings. Each set of choices can then yield a field of rejected possibilities. According to Mary Douglas, it is from this field, through a "reversal" of some sort, that the liminal for this group is often symbolized. For example, high-grid people can go to Club Med, where they will give up the use of money, last names, and all symbols of status for their two-week stay.

The symbols for what is liminal for each group or individual can be related to what is structural. Liminality is a context-dependent quality. Often, the habitual defines order, and then a partial reversal of what is rejected can symbolize the liminal. Liberating enslaved schemata through the liminal experience can bring a new rush of energy to the psyche. Perhaps this is why Jesus planned to use the stone that the builders rejected and why the alchemists thought the *prima materia* in the alchemical work was that which was despised by others, the crude and common sulfur.

In addition, it is important to stress that we always have the possibility of questioning our surroundings. We are not "determined" by them in any causal or mechanical sense. We might think of social pressure working at the same level as the impulse to yawn when we observe other people yawning. The impulse seems to be triggered by our connection with others, but we can suppress it consciously, and if we are intensely focused, it might not affect us at all. In a similar way, we are linked with our social environment and we tend to reproduce it unconsciously, but we also work on it to change it and assert our own views. We are considering particular vectors of social pressure, but these pressures are environmental gradients. We can protest, resist, or leave the societies in which we find ourselves, and sometimes alter them dramatically by our behavior or ideas.

Those who use this theory believe they can show that, whether social groups are in Nigeria or London, certain general attitudes and ways of behaving are typical in each type of informational subculture. For example, in the ++ corner, HIERARCHISTS are people in traditional societies, bureaucratic organizations, and guilds that are hierarchically organized through custom and ceremony. Information is very carefully controlled from one level to the other of such structures. They tend to be conservative and inclusive toward members who conform and cautious toward strangers and new ideas. Their concept of nature, corresponding to their experience, is that there are cultured and civilized areas that need to be preserved by close observation and attendance as well as wild areas outside from which society needs to be defended. Such societies worry about witchcraft, subversives, crowds, or revolts. They prefer slow, gradual, local changes to sweeping revolutionary agendas and have many unspoken rules about protocol, caste, and deference. It is interesting that the medical staff at Gina and Edward's mental hospital tended to fill these requirements. They had a high group identity with their profession and the other medical staff members and were strongly constrained in their behavior by medical ethics, hospital procedure, and state law. They spent an enormous amount of time each week filling out reports showing that they had met these requirements in their daily activities. They were in an environment that was both high-grid and high-group. Perhaps as a result, the medical teams enforced a strict separation between staff and patients through physical ceremonies of lock-up and verbal idioms of pathology. A literal and symbolic glass wall was in place between "Them" and "Us."

Many medical team members fit this template well and were not particularly uncomfortable with their position in the hospital. Some questioned their work and were thinking about alternatives. Perhaps this is partly a question of psychological types. In Myers-Briggs testing in the United States, it was discovered that large numbers of the people who fill roles in hierarchies are "sensation/judgment" types. The "introverted intuitive/feeling" types who make up only one percent of the population (though the vast majority of Jungian analysts) tend to question, look toward the horizon, propose alternatives, or change jobs.

After I worked with patients for a while at the hospital under the observation of the medical team, some of them asked me to give a series of talks to the staff about how I saw mental illness after Jungian training. It was clear I was asking a different set of questions, and I suppose this evoked curiosity. In response, I presented these environmental reflections. Afterward, I had very fruitful discussions with a number of psychiatrists and psychologists, who brought me some of the articles I have been using in these pages. We were able to work on new models together, and imagine other possibilities. The hierarchical environment still had some space for yeasty recombinations of ideas. Staff seminars were held in a low-grid EGALITARIAN environment of equals, where we could question and critique the work we were doing together. The weekly low-grid sessions in which we took turns presenting were fascinating and rejuvenating. One psychiatrist said to me after a session, "You are seeing us as we have forgotten how to see ourselves."

In the +– corner, EGALITARIAN subcultures share information openly and intensively in societies or groups that are densely connected by emotion, communication, interest, or life-style. There is a high level of group identity, but not many rules about what to say or do. The staff seminars at the hospital created this environment. In a larger social setting, one thinks of church sects, political action groups, or small hunter-gatherer tribes that disband seasonally. Here there is a feeling of relatedness at the high group side, but few ceremonies that delineate status or exclusion. The cohesiveness of the group is felt to be fragile, because the identity on which it is based needs to be constantly renewed. Nature in this sector is also felt to be fragile and poised on the edge of disaster. Because I come from northern California, where there are many egalitarian ecology collectives, I have been influenced by this way of thinking and also think of the ecostructure as fragile and endangered.

In EGALITARIAN subcultures, symbols are loaded with cohesive meanings which constantly evolve. Many small and large rituals of group identity and integration naturally arise and become critically important. In this corner are evangelical groups concerned with sin and the end of the world, as well as activist groups with a heightened sense of the urgency of problems of pollution and oppression. Their dialogue with members of the HIERARCHIST (++) group who want to go on doing business as usual is full of misunderstanding and talking at cross purposes, because they cannot agree what actual risk is involved in their different conceptions of nature.

Times of Carnival, *Fastnacht*, and *Mardi Gras* temporarily create an EGALITARIAN environment. It also seems to be the case that each of the rituals of healing discussed in the last section occurs in such an atmosphere. Whereas in the HIERARCHIST subculture, communication is strictly ordered and routed in a somewhat frozen routine, the atmosphere of EGALITARIAN *communitás* and ritual stresses melting, reordering, reconnecting, rethinking, reenacting, and re-creating. Victor Turner has noted that the two environments alternate as phases in many societies.[58] A cultural structure is established and holds until a number of contradictions build up because of life-stage developments or conflicts. Then a liminal period is ritually created. This produces an EGALITARIAN *communitás* phase in which the structure can breathe and recreate itself symbolically. This possibility seems to have been lost in many contemporary urban societies, with their absence of group identity, shared myth, and rituals of integration.

In the -- corner, then, INDIVIDUALIST subcultures are chaotic modern urban environments with low social cohesiveness and the problem of anomie and rapid change. People do not know each other or feel connected with their neighbors, and there are no rules of behavior that guarantee success or acceptance. The job market changes rapidly and thousands of companies close, downsize, and restructure every year. People are thrown back entirely

---

[58] Turner, V., *The Ritual Process*.

on their own resources, in an existentialist reflection on individual choice. The world of nature is there to be mined depending on one's own resourcefulness and ingenuity. There are no powerful rituals or symbols except those that are created and exploited by strong personalities. This is the playground of captains of industry, rock stars, entrepreneurs, media personalities, political lobbyists, and hucksters. It seems to be an extreme and modern setting, very far from the world of our evolutionary past. To survive in such an environment is the norm of "social and occupational adaptedness" that most Western schizophrenics fail to meet. This failure is, in fact, listed in the DSM as a symptom of schizophrenia.

The dominant fantasy of the under-thirty patients I encountered at the hospital was to be a member of a successful rock band. It was as if ordinary life in a contemporary American city was so empty and anonymous, it could not be imagined as a desired life goal. These culture heroes are so important to young people that after the suicide of singer Curt Cobain in a nearby city, hundreds of adolescents in the United States considered suicide themselves, and the suicide rate among them rose dramatically. In England, where teenagers are apparently still literate, local newspapers received a flood of letters about suicide after Cobain's death and the disappearance (and presumed suicide) of singer Richie James. James had often sung about suicide, and his specialty was self-mutilation with razor blades on-stage. The British suicide rate among young men has jumped seventy percent in recent years, and there were over six hundred adolescent deaths from suicide in the year following Cobain's death.[59]

In the –+ corner, the FATALISTS are all those trapped by economic and social conditions in information-poor environments that are exhausting and dehumanizing. Here they are held out of a powerful information nexus in society which might allow them to alter their situations. Many are in a low-group, high-grid world where in order to survive they must work long hours in fields, factories, mines, service industries, or other people's homes, doing low-paid jobs they hate. Often the work is highly repetitive, controlled, and exploitative, enriching someone else in another sector, but leaving those in the –+ corner powerless. There seems to be no possibility of change or escape and at the same time, they may feel no group identity with the social order which contains them. If they are unemployed, they need to negotiate the high-grid government social service sector; or they fall through the cracks and have to live in the dangerous INDIVIDUALIST underworld of street culture. People in this sector tend to experience nature as unpredictable, yielding by luck or chance some good and bad situations in society. It makes sense to play the lottery, gamble, or call for divine intervention. What happens is up

[59] BBC, March 1995.

to fate. Sometimes FATALISTS start talking with each other and decide to join trade unions, political movements, nationalist groups, or millennial religious sects. Then they catapult themselves into the EGALITARIAN sector and press urgently for change in society. Often, they feel despair and somatize their unhappiness, especially in political situations where it could be dangerous to speak their discontent.

It is probably no accident that the incidence of schizophrenia is eight times greater in this type of social environment (though some schizophrenics come from families in other sectors and end up here).[60] Depression and neurasthenia also have a significantly higher incidence in this type of environment.[61] Gina, Edward, Juan, and Nana all were in this sector when they were diagnosed as schizophrenic. José Arnoldo had also moved into such an environment in Chile. The patients in the other two tribal healings discussed above had similarly been thrust toward the low-group sector. Though they remained in their traditional grids, they experienced no longer belonging in the same way to the group. Interestingly, spirit and possession experiences also increase during times of social distress among marginalized and disenfranchized people, "as long as contextual, doctrinal and epistemological features that make spirits possible still hold."[62]

It seems to me that very authoritarian family or educational structures, like the English public school, for example, might also produce a FATALIST atmosphere. There have been a number of studies showing that schizophrenia is more common in families where the parents are dominating, overprotective, rigid, and insensitive to the needs of others. Remember that Gina thought her mother was mean and controlling. In one study at the University of Minnesota Medical School, in-depth interviews about family life were done with 178 schizophrenics, and 150 psychiatrically normal people. The parents of the control group were statistically similar in many ways to those of schizophrenics. About the same number were alcoholics or divorced or hostile to each other. About the same number experienced their mothers as rejecting. The mothers of normal children were significantly worse in a number of ways. The controls experienced their mothers as ambivalent 3 times more often and as indifferent twice as often. More than twice as many of the controls came from poor families. On the other hand, while 81.3% of the mothers of normals were seen as affectionate, only 64.8% of the mothers of schizophrenics were seen as affectionate. Significantly more of the mothers of schizophrenics were seen as overprotecting and dominating. Only 0.7% of the mothers of control group were seen to have these qualities, while

[60] Costello, T.W. & Costello, J.T., *Abnormal Psychology*, p. 226. See also: Gottesman, I.I., *Schizophrenia Genesis*, pp. 76-77.
[61] Scheper-Hughes, N., "Hungry bodies, medicine, and the state," in: Schwartz, T., White, G.M., Lutz, C.A., *New Directions in Psychological Anthropology*.
[62] Mageo, J.M. and Howard, A., *Spirits in Culture, History, and Mind*, p. 21.

13.2% and 10.9% of the mothers of schizophrenics were seen in this way.[63] This suggests that being ignored is less harmful to a child in the long run than being dominated in a FATALIST environment. Of course, this in no way proves the mothers "caused" the schizophrenia. What it does suggest, however, is that highly constrained FATALIST type environments, either in the family or in the social world, may be connected in some way to the stress to which schizophrenia is a response.

We might note here for future reference that when one feels trapped, and surrounding nature and the world are perceived as capricious and unpredictable, one loses the motivation to make sense of them through predictive models. The best strategy in such a situation might be numbing out and going to sleep. Drugs or alcohol could be an inviting alternative. It would be quite helpful to have an explanation for one's fate involving an outside agency – God's will, ancestral haunting, a black box implanted in the brain, an act of Congress. Of course, many people survive and do not become ill in this atmosphere. A special vulnerability has to exist. What is not clear to me is the need to interpret such a vulnerability as an entirely personal matter. In many societies, illness is understood as a call, a sign, a special sensitivity of the spirit that can be useful in regulating group behavior. Like the canaries miners in Appalachia carry into the coal mines to warn them of toxic fumes, the schizophrenic or neurasthenic may be one of the first to react to dehumanizing environments. If we don't have a way to respond to their calls, we miss the possibility of regulating socially toxic customs. The schizophrenic will be isolated and remain outside the social world, or find a way back to society alone without changing it. Without social rituals of healing and integration, we all miss the possibility to periodically rethink our social behavior.

In societies that still can move between EGALITARIAN and HIERARCHICAL structure through ritual, everyone makes adjustments to new elements that can be symbolized and integrated in the dominant myth. If the ancestors are unhappy, or witchcraft has been performed, we can carry out rituals of appeasement that acknowledge and repair the breach. The whole collective is forced to confront the problem and participate in reordering to make amends. The group then functions like the human immune system, which has evolved to recognize a breach in defenses and rush to the scene with containing energies. The immune system is prepared to recognize thousands of invading antigens; perhaps even every conceivable invader can be modeled and recognized. When the antigen meets the antibody, a response is set off in the system that causes many more copies of that antibody to be produced during the next several days. Soon the immune system creates an inner

---

[63] Gottesman, I.I., *Schizophrenia Genesis*, p. 153.

EGALITARIAN society that carries out a ritual of encirclement. Societies that have lost their integrative rituals could be seen as similar to individuals who have developed a problem with immune system response. Because they cannot heal, a process of disintegration sets in. People fall outside "the system" and become hopeless, homeless, jobless, landless, stateless, or soulless.

Finally, then, there is the category of the HERMIT, one who voluntarily or involuntarily steps outside the social order alone. In the best case scenario, the HERMIT begins to see the connection between projected models of the world and the location of the individuals within them. The HERMIT, then, inhabits a space of reflexivity, always connecting knowing and known with evolving inner and outer environments. One can imagine many cultural environments, multiple objective realities each conditioned by and conditioning participants, each arising, surviving for a while, and then becoming extinct. The outsider status of the HERMIT then becomes an acceptable, perhaps even preferable point of view from which to observe rapid and chaotic transformation without dying of it. Or, it becomes possible to maintain two points of view, one conditioned by one's own passionate involvement in a particular body, family, subculture, or economy, and another a detached awareness that everything is transient, relative, and context-dependent. This could be a "middle way." We might think here of the Zen Buddhist ox-herding pictures, where the sage goes off to meditate, has an experience of enlightenment, and then returns to the marketplace with a renewing, relativizing, and vitalizing personality.[64]

The "outsider" is a historical theme in many traditions where creative thinkers have taken time out for reflection. Under this heading, we could place famous examples such as Moses, Mohammed, Milarepa, Gandhi, Mandela, Martin Luther King, Malcolm X, Black Elk, Hildegard of Bingen, St. Theresa, Rabbi Nachman, St. Augustine, Joan of Arc, or Carl Jung. Each went to the margin of the known social world of their time and returned with healing words and energies to an order they had "seen through" in a new way. In the desert, in prison, during critical illness, after unsought visions and visitations, or in acute psychological stress, they began to see the conventions of their traditional environment in a new light. Historian Henri Ellenberger has called this a *maladie créatrice* or creative illness.[65]

Many less-well-known people also have had such an experience. Each of the charismatic healers in the first part of this section must be the product of a period of retreat and discernment. Shamans claim to travel to multiple worlds. Jungian analysts spend years in training on their own analyses,

---

[64] Suzuki, D., "Awakening of a new consciousness in Zen," in: Campbell, J., ed. *Man and Transformation*.
[65] Ellenberger, H., *The Discovery of the Unconscious*.

reflecting on projections, unconscious shadow issues, and alternative constructions of their experience. Schizophrenics, too, often seem profoundly concerned with the issue of a battle of cultural orders to which they can find no satisfactory solution. At the hospital, my role was that of an outsider, and I am also trying to find a solution for cultures in conflict.

It seems that in societies where schizophrenia is regularly healed, there is a place for this outsider status. It is given a meaningful position within the paradigm of the group. It is often the case that there is a notion like the Jungian one of the "wounded healer," so that the occurrence of the illness is interpreted as a calling to become a healer exactly because of the capacity to negotiate the margins of the group. In a myth of the Yoruba religion, which was brought to the Americas through the slave trade, the *orisha* Eshu or Elegba is said to have seen the eyes of ancestors at the crossroads outside his village as a child. No one believed him and he died there. Afterward, disaster struck his village. Eventually, they all went to the crossroads, saw the eyes, and realized they needed to honor the spirit of Eshu. They set up stone markers as ritual sites where the spirit of Eshu could be called forth to see the unseen through divination or inner inspiration. Each individual is held to have his or her own spirit of Eshu that can be accessed through ritual. While Eshu brings powerful insights and energies, his presence prevents him and his followers from shouldering ordinary burdens.[66] Eshu is thus a kind of patron saint of outsiders, giving those who suffer periods of withdrawal from society a meaningful cultural myth to contain their condition. Possession by Eshu can be viewed as an honor that, in time, will bring benefits both to the individual and the community.

One could look at the problem of healing environments for schizophrenia in terms of this grid-group classification system. In each case, the schizophrenic falls out of the social system, losing the connection to the group and eventually is no longer able to function in the grid. In the hospital in the United States, they are treated behind the chain link fence, behind the glass wall of the nurses' station, under a rubric of observation, control, restraint, and seclusion. The grid is thereby intensified until every activity is scheduled and recorded. The goal is objectivity, dispassionate order, and unemotional behavior. The problem is treated as if it were one of melting and an attempt is made to freeze up the ordering environment. The patients are, in fact, returned to a version of the FATALIST environment many of them just fell out of, with even less status, control, and group identity. Most mental patients in the United States and other developed countries feel an enormous sense of shame at needing to be brought to the hospital and they often despise the other patients. They realize that, for the rest of their lives, employers, apart-

---

[66] Thompson, R.F., *Flash of the Spirit*, p. 28.

ment owners, and potential friends will probably reject them when they learn that they are "former mental patients." Sometimes they are scapegoated by their families as well.

This reproduction of an isolating, high-grid, low-group environment may meet the needs of the HIERARCHIST medical staff more than the needs of the patient. HIERARCHISTs are at home in a high-grid world and often feel very uncomfortable in the absence of rules. They naturally want to preserve the whole, while isolating small areas of "local cause" as a problem. The irregularities can then be treated with specific remedies designed to bring them back into line by adapting them to the dominant paradigm. Any suggestion that there is a problem with the paradigm as a whole threatens the very foundation of the structure. The HIERARCHIST naturally defends against this possibility. What if the whole mental hospital approach is dysfunctional exactly because it is too rigidly hierarchical? (I cannot help but wonder what would happen if the doctors, nurses, aides, family members, and patients went out for several nights and lit a bonfire, told each other stories, sang, and danced.)

By contrast, in many healing rituals in rural Africa, India, and Latin America, the patient is brought into an EGALITARIAN environment, and grid is *reduced*. In the liminal or carnival atmosphere, there is much room for fantasy, acting out, and symbol formation. The experience is intense and emotional, filled with numinous symbols, sweaty movement, and physical touching. Brothers, sisters, cousins, and extended family join in. The whole group shares a homeopathic melting in a fragile and treasured ritual journey. The community moves deep into a chaotic region and, with the guidance of the HERMIT healer, is led toward meaning and integration. They return together to a renewed grid and group unity that embraces the patient as a valued member of society with special abilities and vulnerabilities.

Although the Jungian healing examples cited above take place in clinics, they too, seem to operate by reducing grid. In the free, creative work and protected space of the Jungian analysis, there is no demand for conformity or conventionality. Many chaotic experiments can be carried out. In this crucible, an emotional and personal symbol system develops in terms of which the client's meanings can be reintegrated. The HERMIT analyst holds the process, and the clinic provides a supportive and somewhat EGALITARIAN environment. This is especially clear in the work of John Perry with schizophrenics at Agnew State Hospital in California.[67] In all of these cases, a line is crossed at the margin of chaos and order – the edge of chaos – where healing, self-organization, and individuation seem to begin.

---

[67] Perry, J.W., *Roots of Renewal in Myth and Madness: The Meaning of Psychotic Episodes*.

In the socioeconomic system of modern cities, such healing environments would be enormously expensive. Time is money. EGALITARIAN healing environments are labor intensive. The hospital I was in was trying to reduce the time spent in human encounter by computerizing diagnosis. Only a few private clinics and projects in the United States attempt to heal schizophrenics. In Chestnut Lodge, Psychiatrist John Searles saw many of his patients an hour a day for years. Only the very rich can afford to place their relatives in such a clinic. State mental hospitals are under severe budgetary constraints. Buddhist-oriented psychiatrist Edward Podvall set up the Windhorse Project in Boulder, Colorado during the 1980's.[68] There, ten or twenty people were recruited for several months to assist the reintegration of a single former mental patient to the community. They attended many hours of weekly meetings with the patient and paid for and managed housing and meals. After the successful reentry of 15 patients, Podvall stopped to write up his work, which must have been exhausting.

It may be that the problem of schizophrenia in the United States and Europe is related to a lack of valuation of human and spiritual resources. We have a value system that allocates billions of dollars in federal funds to physical infrastructure, space travel, and destructive weapons that probably can never be used without making the earth uninhabitable. Underfunded are schools, food banks, health clinics, libraries, and local social services. These are being cut back or never developed at all in certain neighborhoods. As a society, we are more invested in making fences, roads, dams, machines, buildings, and weapons to defend them, than we are in developing creative and healing environments where human beings and wildlife can thrive. Does something about the group and grid dimensions of INDIVIDUALIST urban life reinforce these priorities?

Jung believed that the anarchic low-group, low-grid information environments of modern cities, with their loss of traditional symbols and rituals, created a culture of amorphous mass. In these societies are many people with "mass psyches," vulnerable to psychic infection because they are unintegrated either by outer ritual or conscious inner processes. In *The Psychology of the Transference*, he wondered if we could understand two tendencies in human culture that I see as comparable to the anthropological analysis of high-group and low-group.[69] He saw high-group as produced by a affiliative "kinship libido" that led people to desire close bonds with others, an "endogamous" tendency toward making every kind of connection through body, mind, feeling, and speech. That was limited by the "incest taboo" which limited the relationship between parents and children after a certain age. The conflict between primary family bond and limitations was then solved by an

[68] Podvoll, E.M., *The Seduction of Madness*.
[69] Jung, C.G., *The Practice of Psychotherapy*, Vol. 16.

"exogamous" tendency that led out and away from the family toward exploration, experimentation, and change. Shaping these connections through the rituals of weddings and initiations is a way to create extended family and social order.

In some parts of the modern world, the exogamous tendency has predominated so completely that all social limitations have been swept away. We can marry and divorce anyone and adolescents experiment without mentors or guidance, but we are hungry for kinship, ritual, *communitás*, connectedness, and integration. When demagogues offer us xenophobic substitutes for kinship, we are vulnerable and susceptible because of our unconscious need for belonging. Mass psyches can be infected by agendas of inclusion in a "master race," "ethnic cleansing," "white citizens council," or "aryan brotherhood." Teenagers can join warring gangs. We can participate in brutal campaigns of murder while joining "crusades," "jihads," or "interventions" in the name of great causes like national sovereignty. Writing after World War II, Jung was deeply concerned about where this tendency might be going. He wrote:

> The original exogamous order is rapidly approaching a condition of chaos painfully held in check. For this there is but one remedy: the inner consolidation of the individual, who is otherwise threatened with inevitable stultification and dissolution in the mass psyche.[70]

This social situation, he thought, may create an inner pressure to find personal and psychological rituals of integration. The need would arise autonomously in the psyche, pushing particularly sensitive individuals away from the amorphous mass that society has become, into an inner process. He may be suggesting that the extreme INDIVIDUALIST low-grid, low-group environment actually encourages certain individuals to go through the painful process of becoming HERMITS by breaking away from the mass social constructions dominant in their subculture. Individuals can refuse the call in a society that labels such experiences "irrational," but if they repress such promptings too completely, they may wind up deeply depressed because they have no energy to continue business as usual.

The widespread pattern of the cross-cousin marriage, which preserves family connectedness without incest, is one way of symbolizing an integrative social bond. If this bond is nonexistent in the outer world, an individual could begin to dream of opposed kinship moieties or marriage quaternios, or cross-cousin marriages, instead. Remember Gina's dream of marrying her Russian lover? In this autonomous inner fantasy, Russia and the United States are two warring kinship moities organizing her the inner world. A marriage with her Russian lover could create peace and order.

---

[70] Jung, C.G., *The Practice of Psychotherapy*, Vol. 16, p. 232.

In times of stress and disorder, an autonomous process may be set off in which the individual is driven by unconscious internal pressures to reschematize and reintegrate experience individually, in order to find a deeper bond to the world. There are many documented cases of marriage and world-reordering dreams in analysis, and I have observed them in individuation processes as well. The inner battle and marriage can represent leaving behind the automatic and unconscious quality of the collective point of view, and prioritizing and becoming aware of one's own inner flow of creative models of integration. One "marries" the ego to an inner center of integration, and is less influenced by social pressures. The crucial thing in such cases, Jung noted, was that the individual go through such a process consciously, gaining a new attitude toward the collective. Jung called it "the immunizing of the individual against the toxin of the mass psyche."[71]

If such a process is successful, the individual becomes conscious of collective attitudes in the environment and can recognize habitual ways of thinking as projections or social constructions. The old self-understanding then crumbles in a painful process of reordering and reconceptualizing one's life. The holding bond or creative center no longer present in society is discovered within the human psyche as the "Self." Marie-Louise von Franz calls such a process "recollection":

> The possibility of *integrating* projected contents instead of apotropaically casting them out into extrapsychic space does not arise until symbols of the Self begin to appear. From this center impulses proceed to a contemplative, thoughtful recollection of the personality. The contents now seen to have been projected are at the same time recognized as belonging to one's own psychic wholeness. Consequently, the psychic energy belonging to these contents now flows toward one's own inner center, strengthening it and heightening its intensity.[72]

The point of such a process is not, however, to separate from the human community. Isolation and alienation from others is a mark of failure of the process. People caught up in an environment of mass psyche can only have a formal relationship; once one achieves a recollected inner and personal point of view, there is a possibility of a deeper connection with others. According to von Franz,

> The first stage shows the process of inner unification of the personality in the individuation process. The second stage however, has reference to a special process that always accompanies individuation in a single person: namely, the development of relatedness to certain fellow human beings and to mankind as

---

[71] Ibid., p. 232.
[72] von Franz, M., *Projection and Recollection in Jungian Psychology*, p. 169.

a whole, a relatedness that proceeds not from the ego but from a transcendental inner center, the Self."[73]

If the need for bonding overtakes us at an unconscious level, many kinds
of destructive behavior can result. We can become identified with grandiose
projects of hegemony in the social world, like the idea of manifest destiny
which allowed European settlers to wipe out ninety percent of the indigenous
population on the American continent. Or we can imagine that our small
group is purer or better than others who are "inferior," "primitive," "neurotic," "unscientific," or "infantile." If no one else shares our fantasies, we can
be overwhelmed by the archaic impulse toward reordering in psychosis.
"Recreating the world in a more harmonious pattern" is a schema that arises
frequently in human affairs. Because the inner impulse toward bonding,
kinship, and integration is similar in all cases, according to Jung, we see
common contents enacted differently. The HERMIT having a mid-life individuation crisis experiences the same endogenous tendency as the psychotic.
The need for a "final conflict," harmonious reordering, and "purity" are also
common themes in war, whether in Nazi Germany, Rwanda, or the former
Yugoslavia. Here the lowest level mass psyche takes over the agenda unconsciously. Because the impulse is primitive and unconscious, it can devour our
conscious differentiation. Then torture, mutilation, and murder can seem
like reasonable means to sacred goals.

Jung likens this world-reordering impulse, which appears in the dreams
and fantasies of most individuation experiences, to a dragon.

> The reason why the involvement looks like a psychosis is that the patient is
> integrating the same fantasy material to which the insane person falls victim,
> because he cannot integrate it but is swallowed up by it. In myths the hero is
> one who conquers the dragon, not the one who is devoured by it. And yet both
> have to deal with the same dragon. Also, he is no hero who never met the
> dragon, or who, if he once saw it, declared afterward that he saw nothing.
> Equally, only one who risked the fight with the dragon and is not overcome by
> it wins the hoard, the "treasure hard to attain." He alone has a genuine claim
> to self-confidence, for he has faced the dark ground of his self and thereby
> gained himself. This experience gives him faith and trust, the *pistis* in the
> ability of the self to sustain him, for everything that has menaced him from the
> inside, he has made his own.[74]

It is of interest, then, that Gina's dreams and fantasies, as well as those of
all the psychotic patients reported on by Perry, seem to be spontaneously
organized in patterns similar to those followed in the traditional rituals cited
above. Perry has written extensively on this subject.[75] Gina dreamed that she

[73] Ibid., p. 174.
[74] Jung, C.G., *Mysterium Conjunctionis*, Vol. 14.

had caused the end of the world, but there was the possibility for a renewal of harmony. This could be read as an entry into Turner's stage 1. Here the old structure has collapsed, and a period of isolation and liminality begins. Schizophrenia could be thought of as an autonomous inner enactment of the liminal stage with the goal of creating a more integrated inner personality structure. In stage 2, Gina imagined that there was a battle for her soul between KGB and FBI agents. Kennedy, who was a hero in the old system, might be cast down. A period of chaos followed, including excursions to Africa and other unknown places where lost friends or wild animals could be encountered. Finally, there was the possibility that a renewed order or a "new king," the lover from Russia, might arise. Then there would be a ritual of integration, as in stage 3. A marriage and a new era of harmony might heal the wound, allowing the return to a renewed social environment. The opposite moieties, Russia and the United States, could be united in cross-cousin marriages that bound them as kin while preventing incest. At the most general level, one could extract a common theme.

From this point of view, we could understand at least some forms of schizophrenia as an autonomous healing process set off in the psyche. The organisms and species with the most possibilities for creative modeling may have the greatest potential for long-term survival in rapidly changing environments. People with proclivities toward creative remodeling may be a kind of "wild card" thrown into the population. We know that both the gene pool and the immune system incorporate such possibilities for change. Small mutations occur spontaneously, constantly enriching the mix of adaptive possibilities. The drive toward dismantling of old schemas and reassembling the building blocks in new ways is part of biological life. We could see it as connected with an ongoing process that results in the attainment of ever new and more inclusive levels of modeling than previously attained. When old models can be disassembled and combined in new ways, we increase our computational abilities. We learn to make models of models.

Most biologists believe that the huge increase in brain size in larger mammals is a result of selection pressures on those mammals that live communally. The large brain allows modeling abilities which lead to greater adaptive success. We can not only model our environment, we can model others in our environment modeling their environment. All the models are constantly changing in relationship to each other. It helps us to survive if we can understand and predict how others are going to act in a group process. Monkeys, baboons, whales, and porpoises have enormously complicated social interactions based on kinship ties, dominance, gender difference, and individual personalities. They must have some sort of inner representation of

---

[75] Perry, J.W., *Roots of Renewal in Myth and Madness*.

these relationships because they remember them and are guided by them in their behavior over long stretches of time.

If we could model the state changes and dynamics of such interactive systems, we would have a model of models of models. Complexity theory and my environmental reflections are reaching toward that. We may be drawn to this goal by an inborn impulse toward recreating our models of the world in a more harmonious pattern, perhaps the same tendency or impulse that is working in Gina. When this autonomous process fails in the case of a particular individual, it could be partly because of a lack of environmental support and understanding. The system of cultural constraints fails, the process loses energy and direction, and the individual becomes "sick."

Where the process succeeds, we can see a common theme. An old order or status encounters obstacles or contradictions or problems it cannot deal with. It may become frozen or even come to a standstill preventing growth. We could think of it as retreating too far into the high-grid, low-group region of the FATALIST. This then could precipitate a slide from the structure to a place of creativity where the frozen order melts into a low-grid, low-group chaotic bath. Here new mutational elements can arise. As we move away from chaos we cross a liminal area where reordering and reintegration can happen. Finally, a new more functional and harmonious ordering emerges that is much less frozen as we cross back from the chaotic toward the structured. Can we imagine that Gina's psyche is spontaneously trying to locate a place where healing begins, on the margin of chaos and order? How can we understand the possibility of healing at "the edge of chaos"?

5. Data versus Noise

Scientific concepts attain the status of natural facts in a two-fold process. First scientists create the contexts in which their knowledge claims are accepted as scientific facts and in which their technologies can work. Scientists adopt what I would call a "(re)contextualization strategy" in which their knowledge claims can gain momentum. Second, scientists then conceal the contexts from which scientific facts and artefacts arise, in a process I will refer to as a "decontextualization strategy." One of the reasons why science succeeds in convincing us that it reveals the truth about nature is that the social contexts in which knowledge claims are transformed into scientific facts and artefacts are made invisible.[76]

– Nellie Oudshoorn

Before the subject of healing and the edge of chaos can be approached, a series of objections presented by the medical model will have to be considered. From the point of view of medical science, there has been no proof of the healing of schizophrenia. It is almost impossible to discuss this issue without falling into a series of contradictions.

The DSM-IV differentiates between schizophrenia and schizophreniform disorder.[77] The first can only be diagnosed when the symptoms defining both diseases have occurred for six months or more. If the symptoms disappear before six months, the diagnosis must be schizophreniform disorder (or brief reactive psychosis or possibly schizoaffective psychosis). Many cases of schizophreniform disorder or brief reactive psychosis spontaneously disappear and never reoccur. At the same time, almost everyone who has dealt with schizophrenia agrees that the sooner treatment begins, the more likely there is to be a positive outcome. It is the long, slow evolution that has the worst prognosis. When Perry screened cases for his work, he tried to find patients who were having their first acute episode of psychosis. Families in

---

[76] Oudshoorn, N., "A Natural Order of Things? Reproductive Sciences and the Politics of Othering," in: Robertson, G., Mash, M., Tickner, L., Bird, J., Curtis, B., Putnam, T., *Future Natural*, p. 124.

[77] American Psychiatric Association, *DSM-IV*, Sections 295-298.

Africa or Latin America are likely to take their relatives to healers as soon as possible after onset wherever such healers are readily available and there is no social stigma attached to visiting them. When the condition is allowed to develop insidiously for years, it may become an embedded response that is extremely difficult to change.

If it is the case that schizophrenia can be healed only if the healing takes place within the first few months of onset, *we can never prove it,* according to the definitions of the medical model. If a healing ritual of any type is performed and the symptoms disappear, *there was never any schizophrenia,* because the symptoms did not last six months. Thus, there could have been no healing of schizophrenia. When it is said that schizophrenia is an incurable disease, we have asserted an untestable hypothesis. It is possible that the primary difference between schizophrenia and schizophreniform disorder is not in the patients, but in the environmental response to the illness. This is also not testable as long as the two conditions are defined as separate entities. The medical model regards environmental information as "noise" to be disregarded.

One of the hallmarks of scientific theories as opposed to other types of cultural modeling systems is supposed to be that scientific paradigms yield testable hypotheses. This definition has been challenged in the anthropological literature because it is possible to point out many cases of scientific beliefs, with the status of theories, that are held without any possibility of testing.[78] At some point every scientific and cultural theory falls back upon the unexamined "indigenous psychology" of the culture of its founders. If we are in a HIERARCHICAL culture that experiences nature as divided between an ordered and good part and a rejected and "polluted" bad part, we are going to be living in a different "natural world" than the INDIVIDUALIST environment where nature is neutral and there to be exploited. The EGALITARIAN concern with fragility and urgency will not necessarily be shared by either. Modern psychological anthropology asks us to rethink our own assumptions, our ways of knowing and formulating facts, our construction of "truth." In an age of cross-cultural engagement, it is no longer possible to naively assume that "objective reality" is not culturally contextualized. We are forced to be aware of the "subjective" part of the "objective."

Medical and psychological anthropologists are currently trying to sort out what portions of scientific and medical technique hold up across cultures. It is extremely difficult, however, to formulate these questions. For example it has been held that up to thirty to sixty percent of medical cures in the West are actually related to placebo effects stemming from the interaction between doctors and patients rather than from the medicines dispensed.[79]

---

[78] For example, see Shweder, *Thinking Through Cultures*.

That means we don't even really understand charismatic healing in our own medical system. We assume that the medicine is "objectively" efficacious, ruling out subjective interactions in a way that makes them untestable. This has been a general prejudice in Western medicine for centuries. It can be traced back to the development of science in Europe under the vigilance of the Church, which could allow the development of material technology only if her hegemony in spiritual matters was not threatened. Unfortunately, mental illness and healing take place in an environment where subjective factors are central. The DSM's isolation of schizophrenia and schizophreni-form disorder as distinct, heterogeneous functional disorders directs our attention toward "objective" symptom control and away from subjective environmental reflection.

But even the objective aspects of medical science have been called into question, because every science is based on a decision about what to look at and what is unimportant. Psychiatrist Albert Scheflen put the problem this way:

> Let me summarize this point as briefly as possible. We have a strategy of science which depends on a careful description of situations and behavioral patterns, *but we have virtually no data base.* At worst we have nothing but papers and books full of inferences; at best we have a reductive view of *"the* stimulus," and *"the* response" or of *the* upsetting factor and *the* stated emotional response. ... But no amount of statistics can prove the validity of an inference, and a consensus is only a measure of reliability within a particular doctrine. Fifty million Frenchmen can be wrong, and the objections of a hundred million American fundamentalists, do not demolish the value of Darwin's work on evolution. In short, *a psychological inference, in the absence of a careful analysis of situation and behavior patterns, is nothing more than a recitation of doctrinal belief.*[80]

Mental illnesses are assumed to be objectively discrete and context independent like a local infection in the medical model. This assumption has been called into question as well. Medical anthropologist Byron Good of the Harvard Department of Social Medicine has written up research he and a colleague did on the newly named "panic disorder," which was presented as an endogenous, context-independent illness occurring spontaneously.[81] They discovered that the adults who had the symptoms had financial difficulties, life-threatening illnesses, or serious family problems that produced fear and worry. There was no way to separate the panic from the context. Medical

[79] Worthman, C.M., "Cupid and Psyche," in: Schwartz, T., White, G. M., & Lutz, C.A., eds., *New Directions in Psychological Anthropology*, p. 167.

[80] Scheflen, A.E., *Levels of Schizophrenia*, p. 115.

[81] Good, B.J., "Culture and psychopathology: Directions for psychiatric anthropology," in: Schwartz, et al., *New Directions in Psychological Anthropology*.

anthropologists Arthur Kleinman, Nancy Scheper-Hughes, and P. J. Guarnaccia explored the high incidence of neurasthenia or "nervios" among the poor in China, Brazil, and Puerto Rico.[82] Psychiatrists have been treating the disease with tranquilizers as if it is a personal deficiency. The anthropologists, exploring the context, discovered that these were environments of chronic hunger and political oppression. Because it was dangerous to say this out loud, distress was expressed through somatization. By locating the disorder in the body of the individual, the medical categories and the establishment that promoted them were helpful in silencing protest and maintaining the political power structure.

The schemata through which we understand schizophrenia or any mental illness are not universal, objective, or context-independent either. Every medical system occurs in a specific society where there are certain rewards and punishments for conformity and rebellion. Scientific medicine has elected to deny or try to rule out local environmental influences on its schemata, its healing, and on the discrete objective entities it wants to isolate and study. In order to be accepted, medical results must be *replicable* in many different contexts regardless of environmental differences. Those diseases like bacterial infections that can be traced to specific sources regardless of cultural environment meet this requirement. Schizophrenia has so far resisted discrete causal location in lesions, family structure, or genes. Yale population geneticist Neil Risch has commented on the "remarkable consistency of such inconsistent findings in the recent history of linkage analysis of common neuropsychiatric disorders."[83] In spite of this contrary indication, the dominant paradigm remains the same, because it is never tested by any particular results.

It is exactly this requirement of replicability that the examples of the healing of schizophrenia in the last chapter can never meet. Each charismatic healer is the product of a particular culture at a particular time. Place the Mapuche healer in Nigeria, or the Nigerian healer in Chile, and they are no longer charismatic healers. In the new environment, they can be tourists, or colleagues, or exotic international visitors, but in most cases, they probably cannot translate their cultural healing idiom. From the point of view of the Western medical model, each of the narratives of healing I presented in the last section is "anecdotal"; they cannot be replicated in other contexts by their very nature. We can never be sure that what happened in the other culture was "really" schizophrenia or "really" healing. Even in the cases of

---

[82] Scheper-Hughes, N., "Hungry bodies, medicine and the state," in: Schwartz, et al., *New Directions in Psychological Anthropology*. Also: Kleinman, A., "Neurasthenia and depression: A study of socialization and culture in China," *Culture, Medicine, and Psychiatry* 1982, 6:117-190; Guarnaccia, P.J., Good, B.J. & Kleinman, A., "Culture and Psychopathology in Latin American Cultures," *The American Journal of Psychiatry*, 1990, 11:1, 449-1, 456.

[83] Gottesman, I.I., *Schizophrenia Genesis*, p. 245.

"healed schizophrenia" reported by Jungians in Western psychiatric clinics, cases in which the illness persisted for many years and thus cannot be classified as schizophreniform disorder, doubts persist. Wherever schizophrenia is considered incurable and the healing is not replicable in other clinics, every reported case remains "anecdotal." It is always possible that the original diagnosis was wrong, or that we are dealing with some atypical phenomenon.

This requirement of replicability postulates for science an idealized and inferred background of Newtonian space-time, objectively spread out like a backdrop in all parts of the data to be studied. The location, culture, mood, and point of view of the researcher are to be eliminated from the objective product – scientific research. But what if something like the relativity Einstein noticed in physics operates at the level of culture? What if no one ever achieves the culture-free objectivity scientists imagine themselves to have? What if certain types of experience can only happen in specific cultural contexts, and the very notion of the "objective observer" as voyeur immediately destroys the possibility of such an experience. Then there would be experiences that forever escaped the individual who attempted to go through life with a detached and disembodied point of view. Like King Midas, who turned every object he touched to gold, such individuals may transform emotional processes to intellectual products and thereby completely miss crucial aspects of lived experience.

Science is made by scientists, individual men and women living at a specific time and place. They are no freer than other people of motives of possessiveness, territoriality, envy, or greed. The choices made about what to study and how to design experiments are always made in specific social contexts, and often based on available funding. Although medical researchers present themselves as (and may at a conscious level, believe that they are) impartial observers of pure scientific data, sociologists are looking at their choices with many questions.

Byron Good has written about the recent history of psychiatric diagnosis, which in his view has gone through major changes in the last twenty years. Though these changes were presented in medical literature as a quest for greater reliability and clarity in procedures, other pressures can be seen as well. Good points to pressures from the pharmaceutical industry for example. "By the late 1960's, pharmaceutical agents with specific effects on psychosis, depression, mania, and anxiety had been developed. Clinical trials of these drugs depended on reliable diagnostic criteria, as did genetic and psychophysiological research."[84] There were also social pressures. Owing to social and political criticisms of mental hospitals, many mentally ill people

---

[84] Good, B.J., "Culture and psychopathology," in: Schwartz, T., et al., *New Directions in Psychological Anthropology*, p. 184.

started to be seen in outpatient clinics. In the economic pressure of this context, the major treatment could only be medication. Then there was a "sharp rise in third-party reimbursement of psychiatric services" that "provided a spur to the integration of psychiatric diagnostic practices with those of other medical subspecialities."[85] Families of mental patients also put pressure on psychiatry, because they did not like the research on family etiologies. They helped to support "a narrow biological definition of psychobiology that removes all responsibility for madness from individuals and their families."[86] The result of these social pressures is that important changes in psychiatric practice have occurred.

> During the last twenty years, psychiatry in Europe and North America has undergone the most extraordinary paradigm shift of this century. Journal publications, research dollars, and treatment orientations all reflect a shift in dominance from psychoanalytic discourse to biological, from a focus on psychological processes to classification of symptoms, from a primary interest in affect and its economy to cognition, and from investments in community psychiatry to biological research and pharmacological treatment.[87]

What is so interesting is that the WHO studies quoted in a previous section were published during this same twenty-year period, yet they seem to have fallen into a vast silence in terms of response in the psychiatric community. In that research, only fifteen percent of schizophrenic patients in developing countries remained on medication during most of the two year follow-up period, while almost sixty-three percent of them had a full remission. Yet, current American texts on schizophrenia continue to hold out neuroleptic medications that correct chemical imbalances in the brain as the *sine qua non* of treatment. For example, a recent textbook on psychology states:

> The most compelling evidence suggesting that biochemical factors are involved in schizophrenia stems from a series of discoveries over the last 40 years that particular drugs affect the occurrence of the disorder's symptoms. The one thing that these drugs have in common is that they appear to exert their influence on one particular neurotransmitter, dopamine. The idea that dopamine plays a central role in schizophrenia has come to be called the dopamine hypothesis. According to the dopamine hypothesis, schizophrenia is due to excessive dopamine activity at particular receptor cites in the brain. Such overactivity may be due to either the presence of too many postsynaptic receptors or hypersensitivity of the receptors to dopamine.[88]

[85] Ibid., p. 184.
[86] Ibid., p. 185.
[87] Ibid., p. 181.
[88] Buskist, W., *Psychology: Boundaries and Frontiers*, p. 558.

The choice to focus on what is going on in the brain when patients are treated with drugs and to exclude evidence that drugs may be irrelevant to the healing of schizophrenia is not scientific in any ideal sense. It is almost as if some medical research into schizophrenia is saying, "Don't bother me with the facts." The ideal approach from a scientific perspective would be to conduct a careful investigation of both kinds of treatment simultaneously. Medications should be used where they can help, but they should not be used ideologically to exclude other modes of treatment. We need to develop techniques to look at what has been regarded as "noise," the cultural and environmental contexts of schizophrenics, health practitioners, and researchers, in a way that incorporates this data into our models.

Good finds it striking that there has been almost no anthropological response to these important changes in psychiatry.[89] He hopes there will be research into the sociology of these changes, and outlines some of the issues this research should pursue. Meanwhile, a beginning has been made in a book which came out in 1992 entitled, *The Selling of the DSM: The Rhetoric of Science in Psychiatry*. Here, the questionable underside of the process that led to the complete overhaul of diagnostic procedures in psychiatry in the last twenty years is examined. Basically, its authors, psychologists Kirk and Kutchins, argue that these changes had more to do with politics than science. The impulse for change, they claim, came from the fact that the profession of psychiatry was losing ground. It was being marginalized in the medical profession and had been reduced to twenty percent of mental health professionals. The core concepts of "mental illness" were under attack by both insiders and outsiders. By defining a new field of biopsychiatry, in which only psychiatrists could administer healing medications, psychiatry could regain lost ground. Biopsychiatry, they state,

> involves the search for physiological, genetic, and chemical bases for mental disorder and the development and use of psychopharmacological agents for treatment. ... Biopsychiatry is an attempt to secure a more powerful base for psychiatry within the jurisdiction of both medicine and mental health.[90]

In order to carry out its agenda, diagnostic categories needed to be redefined as discrete diseases with index symptoms which could be replicated for research purposes. The idea was to devise "an 'atheoretical' diagnostic system that emphasized specific descriptions of objectively observable behaviors."[91] Dr. Robert Spitzer, of the New York State Psychiatric Institute of Columbia University, was appointed head of the project to produce the DSM-III. According to Kirk and Kutchins, a small homogeneous group of five

---

[89] Good, Ibid., p. 181.
[90] Kirk, S.A., Kutchins, H., *The Selling of the DSM: The Rhetoric of Science in Psychology*, p. 10.
[91] Ibid., p. 77.

people with a behavioral approach to diagnosis made all the essential decisions about the structure and contents of the new DSM. By 1980, the task force was made up of fifteen psychiatrists and four consultants. Members of the American Psychological Association were completely excluded from the process. Its president, Theodore Blau, wrote in a letter to the Task Force: "Candidly, the DSM-III ... is more of a political position paper for the American Psychiatric Association than a scientifically-based classification system."[92] Even dissenting psychiatrists were excluded from the process. There were many questions during this period about the inclusion of minorities and women on the Task Force and committees working on the DSM project. At one point, a committee of Black psychiatrists asked directly for representation on the Task Force. Kirk and Kutchins claim that Dr. Spitzer refused, suggesting "that there was no Black psychiatrist among the 18,000 members of the APA with adequate expertise to meet his criteria for membership on the DSM-III Task Force."[93]

It seems, then, we are at an impasse in considering this set of problems. We cannot show that schizophrenia has been healed, but we also cannot show that it has not been healed. No one has been able to find a local cause, but we cannot prove that no local cause exists. This is the encounter of two incompatible paradigms, similar to the encounter of two cultures. The Western medical practitioner explains that there are no spirits of ancestors to cause or cure illness. The "Other" explains that indeed there are. Where can we go from here? Do we have to wait for a schema to become extinct?

[92] Ibid., p. 115.
[93] Ibid., p. 102.

6. Human Information Processing

Connectionist conceptions of the cultural do not merely operate within the parameters of a humanist discourse of individuals and societies, but collapse distinctions between human life, natural life, and the artificial lives of economies, on-line libraries and complex systems of every kind. Cultures are parallel distributed processes, functioning without some transcendent guide or the governing role of their agencies. There is no privileged scale: global and molecular cultures cut through the middle ground of states, societies, members, and things. There is nothing exclusively human about it: culture emerges from the complex interaction of media, organisms, weather patterns, ecosystems, thought patterns, cities, discourses, fashions, populations, brains, markets, dance nights and bacterial exchanges. You live in cultures, and cultures live in you. They are everything and the kitchen sink.[94] – Sadie Plant

The problem of competing paradigms can be viewed from an evolutionary perspective. We are biological organisms trying to model and predict our world. To what extent can any cultural model claim a privileged perspective over any other? Every schema directs attention toward some data and ignores other input as irrelevant. What is central in one model is "noise" for another. A whole science can be built up in an area formerly relegated to random unrelated effects, as in the mathematical theory of non-linear dynamics. In the local cause model of schizophrenia, regional ecostructures are noise. The goal is to find a replicable cause no matter what type of relational region schizophrenia is found in. But how can we establish that our scientific models have divided data from noise in the most fruitful way? This has been debated in modern philosophical literature for several hundred years.

Anthropologist Richard Shweder has attempted to sum up this debate in his most recent book, *Thinking Through Cultures*. He suggests we think of our theories as "reality posits."[95] They attempt to grasp the "real world" that is

---

[94] Plant, S., "The Virtual Complexity of Culture," in: Robertson, G. et al., *Future Natural*, p. 214.

present in our surroundings, but we never succeed in representation because we are bodies with a limited point of view.

The "real" arises within with our cultural paradigms, which shape our personalities, as well as our social and intellectual environments, as part of early childhood neuronal development. The human phenotype is formed partly in and partly out of the womb. Biologists now understand childhood development through "maintenance-loss" models.[96] For example, it has been shown that children under two can distinguish many more sounds than the adults in their environment. The adults then reinforce one set of sounds that form the language they are using.[97] Neurological networks for distinguishing these sounds are built up through continual re-use. Others are extinguished. It is thought that our ability to express various emotions, to notice patterns, and to discriminate environmental input is formed through maintenance-loss in childhood. Each culture helps its new members establish thresholds for discrimination, because choices must be made in directing our attention. As the structure of our neocortical neurons develops through childhood, we gain voluntary control of some of our impulses at the same time as the neurons gain ability to inhibit messages from older portions of our mammalian brain. Each culture develops characteristic phenotypic "complexes" out of the field of genotypic possibilities. Analyst Michael Fordham's notion that our personality structure "deintegrates" from a previous unity is supported by current neurophysiological research.[98]

Children, and all biological organisms, are born with the capacity to make models that anticipate, predict, and allow for feedback and correction. Philosopher Karl Popper has written:

> I assert that every animal is born with expectations or anticipations, which could be framed as hypotheses; a kind of hypothetical knowledge. And I assert that we have, in this sense, some degree of inborn knowledge from which we may begin, even though it may be quite unreliable. This inborn knowledge, these inborn expectations, will, if disappointed, create our first problems; and the ensuing growth of our knowledge may therefore be described as consisting throughout of corrections and modifications of previous knowledge.[99]

We are more pliable as neonates than as adults. Though we continue to grow, early experience reinforces some neural pathways and extinguishes others. After this occurs, new experience can never again happen on an open field where all expectations are equally present. It is as if only the child can truly be a scientist in the ideal sense of being quite open to the new. There

[95] Shweder, R., *Thinking Through Cultures*, p. 35.
[96] Ibid., p. 6.
[97] See Werker, J., "Becoming a native listener," *American Scientist*, 1989, 77:54-59.
[98] Fordham, M., *New Developments in Analytical Psychology*.
[99] Popper, K.R., *Objective Knowledge: An Evolutionary Approach*, p. 258.

are maturational windows that close off as the child becomes older. During these time periods of open maturational windows, the susceptibility to certain kinds of learning is dramatically increased. The "imprinting" periods of baby geese described by ethologist Konrad Lorenz are an example of a maturational window. When baby geese spent this short day-long imprinting period in early life with Lorenz instead of their biological mother, they later followed Lorenz around and imitated his behavior. Human children have many maturational windows. If they don't hear speech or exercise physically at crucial periods, they will be mute or awkward as adults. No amount of later learning can fill this particular gap, though other learning is still possible.

It seems we have a type of maturational window in certain periods of our adult life. The mid-life crisis could be thought of as a maturational window for new growth. Traditional healing rituals described earlier seem to be treating schizophrenia as a kind of maturational window during which a person is ready to be culturally and emotionally imprinted. The tendency toward integration with its "recreate the world in a more harmonious pattern" schema could occur at certain phases of life when old ways of doing things are no longer working well. The liminal period described earlier in both ritual and personal experience may reflect the occurrence of a new maturational window that, if successful imprinting occurs, allows for a return to the social world with new energies and a new role. Such maturational windows can be thought of as "phase changes" that occur within the organism either as a result of development, as in adolescence, or in response to various stressors in the environment. We can imagine that some individuals are more vulnerable to this process as a result of genetypal or phenotypal encoding than others.

If we had to imagine what might be happening within neurological networks during such a period, we could think of the window as an inner problem of high grid. A previously highly canalized structure of networks could develop to a point where it went through a phase change, some kind of catastrophe that plunged it into a low-grid or low-group state. We know that the neocortex extinguishes a great deal of input from other bodily systems by setting up thresholds for consciousness. We only "notice" consciously whatever input rises above these thresholds. For example, we screen out lots of background noise and only pay attention to unusual noises we are not habituated to. One could imagine that, if many thresholds were breached by new information at once, there would be a possibility of overload. Messages might flood the channels, erasing the grid and causing a phase change. A phase change between high-grid and low-grid might be one way to model schizophrenia. A phase change between low-group and high-group might be a way to model healing. These possibilities will be discussed more fully in Chapters 11 and 12.

Dendrites and axons in the neurological structure (like the antigens and antibodies in the immune system), can be compared to individuals in a social group. We could think of the interaction of dendrites and axons using the same categories we used for the interactions of human beings in social groups. The idea is that something about the system of relations is the same even when what is related is different. In the field of genetics, the feature we are considering is called *epistasis*, a complex calculation of how many elements are connected, how many connections there are among them, and how rapidly they are changing. Neurological networks can vary in these ways as well. If the networks fall into a low-grid state when the individual whose brain they are in is isolated and without emotional input, that could produce a low-grid, low-group or low-coherence chaotic (INDIVIDUALIST) connectivity. In this environment, the canalization (HIERARCHY) of messages is lost or overrun, and every node can connect at random with many others. The system can move toward chaos and fall apart or remain disconnected. If the low-grid state is "welded" by emotional input, personal attention, or ritual, a low-grid, high-group or high connectivity (EGALITARIAN) state could be produced where imprinting and healing can occur. In order to understand such a possibility, we will have to learn more about the behavior of connected systems in the next chapter. Under normal circumstances, however, we must assume that adult neurological networks become highly canalized as experience grows. The paradigms that are encoded in this canalization are resistant to change because every reinforcement strengthens their hold, whether the individual is a scientist or a shaman. This resistance is abetted by cultural ritual, speech, and symbols in a process that has been called "semiotropism."[100]

We can imagine the diagram used previously to map grid and group in societies in a more general form that could map many types of information flow in connected systems or epistasis. The ++ sector could be any network of highly canalized relations; the + – sector, a bounded and individually related group; the – – sector, an unbounded arena where many different types of connectivity could form and reform; and the – + sector, an area excluded from the group, but frozen by a strong grid. The liminal area at the edge of chaos would be the area of maximum evolvability of the system. The new diagram would look like Figure 6.1.

The reason why we can model both human societies, the immune system, and neurological networks by using a diagram with the same dimensions is that all are information-processing systems. Each node in either scale,

---

[100] Laughlin, C.D., McManus, J., d'Aquili, E.G., *Brain, Symbol, and Experience*.

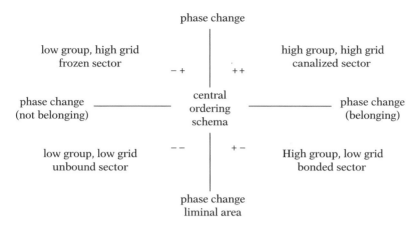

Figure 6.1 – Bonded / Unbound

whether a person, an antibody, or a nerve cell, is doing a kind of computation. A schema is held out to the world for informational input that results in various behaviors, feedback, and alteration of the original schema. When information is hoarded and controlled in a highly canalized system, whether in a fascist dictatorship, a neurological network, or a rigid personality in the (++) sector, many experiences are pushed out of the information system. There is then an attempt to bind them in the excluded (–+) sector. There is always a danger they will go through a phase change and get out of control in a low-grid region.

Intuitively, it is easiest to imagine these differences at the scale of human interaction. In modern industrial society, for example, control over wealth, resources, and information is held by a small stratum of the population, which in the United States has been calculated at about one to five percent. The infrastructure for containing the excluded sector is beginning to fail. In some neighborhoods, almost half the young people leave school without finishing. The United States has the largest prison population, as a percentage of population, in the world.[101] Drug addiction is an epidemic in certain areas. Whole social ecostructures can go through phase changes leading to riots. The destruction of the Berlin wall, the demonstrations of the democracy movement in China, and the revolution in Nicaragua could all be seen as a phase change from a rigid high-grid information-processing system to low-grid connectivity.

At the same time, there are counter-movements toward the creation of new information channels. Young people from different cultures are finding ways

---

[101] See, for example, Hollinger, D.A., *Post-ethnic America: Beyond Multiculturalism*, p. 165-172.

to communicate through sharing their music and rhythms. "World music" tours draw tens of thousands of listeners who become linked by common sentiments. Video and audio tapes are passed from hand to hand in an underground network of subversive messages, even in countries where they are banned. The phenomenal growth of the Internet computer network in the last few years seems to be creating a new linkage schema. Human rights activists are now using it to publicize arrests or torture that used to occur in secret. In many countries, human rights movements have been organized through the international use of Internet. The governments would like to ban them but cannot, because the network is also used for scientific research. The new communications networks feed back into the societies that produced them and cause changes in structure other than those for which they were intended.

Human beings are different from currently existing computers because our "hardware" is living tissue already organized in a nested hierarchy of information-processing systems. When our human information-processing units solve a new problem, the feedback alters the hardware! When I learn a new language, for example, I am reprogramming my neurological networks at the same time that I learn to communicate. I have learned a new system of computation that changes my relationship to the environment and myself. In this sense, both the Internet and my personality are phenomena of "intrinsic emergence."

Sometimes "emergence" is defined to mean that an observer notices a pattern that was unexpected. Defined in this way, emergence always needs an outside observer to exist. "Intrinsic emergence" is a type of emergence in which the pattern is "noticed" in a way that results in a greater computational ability for the information system in which it occurs. When I learn another language, I can orient myself and follow directions in a previously foreign environment. Many possibilities result from my attention to these new patterns. Mathematician James Crutchfield defines intrinsic emergence in the following way: "Intrinsic emergence (must) be defined in terms of the 'models' embedded in the observer. The observer in this view is a subprocess of the entire system. In particular, it is the one that has the requisite information processing capacity with which to take advantage of the emerging patterns."[102] While I write these words, I am noticing patterns that are redefining the way I will see the world in the future, and some change must also be occurring in my own brain as a result. When I am finished, my personality will be a little different than it was when I started. Human personality is in a constant state of intrinsic emergence. It is never a finished whole.

---

[102] Crutchfield, J.P., "Is anything ever new? Considering emergence," in: Cowan, G.A., Pines, D., Maltzer, D., eds., *Complexity: Metaphors, Models, and Reality*, p. 519.

Apparently, the biological organism is made up of a series of nested information-processing systems, in which each emergent level feeds back into those fixed earlier both in ontogeny and phylogeny. The earlier in life maturational windows occur, the more fixed and difficult to change is the encoding. The feedback systems have been reinforced so completely, it is almost impossible to override them from above. Models that are learned late in life can be changed much more easily than those first developed. It seems it would be very useful to have several different modeling systems that could change at different rates. Some could be slow and steady and homeostatic, some rapidly changing to account for short-term crises and changes, and still others deeply integrative to make sure it all works together. It may be that the neocortex has developed through evolution because it is so useful to some-times be able to model the environment as an inner representation of a "detached observer" with ever greater computational abilities. With each increase in brain size, organisms seem to gain more possibilities of "as-if" thinking. It is the late-developing human abilities that provide so many possibilities of reflection, choice, and voluntary control. Of course, it is possible for this detached as-if thinking to become so overdeveloped that it becomes difficult to make any choice or commitment at all.

Our breathing and blood circulation occur automatically. They are regu-lated through inner homeostatic schema we usually pay no attention to. Established early in life, they go on functioning without major changes. Dreams are also outside our conscious control and appear to be an integra-tive modeling system that cycles every twenty-four hours. Fear and pain erupt only occasionally apart from conscious choice, but how we react is sometimes within our control. A whole system of nested hierarchies of models exists in an adult human based on an initial set of possibilities. All biological life forms are now thought to share this feature. This could mean that in fact there is never a strictly local cause in any biological system. Every event takes place in a bioregion with many levels of interconnected informa-tion processing. In this way of thinking, we are ecosystems within ecosys-tems. Victor Turner expressed this insight as follows:

> If one considers the geology, so to speak, of the human brain and nervous system, we see represented in its strata – each layer still vitally alive – not dead like stone, the numerous pasts and presents of our planet. Like Walt Whitman, we "embrace multitudes." And even our reptilian and paleomammalian brains are human, linked in infinitely complex ways to the conditionable upper brain and kindling it with their powers. Each of us is a microcosm, related in the deepest ways to that lovely deep blue globe swirled over with the white whorls first photographed by Edwin Aldrin and Neil Armstrong from their primitive space chariot. ... [103]

As a result of our social experience in a given culture, we gradually build up a stable paradigm for interpreting the world that is reinforced by significant adults. Of course, every child has his or her own particular attitude toward this process, combining elements of rebellion, ingenuity, creativity, and consent. Each culture attempts to enforce shared models, which it uses to address, name, and ritualize selected elements encountered in experience. Thinking, human culture, science, and in fact, all social activity are made possible by shared models. They have a built-in conservativism, because if they changed too fast, we would lose the ability to communicate.

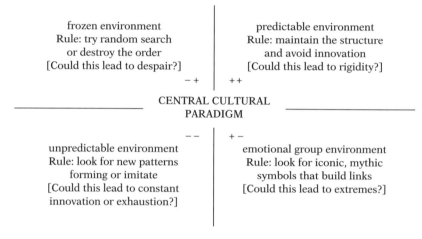

frozen environment	predictable environment
Rule: try random search	Rule: maintain the structure
or destroy the order	and avoid innovation
[Could this lead to despair?]	[Could this lead to rigidity?]
− +	+ +

CENTRAL CULTURAL
PARADIGM

− −	+ −
unpredictable environment	emotional group environment
Rule: look for new patterns	Rule: look for iconic, mythic
forming or imitate	symbols that build links
[Could this lead to constant	[Could this lead to extremes?]
innovation or exhaustion?]	

Figure 6.2 – Environment / Strategy

It may be that human beings have a "learning bias" toward rejecting what is odd and accepting what conforms to the current paradigm. This pressure toward conformity with the thinking of our teachers is adaptive for culture as a whole when the outer environment changes slowly. If the outer environment begins to change rapidly, conformity may not be the best strategy. Innovative individualistic thinking may work better in chaotic environments. Different people may have abilities that allow them to do better in certain environments than in others. This would account for psychological types. The population of human beings has probably been selected over eons for the adaptability that would allow us to react differently under different conditions. The bias, represented by the familiar saying, "When in Rome, do as the Romans do," would amount to what Jung calls collective consciousness. A counter pressure exists for us to rethink everything anew. Some people may

---

[103] Turner, V., *Body, Brain, and Culture*, p. 117.

be more open to the pressure of imitation than others. We could then imagine different types of learning in our diagram of grid and group depending on the character of the environment and the individual as shown in Figure 6.2.

Cultural paradigms then, are the result of forces for change and stability impacting individuals at any given moment. They are in a constant process of accommodation to the environment, which, however, must occur gradually if there is to be a continuing shared language. At the same time, different paradigms compete like species in an ecostructure. Over time, some become extinct. They are gobbled up by others the way the huge variety of regional languages and dialects in Europe have been gobbled up by standard English, German, French, and so on.

Each cultural model is a different symbolic structure that intends as its "signified" the "real" world. Shweder suggests, however, that the "really real" is always transcendent.

> Transcendent realities can be imagined but never seen or deduced, for they are constructions of our own making, which sometimes succeed in binding us to the underlying reality they imagine by giving us an intellectual tool – a metaphor, a premise, an analogy, a category, – with which to live, to arrange our experience, and to interpret our experiences so arranged. ... The fact that you cannot get beyond appearances to reality with the methods of science or the rules of logic (or for that matter, through meditative mysticism) does not mean that you should stop trying to imagine the really real, or that the imagination *must* be disrespectful of sense data or deductive logic, or that "anything goes."[104]

All cultural paradigms are based on our construction of the world, but our range of access to the "really real" is limited by our biological structure. Many writers have tried to imagine how the world would seem different if we were beings with different types of sense organs. Biologist Adolf Portmann pointed out that different organisms have eyes equipped to distinguish different modalities of light. Bees can see ultraviolet, and are much more able to see colors at the blue-violet end of the spectrum. Red is hardly distinguishable to them, but green leaves and white flowers reflect ultraviolet light. We humans distinguish clearly at the red end of the spectrum and cannot see ultraviolet. He writes, "The statement given by our perceptual equipment is quite different from that of flies or bees, and thus it is quite inadequate for true cognition of the world around us, let alone being an instrument for constructing a 'correct' picture of the world."[105]

---

[104] Shweder, R., *Thinking Through Cultures*, p. 361.
[105] Portmann, A., "Color sense and the meaning of color from a biologist's point of view," in: *Color symbolism*, Zürich: Eranos Excerpts, 1977, Spring, p. 9.

British writer Peter Redgrove is fascinated with all the modalities of sensation and communication there are in the animal world, giving them the possibility of "touch like sight."[106] Birds orient their night flight with some kind of geomagnetic orientation. Snails, crickets, fish, and whales are also sensitive to it. Bats, whales, and dolphins use a system of echo-location sonar. Electric eels perceive by electrifying their environment. Clams, hydra, and sea anemones have light-sensitive skin. The sense of smell in many animals is over two hundred times more sensitive than that of humans. Dogs can smell the "odor fingerprints" of individual human beings. Starfish smell clams through many layers of sand. Salmon find their way by smell through thousands of kilometers of ocean to the place they were spawned. Moths can see infrared (IR) heat radiation. "We cannot see it, because the lenses of our eyes have neither the correct shape nor material. If we could see in the IR, a cornfield in the moonlight would look like a vast array of fluorescent lights."[107]

Sir Cyril Burt wondered in his essay, "Psychology and Parapsychology," how much of the way we construct the world is based on the irregularities of human sensation. He noted that our sense of touch is sensitive to a stimulus of 0.1 gram or about 10^{20} ergs. "On the other hand, the eye in rod vision is sensitive to less than 5 quanta of radiant energy, about 10^{-10} ergs." He thought this difference gave us the impression that the world is divided into two different modalities, mass and energy, matter and mind.

> Had the perception of mass been as delicate as the perception of energy, the identity of the two would have seemed self-evident instead of paradoxical. When seeing light, we should at the same time have felt the pressure or impact of the photons; and mass and energy would from the outset have been regarded as merely two different ways of perceiving the same thing ... [108]

We seem to be left with multiple ways of "constructing reality." The purpose of our models may be less to create homologies or exact replicas of "the real," than to allow testing and feedback about the environment. Each culture, each symbol system, each paradigm is a way to come to grips with the world. Perhaps the important question about each model is not, "Is it true?", since we can never know the answer, but rather, "What does it allow us to do, imagine, predict, work on, change, or cure?" As long as a paradigm works to bring coherence to experience, it is constantly reinforced. Perhaps we are born with some kind of "fail-safe" program to deal with the rare eventuality in which we have to throw an entire worldview overboard.

---

[106] Redgrove, P., *The Black Goddess and the Unseen Real*.
[107] Ibid., p. 42.
[108] Burt, Sir C., "Psychology and parapsychology," in: Koestler, A., ed., *The Roots of Coincidence*, p. 35.

All paradigms, however, are myopic. They are based on near-sightedness to a greater or lesser degree, because we can only work with the limited portion of the world that can come into our perception and the limited portion of the world that is recognized by our culture of birth. When we as humans correct for our perceptual myopia with tools or scientific instruments, we construct our theories within the same cultural limitations, introducing another level of myopia. We can never get rid of the problem of myopia, because it is built into the human perceptual and cognitive apparatus. But we can know it is there and allow it to relativize our certainties. Then we have to become aware that our schemata are context-dependent and that science, religion, culture, and even our personalities are cobbled together out of context-dependent building blocks.

Not all scientists and philosophers of science have been willing to accept this conclusion. American philosopher Richard Rorty in his book, *Philosophy and the Mirror of Nature,* carries out a long argument on this theme. "I have tried to show how the urge to break out into an *arche* beyond discourse is rooted in the urge to see social practices of justification as more than just such practices."[109] Rorty suggests we must each learn the social practices of justification, the "natural" science and indigenous psychology of our own culture, as we come into adulthood, because it is there we must make our lives.

Of course, we can also challenge these norms. In this book, Rorty does not deal with the power and privilege problems which must occur when different subcultures with competing value systems are trying to occupy the same ground with opposed social practices of justification. According to Shweder, these are normally kept apart by "contextualization." "When you live in the same world all disagreements are matters of error, ignorance, or misunderstanding. When you live in different worlds there is far more to a disagreement than meets the eye."[110] Hopefully, there are some liminal and dialogical situations where these differences can be settled more by discussion than raw power struggle. Self-deceptions about universality can only hinder the process. In Rorty's view:

> Objectivity should be seen as conformity to the norms of justification (for assertions and actions) we find about us. Such conformity becomes dubious and self-deceptive only when it is seen as something more than this – namely, as a way of obtaining access to something which "grounds" current practices of justification in something else. Such a "ground" is thought to need no justification, because it has become so clearly and distinctly perceived as to count as a "philosophical foundation." This is self-deceptive not simply because of the general absurdity of ultimate justification reposing upon the

[109] Rorty, R., *Philosophy and the Mirror of Nature*, p. 390.
[110] Shweder, R., *Thinking Through Cultures*, p. 18.

unjustifiable, but because of the more concrete absurdity of thinking that the vocabulary used by present science, morality, or whatever has some privileged attachment to reality which makes it *more* than just a further set of descriptions.[111]

Unfortunately, there is still no consensus on the question of multiple models for constructing reality in contemporary scientific and philosophical circles or in Western society which becomes more multicultural daily. Instead, a fragmented debate is raging in, for the most part, separated and unintegrated social institutions and academic disciplines. Shweder sums up the current philosophical situation as follows:

> Some claim that reality posits that are rational or realistic or reality finding are those in which subjectivity has been reduced to zero. That means that perfect rationality or realism (subjectivity set at zero) consists in a perspective-free ("unbiased") witnessing of the world. The idea is one of stepping completely out of our mind, personality, and position in the social order, so as to see the world as it really is, as a thing in itself, uncontaminated and undistorted by projected traces of our intellectual point of view, wishes, desires, goals, emotions, and interests.
>
> Others agree, but argue that since that is impossible, rationality and realism can never be achieved. As that argument goes, perspective free perception is a god-like state of mind unattainable by human beings. Others argue that the least we can try to do is strive to be godlike, correcting for projections and distortions wherever possible. Still others argue that perhaps it is our prejudices that make it possible for us to see; perhaps our prejudices even make it possible for us to see some things as they really are.[112]

This discussion about multiple perspectives had not yet reached as far as the medical treatment team meetings at the mental hospital where I worked. There, the medical model was considered to be a universally and objectively applicable system of categories that accurately and uniquely determined reality. Our goal was to apply it with rigor. Perhaps it was the HIERARCHICAL (++) hospital environment that created social conventions requiring agreement and uniformity in the treatment team. The creative modeling was all happening on the other side of the glass wall and was labeled delusional. We were trying to contain it, medicate it, and eliminate it because we were seeing it as connected with disease. Health was unconsciously equated with paradigm conformity. What we really wanted was that the mentally ill think like us, dress like us, talk like us, and live like us. We just didn't know how to accomplish this end. We were not prepared to deal with their phase changes in any other way.

---

[111] Rorty, R., *Philosophy and the Mirror of Nature*, p. 361.
[112] Shweder, R., *Thinking Through Cultures*, p. 357.

Our failure was nowhere more pronounced than in our encounters with the "fantasy worlds" of the schizophrenics. There was no room in the medical model to think of mental illness as an attempt at a transformative process in itself. In the local cause notion, the transformation that caused schizophrenia had happened in the past and needed to be corrected in the present, if possible, by a return to the *status quo ante*. What was wanted was a restoration of a previous level of functioning. Schizophrenia was perhaps being imagined as the result of a faulty internal computer program. A programming error of some sort not yet located had resulted in an output distortion. Perhaps the medications would search and destroy the brain malfunction. When the medications didn't work, the malfunction would be understood as chronic. If schizophrenics are driven by an urge to transform themselves and their environment, a biological force was meeting an immovable object. The entire HIERARCHICAL hospital was set up in a way to prevent its restraints from being changed or trespassed by patients. The maturational window, if it existed, was not being used.

Because the hospital paradigm occurs in an evolutionary environment where paradigms must compete like species, it takes its place in an ecostructure that is constantly changing. New discoveries in biology are evolving in the background of medical research. The development of psychological anthropology and cultural theory raises new issues and allows new ways of posing problems. At a more concrete level, thousands of patients and their families have formed associations and complained to their state governments about the treatment they have received at mental hospitals. In the United States, several well-known novels and films, like Kesey's *One Flew Over the Cuckoo's Nest* and Wiseman's *Asylum*, have raised public concerns. At the same time, state governments are feeling budget limitations and looking for areas in which to make cuts.

The end result of these pressures on the particular hospital where I worked is that it closed. Like other dinosaurs of the past, it has become extinct. Patients in that state are now sorted into the "criminally insane," who go into a kind of prison-hospital, and "the rest." Most of the former patients from our hospital ended up housed in group homes in the community. They are brought periodically to regional health centers for therapy. A new model of treatment is evolving and many symbolic schema are competing for a niche. The intellectual landscape is changing as we try to recompute our internal schemata. Many people at once are reaching for new ways to add things up.

7. Connectionist Models

From the crack of the big bang a hot universe runs down for ten billion years or so. About two-thirds along in its history something clicks, and an insatiable force begins hijacking the slipping heat and order into local areas of higher order. The remarkable thing about this hijacker is that it (a) is self-sustaining, and (b) it is self-reinforcing: the more of it around, the more it makes of itself. ... The rising flow uses its short moment of order to snatch whatever dissipating power it can to build a platform upon which to extract the next round of order. It saves nothing and spends all. It invests all the order it has to amplify the next round of complexity, growth, and order. In this way it taps chaos to breed antichaos. We call it life.[113]
– Kevin Kelly

What if we were to think about human consciousness, mental illness, and health without the local cause paradigm? Different models can illuminate new aspects of a structure and suggest promising directions for research on unsolved problems. Complexity theory has offered new schemata that allow a radical rethinking of how the biological organisms developed in the natural world. In effect, it requires a new synthesis, even a new paradigm in scientific thought.

Western scientific models have tended to think of the development of biological organisms as dominated by a kind of central control mechanism, usually the genetic code, which allows occasional random mutations. Perhaps this is partly because science developed in a hierarchical monotheistic culture that put a lot of stock in a "First Cause" that was considered single, whole, and undivided. Genes can be thought of as "first causes," like the theorems in Euclidean geometry from which one can deduce a proof. A mistake in writing out the theorems can produce faulty conclusions. In the computer age, we can formulate this difficulty as an error in programming. A small error in the operating program of a can produce devastating catastrophes in computer output. "Garbage in, garbage out."

---

[113] Kelly, K., *Out of Control*, p. 417.

In the new model, many biological processes are understood through the model of parallel rather than linear computer programs. In parallel processing, each node in a network responds simultaneously to others which are responding to it. The nodes can have many or few connections, yielding many different types of behavior in the system. It is impossible to predict what will happen in a large network because there would never be time to compute all the possibilities. On the other hand, surprisingly, parallel processing systems can produce order on their own. The grammar of this order can be studied, even if no state of any particular network can be predicted. The study of this grammar has come to be called "complexity theory," because it is about of the behavior of complex systems. A subset of these systems are "self-organizing," in that order evolves as the system "learns" to regulate itself through positive feedback during its ongoing encounter with its internal environment. Physicist Murray Gell-Mann summarizes the difference between mechanical systems and self-organizing systems as follows: "Complex adaptation is to be contrasted with simple or direct adaptation, as in a thermostat, which just keeps mumbling to itself, 'It's too cold, it's too cold, it's too hot, it's just right, it's too cold,' and so forth."[114] In complex adaptation, the system feeds back information about the environment as its computations and "feedforward" predictions (or models or schemata) become ever more sophisticated. If the environment changes precipitously, or if the self-organizing system becomes frozen in its modeling capabilities, its order may fall apart or die out. In computer simulations, survival means continuing to change from one computation state to another. When a self-organized system in a computer model falls into the basin of a point attractor and begins to arrive at the same "conclusion" over and over, it is "dead." If it could be shown that this model fits noted regularities in evolutionary development, we would have a way to think about self-organization in nature. According to biologist Stuart Kauffman:

> "It is therefore a major initial point to realize that, in whatever sense the genomic regulatory system constitutes something like a developmental program, it is almost certainly not like a serial-processing algorithm. In a genomic system, each gene responds to the various products of those genes whose products regulate its activity. All the different genes in the network may respond at the same time to the output of those genes which regulate them, In other words, the genes act in parallel. The network, in so far as it is like a computer network at all, is like a *parallel-processing network*.[115]

---

[114] Gell-Mann, M., "Complex adaptive systems," in: Cowan, G.A., Pines, D., & Meltzer, D., eds., *Complexity Metaphors, Models, and Reality*, p. 20.
[115] Kauffman, S.A., *Origins of Order*, p. 442.

The idea that complex self-organizing systems arise spontaneously in the natural world has been explored in a number of scientific fields in the last twenty-five years. One well-known landmark in this exploration was the 1977 presentation of a Nobel Prize to chemist Ilya Prigogine for his work on the thermodynamics of nonequilibrium systems (open systems). This led to a realization that Newtonian science, the dominant Western scientific idea of the last 300 years, was based on a special subset of systems in the universe called "closed systems." In *Order Out of Chaos*, written by Prigogine and Isabelle Stengers,[116] the rethinking of these ideas in the light of the new discoveries was begun. Alvin Toffler wrote in the Introduction to the English edition:

> "The importance of this book is not simply that it uses original arguments to change the Newtonian model, but also that it shows how the still valid, though much limited, claims of Newtonianism might fit compatibly into a larger scientific image of reality. It argues that the old "universal laws" are not universal at all, but apply only to local regions of reality. And these happen to be the regions to which science has devoted the most effort.[117]

The Newtonian model "tended to emphasize stability, order, uniformity, and equilibrium. It concerned itself with closed systems and linear relationships in which small inputs uniformly yield small results."[118] But closed systems, it turns out, form only a small part of the physical universe. Prigogine's work:

> shifts attention to those aspects of reality that characterize today's accelerated social change: disorder, instability, diversity, disequilibrium, nonlinear relationships (in which small inputs can trigger massive consequences) and temporality – a heightened sensitivity to the flows of time. ... Most phenomena of interest to us are, in fact, open systems, exchanging energy or matter (and one might add, information) with their environment. Surely biological and social systems are open, which means that the attempt to understand them in mechanistic terms is doomed to failure.[119]

In Prigogine's original work, he dyed two different gases different colors, and slowly increased their rate of entry into a closed chamber. When the gases first entered the chamber, random patterns of color formed and fell apart. Then, at a certain rate, the colored gases began to pulse – first one color for a few seconds, then the other – in rhythmic patterns Prigogine called "limit cycles." This model, now observed in laboratories all over the

---

[116] Prigogine, I., & Stengers, I., *Order Out of Chaos*, p. xiv.
[117] Ibid., p. xiv
[118] Ibid., p. xiv.
[119] Ibid., p. xiv.

world, was named a "Brusselator," since the work was first done in Brussels. Prigogine and Stengers describe the work as follows:

> Whatever the initial conditions, it approaches the limit cycle, the periodic behavior of which is stable. We therefore have a periodic chemical process – a chemical clock. Let us pause a moment to emphasize how unexpected such a phenomenon is. Suppose we have two kinds of molecules, "red" and "blue." Because of the chaotic motion of the molecules, we would expect that at a given moment we would have more red molecules say, in the left part of the vessel. Then a bit later, more blue molecules would appear, and so on. The vessel would appear to us as "violet," with occasional irregular flashes of red or blue. However this is not what happens with a chemical clock; here the system is all blue, then it abruptly changes its color to red, then again to blue. Because all these changes occur at regular time intervals, we have a coherent process. Such a degree of order stemming from the activity of billions of molecules seems incredible, and indeed, if chemical clocks had not been observed, no one would believe such a process is possible. To change colors all at once, molecules must have a way to "communicate." The system has to act as a whole. We will return repeatedly to this key word, communicate, which is of obvious importance in so many fields, from chemistry to neurophysiology. Dissipative structures introduce probably one of the simplest physical mechanisms for communication.[120]

The dissipative structures, as they are called in Prigogine's work, can be both time and space dependent, so that regular "chemical waves" pass through the system. The structures can also exhibit time-independent behavior causing stable structures to appear in different regions. For Prigogine, these results were astounding because they were not explicable in terms of the current scientific paradigm:

> Here we must pause once again, this time to emphasize how much the spontaneous formation of spatial structures contradicts the law of equilibrium physics and Boltzmann's order principle. Again, the number of complexions corresponding to such structures would be extremely small in comparison with the number in a uniform distribution. Still nonequilibrium processes may lead to situations that would appear impossible from the classical point of view.[121]

One way to conceptualize this intuitively has been through a model of the dynamics of water. If water is fed into a channel through a hose, say, we can find out what happens at different levels of energy input by opening the hose valve to allow water to run in at different rates. If the rate is slow, the water will run through the channel in a smooth sheet, forming a stable pattern. If

[120] Ibid., p. 148.
[121] Ibid., p. 150.

we increase the flow significantly, a series of whirlpools will form that maintain their patterned structure even though continuously new molecules of water flow through each whirlpool. If we increase the flow still more, the water will flow through the channel with turbulence, forming no patterns at all. The process can be reversed as well. When the flow is diminished the whirlpools will form again. As it happens, we know from everyday experience that water also has several distinctive phase transitions. When frozen, it can form ice, when heated, steam; it can form fog on land and rain or snow in the air. These phase transitions represent differences in quantity that become difference in quality at another level. A lowering of water temperature past 32°F causes an emergent quality – ice; and a raising of the temperature above 212°F causes boiling and a transition to steam. These phase transitions are sharp and sudden, and are called "first order phase transitions."

We could plot all these transformations of water on our now familiar dimensional diagram as is shown in Figure 7.1.

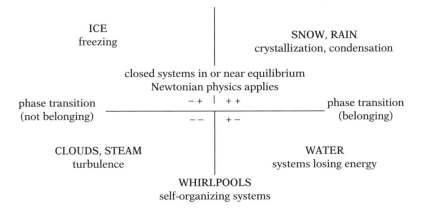

Figure 7.1 – Phase transitions

Self-organized structures like whirlpools occur naturally. They happen not because individual molecules have special properties, but because a whole network of such molecules reaches a certain state of connectivity. Whirlpools exhibit self-organization, but they are accidental and subject to outside conditions. They have no control over their energy sources. We do not think of them as alive. The whirlpools are complex systems, but not complex adaptive systems (CAS). How could we understand biological life forms as capitalizing on this natural form of self-organization? We would have to imagine that a whirlpool learns to learn, and gradually works its way up to the water tap which is its source, taking control of its output. Then the whirlpool would have a feedback system to monitor the right amount of water to keep itself in existence.

In his 1993 book, *The Origins of Order*, Stuart Kauffman, attempted to sum up twenty years of work on this problem. The major issue in the neo-Darwinist evolutionary scenario was the idea that complex adaptive life forms could have arisen merely through random trial and error, without some principle of internal organization. For many biologists there seemed to be a missing piece in the puzzle of the development of complex life forms. There had to be other undiscovered sources of order, which Einstein had called "secrets of the Old One."[122]

Michael Waldrop interviewed many of the major theorists of the new complexity sciences in his recent book in *Complexity*. Waldrop explains biologist Stuart Kauffman's reasoning:

> Kauffman was also troubled by people's tacit assumption that detail was everything. The bio-molecular details were obviously important, he knew. But if the genome really had to be organized and fine-tuned to exquisite perfection before it could work at all, then how could it have arisen through the random trial and error of evolution? That would be like shuffling an honest deck of cards and then dealing yourself a bridge hand of 13 spades: possible, but not very likely. ... There had to be more to it than that, he thought. "Somehow I wanted it to be true that the order in genetic regulatory systems was natural, that it was quasi-inevitable. Somehow the order would just be there for free. It would be spontaneous." If that was the case, he reasoned, then this spontaneous self-organizing property of life would be the flip side of natural selection. The precise genetic details of any organism would be the product of random mutations and natural selection working just as Darwin had described them. But the organization of life itself, the order, would be deeper and more fundamental. It would arise purely from the structure of the network, not the details. Order, in fact, would rank as one of the secrets of the Old One.[123]

Biologists realized that, in the natural world of evolution, no gene ever operated independently. What was needed was a way to model epistasis, the whole network of interactions which were going on simultaneously. If there was something special about the particular gene or neuron to be modeled, evolution would take eons to hit upon it by random mutations. But if something in random networks produced a stable order, then such orders could be fairly common in the world. In the 1970's, Kauffman began to work on the circuitry of random networks in computer models. Each node could be thought of like a light bulb, as either on or off. Every light bulb switch could be connected to one, two, or infinitely many other light bulb switches, so that when the first went on, the next went on, and so on. The light bulbs

[122] Waldrop, M.M., *Complexity*, p. 108.
[123] Ibid., p. 105.

could be genes, or any nodes in any network. He quickly discovered that if there were very many connections between switches, the network was "as densely tangled as a plate of spaghetti, so that every gene was controlled by lots of other genes, then the system would just thrash around chaotically."[124] If each gene were controlled by only one other gene, the network would be too simple. "It would be like a billboard where most of the bulbs just pulsed off and on like mindless strobe lights."[125] But he discovered that a two-input network of 100 genes would quickly settle into orderly states. Most of the light bulbs remained either on or off in frozen regimes, and the rest cycled through a handful of configurations. This work suggested that there was some form of order that was innate to networks, to connectedness and exchange of energies, and was as basic in the universe as number itself. He soon discovered a mathematical regularity: the number of stable cycles was roughly equal to the square root of the number of nodes in the system. This work modeled complex networks, but still lacked the feature that made them "adaptive."

An important next step was to figure out how such a network might have worked historically in the development of biological evolution. A number of people experimented with aspects of this problem simultaneously during the 1970's. Modern biotechnological laboratories were having a difficult time synthesizing protein molecules, because they are enormously complex objects involving a chain of hundreds of amino acid building blocks in a precise order. If we imagine that life began accidentally in some kind of primal soup of chemicals three to five billion years ago, such complex molecules would have had to develop through random interactions. Statisticians and creationists alike had calculated that it would have taken far longer than the lifetime of the universe to produce even a single complex protein molecule by this method.

It could have produced some simple small molecules, however, and among these might have been catalysts that speeded up the production of certain molecules and retarded the production of others. A catalyst could speed up the production of molecule #1, which then led to the formation of another catalyst. Eventually a closed circle could be formed (like a whirlpool in a water channel) in which the last catalyst led to the formation of the first.

> If the conditions in your primordial soup were right, then you wouldn't have to wait for random reactions at all. The compounds in the soup could have formed a coherent, self-reinforcing web of reactions. Furthermore, each molecule in the web would have catalyzed the formation of other molecules in the web – so that all the molecules in the web would have grown steadily more and

---

[124] Ibid., p. 109.
[125] Ibid., p. 110.

more abundant relative to the molecules that were not part of the web. Taken as a whole, in short, the web would have catalyzed its own formation. It would have been an "autocatalytic set."[126]

The mathematics to model the idea of an autocatalytic set had been around since the invention of computers in the 1940's. John von Neumann had experimented with self-reproducing programs called cellular automata, and a number of people had worked on programs that had nodes or agents that could recombine according to simple rules, gradually building up complex structures that would at some degree of complexity begin to reproduce themselves in periodic cycles. These had been applied in a number of different disciplines: to neurological networks, gene structures, economies, chemical reactions, game theory, and so on. Eventually, Doyne Farmer, a Los Alamos physicist, was able to write a paper called, *A Rosetta Stone for Connectionism*,[127] showing that all of these programs could be translated into each other, and all had to do with the mathematics of networks, where very simple networks of nodes (whether light bulbs, polymers, strings of binary numbers, neurons with off-on switches, economic agents who must sell or buy) could generate surprisingly complex outcomes. The key was that the nodes had to be programmed to adjust to feedback, to learn to adapt in a changing environment. The new programs involved parallel rather than sequential processing. Many different computations had to take place simultaneously before each state change of the system.

Since the early 1960's, a number of researchers have been probing the underlying hypotheses of the neo-Darwinist selection/drift filter in evolutionary biology and attempting to model systems in nature that were self-organizing. Kauffman questioned the inattention of contemporary evolutionary theory to the contribution of the organism toward its own evolution. "Restated, perhaps there are properties of organisms which recur, not by virtue of selection, but by virtue of being inherent properties of the building materials. Such properties would constitute ahistorical universals."[128] He was convinced that there is such an unrecognized contribution.

> However, the possibility that divergence, directional change, or stasis in the face of arbitrary mutational events might be partially due to the constraining self-organizing features of organisms has not been incorporated as a truly integral part of contemporary evolutionary theory.[129]

---

[126] Ibid., p. 123.
[127] Ibid., p. 341-342.
[128] Kauffman, S. A., "Self-organization, Selective Adaptation, and It's Limits," in: Depew, J. and Weber, B.H., *Evolution at a Crossroads*, p. 169.
[129] Ibid., p. 169.

Today, this idea is being widely discussed, and new models of the origin of life are being proposed. The new research postulates that the development of life forms can be understood as a combination of the Darwinian principles of random mutation and natural selection in combination with self-organizing features in the deepest structure of the natural world. According to Ervin Lazlo, founder of the General Evolution Research Group of the U.N., in his 1987 book, *Evolution: The Grand Synthesis*, we can understand all structure in the world as self-organizing.[130] The new research into complex systems has required a revolutionary shift in point of view, according to Lazlo. In the past social scientists studied "statistics instead of dynamics; structures and states instead of processes and functions; self-correcting mechanisms instead of self-organizing systems; conditions of equilibrium instead of dynamic balances in regions of distinct disequilibrium."[131] Lazlo believes it is now possible to work out a "Grand Evolutionary Synthesis," showing how life forms develop from the simplest autocatalytic chemical reactions to complex human societies. "A grand synthesis of the myriad forms and processes of evolution is possible because, as the sciences of complexity now discover, evolution is nevertheless singularly consistent: it brings forth the same basic kind of entity in all its domains. This entity is a system of a particular kind ... "[132] These systems, which Lazlo calls "systems in the third state" are called "complex adaptive systems" (CAS) in American research journals.

Biological life forms are only one example of self-organizing complex systems that can be observed in the nature world, constructed in laboratories, and understood and modeled with current mathematical theory developed since the 1960's. The conditions for complex systems arise spontaneously in the natural world anywhere that interconnected networks of multiple agents act in parallel. Under certain very specific circumstances of connectivity, these networks begin to generate autocatalytic structures, that is, growing creative patterns that have the capacity to reproduce themselves and adapt to changing conditions through feedforward models and feedback. They are able to make use of energy sources in their environment to sustain themselves as well as to grow and develop, so they do not move toward a state of entropy. Many natural phenomena can be modeled as complex systems: ant colonies, flocks of birds, molecules, DNA, immune systems, brains, cells, ecological niches, social systems, economies, or scientific communities. In complex systems nothing is fixed, but all the agents are reacting to each other's actions in a constantly changing landscape.

---

[130] Laszlo, E., *Evolution*, p. 49.
[131] Ibid., p. 19.
[132] Ibid., p. 20.

There is no master control: the organized pattern arises from complex "strategies" of competition and cooperation worked out in response to changing conditions. These strategies are myopic. They are not conscious and do not depend on anything like human foresight, but they function by making active "predictions" or if-then connections based on internal information models and then winning or losing strength in the system based on the success or failure of the model. Outcomes are never predictable in principle, because the number of combinations and changing factors are too large to calculate. This type of organization is sometimes called distributed intelligence.

Each complex system eventually has many hierarchical levels of order, with cooperating agents at one level becoming the building blocks for agents at higher levels. The building blocks are constantly revised and rearranged as the system adapts to new orders of combination in the environment. Therefore, there is perpetual novelty in complexity. New levels of emergent order can arise that could never have been predicted.

The theory has been interestingly applied in economics. Some economists, for example, wondered how certain technologies seem to arise and lock in to economic development, not because they are the best technologies, but because they happen to be in a critical place at a critical time. The classic example of this is the QWERTY keyboard, which is currently in use all over the English-speaking world on typewriter and computer keyboards. (QWERTY is spelled out by the first 6 keys on the left top row of the keyboard.) Actually it was invented by engineer Christopher Scholes in 1873 to slow down typists who tended to jam early typewriting machines if they typed too fast. But that meant that all the typists around when Remington first mass produced typewriters knew the QWERTY system and wanted machines that allowed them to use it. Then, when other companies began to produce typewriters they also used QWERTY keyboards, so the system locked in. It was as if the mere existence of a pattern at the right time and place could draw off energy from the system to strengthen itself through positive feedback. Was this a kind of a phase transition? Could economic systems be seen as complex systems? And could the dynamics involved be described in mathematical terms? Economists working on these problems during the 1970's began to suggest that technology functions not as a commodity but as a complex ecosystem, a highly interconnected web. As in biological evolution, technological webs can go through periods of creativity and extinction.

Writing in *Scientific American* in 1986, a group of physicists summed up the implications of the newly developing "science of complexity" or "chaos theory" as it was called then:

Chaos brings a new challenge to the reductionist view that a system can be understood by breaking it down and studying each piece. This view has been prevalent in science in part because there are so many systems for which the behavior of the whole is indeed the sum of its parts. Chaos demonstrates, however, that a system can have complicated behavior that emerges as a consequence of simple, nonlinear interaction of only a few components. The problem is becoming acute in a wide range of scientific disciplines, from describing microscopic physics to modeling macroscopic behavior of biological organisms. ... For example, even with a complete map of the nervous system of a simple organism. ... the organism's behavior cannot be deduced. Similarly, the hope that physics could be complete with an increasingly detailed understanding of fundamental physical forces and constituents is unfounded. The interaction of components on one scale can lead to complex global behavior on a larger scale that in general cannot be deduced from knowledge of the individual components.[133]

In 1984, physicist Stephen Wolfram worked out that computer models of complex systems seemed to fall into four classes. Class 1 rules produced models that went dead in just a few computation sequences. They produced what mathematicians call "point attractors." Class 2 rules settled into repeating patterns, with just a few random changes, referred to as a "periodic attractors." Class 3 rules produced chaotic systems that never settled down. Class 4 rules, however, produced something very new and surprising – "coherent structures that propagated, grew, split apart, and recombined in a wonderfully complex way." In mathematics, they were expressed as deterministic chaos or fractals, held together by "strange attractors."[134]

A few years later, Los Alamos computer analyst Chris Langton discovered he could correlate these rules with numerical values. He programmed his cellular automata programs to try out different values of lamda, which represented the percentage of cells that would still be developing in the next generation of computations. At 0.0 he discovered systems with Wolfram's Class 1 rules. At 0.5 he discovered Wolfram's Class 3 rules. However, there turned out to be a critical value – about 0.273 – at which the system behaved in a dramatically new way, like Wolfram's Class 4 rules. This region began to be called the "edge of chaos," the place where complex adaptive systems (CAS) begin to evolve.

Langton, interested in trying to find a program that would model the development of life forms, or artificial life, searched for what in the natural world might correlate with this discovery. Eventually, he was able to correlate the mathematical model of "the edge of chaos" with second-order phase

[133] Crutchfield, J.P., Farmer, J.D., Packard, N.H., Shaw, R.S., "Chaos," in: *Scientific American*, December 1986, p. 56.
[134] Waldrop, M.M., *Complexity*, p. 119.

transitions. First-order phase transitions, like the transformation of water to ice when cooled, are very common in nature. Second-order transitions are relatively rare under the temperature and pressure conditions of the biological environment where humans live.

> They are much less abrupt, largely because the molecules in such a system don't have to make that either/or choice. They combine chaos and order. Above the transition temperature, for example, most of the molecules are tumbling over one another in a completely chaotic fluid phase. Yet tumbling among them are myriads of submicroscopic islands of orderly, latticework solid, with molecules constantly dissolving and recrystallizing around the edges. These islands are neither very big and very long lasting, even at a molecular scale. So the system is still mostly in chaos. But as the temperature is lowered, the largest islands start to get very big indeed, and they begin to live for a correspondingly long time. The balance between chaos and order has begun to shift. Of course, if the temperature were taken all the way past the transition, the roles would reverse: the material would go from being a sea of fluid dotted with islands of solid, to being a continent of solid dotted with lakes of fluid. But right at the transition, the balance is perfect: the ordered structures fill a volume precisely equal to that of the chaotic fluid. Order and chaos intertwine in a complex, ever-changing dance of submicroscopic arms and fractal filaments. The largest ordered structures propagate their fingers across the material for arbitrarily long distances and last for an arbitrarily long time.[135]

The diagram we have been using to illustrate the different aspects of complexity has a mathematical expression at the highest level of abstraction. We can lay Wolfram's rules roughly onto our previously mapped 4 sectors in Figure 7.4. This suggests that the phase changes of water and other substances, the differences in societies, the neural, immune system, and genetic structures we have been discussing, all can be modeled as expressions of a fundamental feature of number and connectivity disclosed in parallel processing systems. This grammar of information processing is like a computational code of life itself. The schemata that we use to understand complexity can give order to our scientific models of the perceived world. Mathematics and complex systems seem to be some kind of basic substrate of thinking and perception as well as fundamental in our world construct.

This location at the edge of chaos, then, is the maximum point of creative but semistable reordering before turbulence in all complex systems. It is believed by some theorists that complex adaptive systems, and all biological species, tend to evolve toward the edge of chaos. CAS that are able to survive competition for resources and maintain stable structures do so because they

---

[135] Ibid., p. 229.

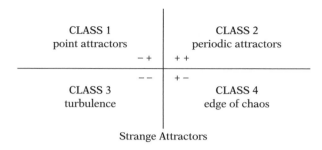

Figure 7.4 – Wolfram's rules

handle new information better. That is, the processes at the edge of chaos somehow represent computational and self-organizing skills that allow evolutionary success in landscapes particularly suited for evolutionary development. Stuart Kauffman suggests:

> But it is also plausible that systems poised at the boundary of chaos have the proper structure to *interact* with and internally *represent* other entities of their environment. In other words, complex living systems must "know" their worlds. Whether we consider *E. coli* swimming upstream in a glucose gradient, a tree manufacturing a toxin against an herbivore insect, or a hawk diving to catch a chick, organisms sense, classify, and act upon their worlds. In a word, organisms have internal models of their worlds which compress information and allow action.[136]

Essentially, models classify system states as "the same" or "different." Whether we are talking about one-celled organisms, nerve cells, adult human beings, or parallel-processing computer models, all survive by forming schemata against which to test ongoing experience, and then using feedback to alter the models. These schemata order experience in the same way as the frozen portions of informational networks create areas of "the same" in an ocean of "difference."

Many complexity theorists hold that those biological life forms that have evolved for millions of years are likely to be close to an "edge of chaos" in terms of computational abilities, both individually and as a group. It may be that phase transitions are built into their structure as a possible gambit under certain circumstances. It is thought they maintain themselves at a subcritical state that is at the edge of order and stability, but sometimes go over into the edge of chaos to go through a creative reordering phase. It is also possible to go too far into an ordered, frozen region into a critical state where no learning can occur. In the critical state, a small perturbation could

---

[136] Kauffman, S.A., *Origins*, p. 232.

potentially cause a big transformation because the system has grown inflexible. Ecosystems that have achieved some control over their interactions and evolvability would best be able to "ride" changes in the environment and adapt to them. They can evolve their can evolvability. According to Kauffman:

> Real ecosystems are not totally connected. Typically, each species interacts with a subset of the total number of other species; hence the system has some extended web structure. We can now extend our own results to such ecosystems. The supposition that selection can act on a coevolutionary system to control its connectivity, and therefore its dynamics, points in a very interesting direction. It might be the case that coevolving ecosystems tend toward a state of "self-organized criticality" in which parts of the ecosystem are frozen for long periods, such that the species in the frozen component do not change, while other species continue to coevolve.[137]

The human body is such a coevolving ecosystem, with some systems – breathing, heartbeat, – controlled by more or less frozen structures, while other systems – immune reactions, dreams, thinking – are free to continue evolving. If the tendency toward coevolution is part of the ordering process at the edge of chaos, then societies, schemata, neural networks, economies, and even psyches would be going through a constant process of integration. Frozen islands would be maintained in a sea of intercommunicating networks that organized around them into new structures. There would be a kind of tacking back and forth between too much order and rigidity, and too little. These adjustments could then feed back into the system, altering its structure and causing emergent patterns. Kauffman sums up this scenario as follows:

> We have now seen that the transition region between order and chaos gives rise to the most complex dynamics. In addition, tentative evidence supports the hypothesis that parallel-processing systems coevolving to carry out complex tasks, such as the mismatch game, do in fact evolve both from the ordered regime and from the chaotic regime, toward the edge of chaos. Thus we are led to a bold hypothesis: Living systems exist in the solid regime near the edge of chaos, and natural selection achieves and sustains such a poised state. ... Boolean systems, and by extension some large family of homologous nonlinear dynamical systems, with nearly melted frozen components can carry out the most complex, yet controllable behavior. They can adapt by accumulation of successive variations precisely because damage does not propagate widely. Useful alterations in the behavior of one functionally isolated island can accumulate with alterations in another island. Furthermore, evolvability is high in networks near the order-chaos boundary because here many muta-

---

[137] Ibid., p. 255.

tions cause minor changes and some mutations cause major changes. In a changing environment, this range of responses causes adaptive buffering.[138]

The critical state has been modeled by physicist Per Bak and colleagues as a sand-pile on a round table onto which sand is falling one grain at a time from a central location above the table. At the beginning of the process, the grain can fall anywhere on the table and find a stable location. As time passes, a central sand mountain begins to build up on the table. It becomes like a network in which there are so many connections and constraints on information flow that no innovations can happen. At a certain point, the mountain reaches a critical state where no more grains can find a footing. Each new grain then can cause a small or a large avalanche. The general pattern is many small avalanches and a few large ones. Anywhere that this pattern occurs – in earthquakes, traffic patterns, economies, species extinctions, genetic drift –, it is a marker for a system in a critical state.

Reaching this state would cause a complexity catastrophe if each grain of sand represented new learning. It would mean that, after a certain point, new ideas could not find a footing on the pile and might cause an avalanche carrying away with them many successful adaptations. The sandpile in a critical state would be like a complex system that is almost frozen. If we imagine the grains of sand as mutations or new learning, those that fall on the table at the beginning have a much greater chance of finding a place. As with the QWERTY keyboard, timing may be crucial. Those falling on the mountain in a critical state may be lost in the system not because of any intrinsic property of the individual grain, but because it can cause overload and runaway avalanches in the structure as a whole. If the sand is wet, the system can go into a supercritical state, where a single last grain can cause massive destruction. In this state many positive innovations will be lost.

One of the strategies that seems to have been useful in the adaption of organisms to the edge of chaos is canalizing, that is constraining future developments by channeling their emergence. We can imagine this in terms of the sand pile, as the capacity of the pile itself to form valleys that could allow new grains to slide down the mountain without disturbing the structure. In biological organisms, the "sandpile" is, in fact, living tissue that reacts when it is acted upon. In searching for solutions, the "living sand pile" could create a "new table top" above it that would freeze development in part of the area below, while allowing a whole new "level" of new adaptations above. Biologist C. H. Waddington has suggested that life forms create "creodes," which are fixed channels of development that constrain future development within a certain range.[139] Creodes would be to evolution what

---

[138] Ibid., p. 280.
[139] Laughlin, C.D., et al., eds., *Brain, Symbol, and Experience*, p. 54.

grammar is to language and rituals are to cultures, a structure which defines and constrains future possibilities. Waddington believes that at each layer of evolution, genes limit possible connections and make others more likely. He pictures these limits as pegs and wires which cause "valleys" or channels to appear in the landscape above. When new experience enters, like a ball or grain of sand, it is more likely to be constrained by a creode. But under external experiences of environmental stress, like a windy day, for example, the ball or the grain of sand may be pushed out of its creode. Then it could fall on the side of the sand mountain and cause an avalanche. The ideal place to achieve evolutionary success might be at a highly canalized subcritical state. Here there are still some possibilities for new growth, new ideas, and new mutations to find fertile territory to take hold; but the possibility of destructive avalanches is held in check under most circumstances. Extended order is traded for unregulated flow. Darwinian natural selection may be working to optimize subcritical states because they are the best place to adapt, but the fact that the mountain forms in the first place is due to the self-organizing feature of complex adaptive systems.

Something like the formation of information processing "creodes" seems to occur in the human nervous system. Biologist D. O. Hebb hypothesized in 1949 that nerve cells become associated in an array or pathway by firing at the same time.[140] When they do this, they seem to register some kind of "gain" and tend to fire as a group again. The gain is a kind of feedback through which the pathway "learns." Once a pathway becomes activated, it is more likely to be activated in the future. Each activation associates some cells and inhibits other connections. Perhaps something equivalent to a dissipative system forms when just the right number of connections is made. Then the self-organizing properties of the system constrain future activity. There is evidence that the spiral waves generated by heart muscles and electrical activity within our brains sometimes operate in this way.[141] Once set in motion, the system is unresponsive to further stimulus until its activity is completed.

The developed neurological networks become a CAS with a high-grid, high-group creode system that keeps it poised at near the edge of chaos under most circumstances. But any living system operates on a changing landscape, where gain is constantly being adjusted. A larger pathway could "eat up" a smaller one, or a pathway could become extinguished by inhibition. The pathways would compete for energy the way species compete for resources. Certain kinds of activities could bring the structure closer to a critical state or closer to chaos.

---

[140] Hebb, D.O., *The Organization of Behavior*.
[141] See Coveney, P. and Highfield, R., *Frontiers of Complexity*.

One could imagine ecostructures within the nervous system with fierce competition and fragmentation, and others with a cooperative strategy of coevolution. Competition has been named the "Red Queen strategy" after the character in Alice-in-Wonderland who must constantly run faster to keep up with others who must also run faster to keep up with her. Red Queen environments exhaust resources and lead in the long run to lowered adaptation. Some cooperative coevolution would be a more successful strategy, but if there were too many cooperative constraints, an environment could become frozen and unable to respond to change. That means that natural selection in certain landscapes might favor those organisms with an integrative function that could hold some features in the landscape in a frozen, canalized regime, while allowing other features to coevolve to the edge of chaos, where new possibilities of creativity are maximized. Organisms must then have evolved with the capacity to adjust their connectivity or epistasis at certain levels. In Kauffman's view,

> Selection, in a kind of selective metadynamics and as if by an invisible hand, may act on individual members of a species to alter the statistical structure of their fitness landscapes and the richness of their couplings to other partners so as to attain ecosystems poised at the phase transition between order and chaos. These structured ecosystems harbor nearly melted frozen components, optimize sustained fitness, and permit propagation of avalanches of coevolutionary change, ringing out the old species and ringing in the new.[142]

With the new model of complex adaptive systems, it is possible to link discoveries in many previously separate academic disciplines and to separate out local features of various systematic endeavors from the general (archetypal) features of CAS. Perhaps the most interesting aspect of this work from a psychological point of view is that the principles being uncovered apply equally to systems we would previously have classified as primarily physical – cells, ant colonies, catalytic reactions – and systems we would have classified as primarily mental or cultural – social systems, human cognition, economies. The differences between physical-somatic CAS and psychic-cultural CAS do not seem to be especially important to the theory, which blurs the line between them. This has caused major debates in philosophical circles over the similarities and differences between human minds and the rest of the natural world.[143] Computer scientist John Holland, quoted by Waldrop, has been convinced for twenty-five years, "that adaptation in the mind and adaptation in nature were just two different aspects of the same thing."[144] Moreover, he was convinced that "if they really were the same thing, they ought to be describable by the same theory."[144] While trying to

---

[142] Kauffman, S.A., *Origins*, p. 261.
[143] See Dennett, D.C., *Darwin's Dangerous Idea*.

work out this theory, he was continually forced to find mathematical expressions for modeling and prediction, as if both psyche and soma, and all growing organisms, shared the need for something like a model or image against which to test experience in order to better adapt to it.

But to Holland, the concept of prediction and models actually ran far deeper than conscious thought – or for that matter, far deeper than the existence of a brain. "All complex adaptive systems – economies, minds, organisms, – build models that allow them to anticipate the world," he declares. Yes, even bacteria. As it turns out, says Holland, many bacteria have special enzyme systems that cause them to swim toward stronger concentrations of glucose. Implicitly, those enzymes model a crucial aspect of the bacterium's world: that chemicals diffuse outward from their source, growing less and less concentrated with distance. And the enzymes simultaneously encode an implicit prediction: If you swim toward higher concentrations, then you are likely to find something nutritious. "It's not a conscious model or anything of that sort," says Holland. "But it gives that organism an advantage over one that doesn't follow the gradient."[145]

What Holland is looking at could be described as a pre-conscious, pre-nervous system, self-organizing tendency at a somatic level in biological organisms. In order to understand this, it is important not to unconsciously import the old Cartesian distinction of "matter" and "mind" as completely separate, basic, irreducible "substances," into the concepts of soma and psyche. The old concept of "matter" treats the natural world as a closed and frozen system in or near equilibrium in the –+ sector of our diagram. In the Newtonian paradigm, "mind" becomes mysteriously inexplicable. Although systems in or near equilibrium do exist in the natural world, they are only one type of system. Living tissue, or soma, is already organized in the +– sector, as an open dissipative system, a complex adaptive system. It has gone through a phase change from mineral to life form, from frozen regime to adaptive living system. "Matter" and "soma" are organized differently and should not be confused. In the new paradigm, both soma and psyche are evolving information processing systems that depend on feedback from the environment. They are both complex adaptive systems poised near the edge of chaos, capable of complicated modeling and going through processes of change, though at different time scales. The somatic bodily processes include the approximately forty-year period of reproduction in which gene mutations can occur. Neurological networks take their basic form over the twenty-year period in which an infant grows to adulthood. The immune system and mental schema change from day to day. We have to begin to understand the

---

[144] Waldrop, *Complexity*, p. 176.
[145] Ibid., p. 177.

human organism as a network of nested systems, each level contained in and containing others.

It seems that there are two rather different modes of transformation in every CAS. In biological species, a current genotype can be changed by a random mutation in DNA. This is modeled in computer programs as "exploration learning" and is very conservative in biological life forms, being protected by many safety devices that function like creodes to constrain possible changes. On the other hand, the basic structure or genotype can remain the same but the strength of different elements could be reinforced, as in the gain achieved when a neural pathway fires. This is called "exploitation learning" and involves reinforcing pathways of linkage and classification within the hard wiring that already exists. Many differences of phenotype in the human being depend on exploitation learning. In fact, humans are evolving to have more and more possibilities of exploitation learning. One thinks here of a child learning mathematics. All the elements are in place already, but they are acting on each other to reinforce some learning pathways and extinguish others.

Philosopher Gregory Bateson thought that exploration learning is like setting the thermostat in your house for a higher temperature when it gets cold in the winter, and exploitation learning is like putting on a sweater if you get cold at that setting. But if you get very cold, you can reset the thermostat.[146] Being able to reset the thermostat is an accomplishment of a different and higher logical type than putting on a sweater. In human beings, it seems that soma, because it is very conservatively constrained, is more connected with exploration learning, and the psyche is more connected with exploitation learning. At the same time, exploration learning seems to be leading to a soma and psyche with greater and greater possibilities for variability in behavior. The evolutionary history of human beings seems to have left open large areas of phenotypal development dependent on exploitation learning. This makes human beings very flexible in dealing with environmental changes. Flexibility is most useful in a rapidly changing environment or to a creature who can rapidly change environments. Humans have the capacity to become acclimatized to both sea-level and high mountain living by habituating to different respiratory and circulatory rhythms. Those who have the most possibilities of acclimatizing to new situations will be the most adaptable. They will survive long enough for exploration learning to produce useful mutations. In Bateson's view, our species is being acted upon by selection to enhance the greatest amount of choice and creativity, consistent with maintenance of order. When we use this creativity, the next period of selection will favor those who use it best. There is an ideal balance for

---

[146] Bateson, G., *Mind and Nature*.

creativity at a poised state between order and chaos as in all CAS. Too much creativity leads to anarchy and chaos. Too little leads to rigidity.

Complexity theory is still a young science and more is known about how computer programs work than how such models apply to the evolution of biological life. It is unclear where and how we might understand parallel processing and feedforward models when we are talking about brain cells or heart muscles. More is known about the schemata of computer modeling systems than about what homologous process is at work in the psyche and soma. In a talk entitled, "Complexity Made Simple," Holland laid out the following seven basic features of all currently known complex adaptive systems.[147]

1. They are based on "aggregation." This can be understood as something like the high group dimension we used in discussing societies. The nodes in each system act together in concert, though no one is sure what the "glue" is in any particular application. Perhaps biological organisms that tend toward aggregation in coevolving systems have survived because the strategy allows higher levels of computation.

2. The systems are "nonlinear." Simple causes do not produce simple results. Depending on initial conditions, small changes can have huge effects that cannot be modeled with conventional mathematics based on trends or statistics. These systems truly leave room for chance and creativity. Nothing is determined by the past.

3. Resources "flow" through the system. There is an unpredictable multiplier effect such that when a certain node is in the right place at the right time with the right model, it can win a jackpot or move into chaos, while its closest neighbor is untouched.

4. The systems are "diverse," with each node in constant change as ever new information flows toward it from the environment. Imitation seems to be built into the adaptive pattern, as each node models successful strategies by its neighbors and tries them out. This gambit may prove less costly than independent research or reinventing the wheel.

5. Every system uses "tags," that is, emblems or recognition signs that allow patterns to be sorted into same and other. These break symmetries by privileging certain patterns over others.

6. The systems all use "building blocks" that are constantly shuffled and rearranged. New inventions are often a recombination of previously used bits. "For example, internal combustion engines employ Venturi's perfume spraying device (carburetor), Volta's sparking device (spark plug), the pistons of a mine pump, the gear wheels of a water mill, and so on."[148]

---

[147] Holland, J., "Complexity made simple," *The Bulletin of the Santa Fe Institute*, 1994, 9(3): 3-4.
[148] Ibid., p. 4.

7. The systems build "internal models" of their world. They are run in "virtual mode" as a "lookahead" to anticipate the future. The systems rely on feedforward and feedback to modify their models. They are in a constant process of intrinsic emergence, where new information alters the structure of information processing itself.

8. Schemata, Psyche, Synchronicity

What is needed is a view of humanity that integrates the human into nature rather than separating us out from it, and a view of nature that stresses its interpenetration into all areas of human experience and cognition, including the artificial worlds of simulation technologies.[149]

– Katherine Hayles

Many complexity theorists have hesitated to take on the implications of these models for human consciousness, but clearly there must be a connection. At a recent workshop entitled, "Complexity: Metaphors, Models, and Reality," psychologist Ben Martin gave a historical overview of the use of the concept "schemata" in philosophy. He then went on to outline how cognitive psychologists are framing human cognition in terms of feedforward models like those used in the theory of complex adaptive systems. Having accepted that human knowledge is myopic, cognitive psychologists propose that we generate correctable internal schemata which we use to scan and test the environment. Martin sums up the work as follows:

> Just as schemata represent world knowledge, a connectionist network can represent environmental information by altering weights so as to change stable states of the system. Just as schemata have variables, a connectionist network can use unit activities, or the activity of ensembles of units to encode features of the environment. The possible state of this unit or ensemble would then correspond to possible values of an environmental variable. Just as the schemata can embed, so a part of the network can represent a subschema of the schema instantiated by the full network. Finally, just as the schemata represent knowledge at multiple levels of abstraction, the ensembles of activity in a network can capture the properties of any information from the environment as long as the parameters of the network are adjusted according to the proper learning procedure.[150]

---

[149] Hayles, K., "Towards a Conclusion," in: Cronon, W. ed., *Uncommon Ground*, p. 465.

In the discussion of this paper, the workshop participants were trying to make models of themselves modeling complex adaptive systems modeling the world: models of models of models, as in building blocks within building blocks. At the end of his talk, Ben Martin gave a list of the basic features of cognitive schemata, and not surprisingly, the list dovetailed neatly into Holland's list of basic features of all complex adaptive systems. Very similar features were being called by slightly different names. Holland's "aggregation" became "assimilation" and "inclusiveness." Holland's "tags" became "summarization." Holland's "building blocks" became "recursiveness."[151]

In his 1979 book, *Mind and Nature*, Gregory Bateson was reaching for a model which placed the development of mind within the context of evolutionary biology. He tried to work out what basic features would be required for mind to function, and came up with a list of six tentative items, again very much like Holland's list. He also suggested that, in the future, based, perhaps, on G. Spencer-Brown's *Laws of Form* or on René Thom's catastrophe theory, "deep restructuring of the foundations of mathematics and epistemology may come."[152] He certainly would have been very excited about complexity theory, and it is regrettable that he died just before the decade in which its development burgeoned. Bateson saw that mind must depend on something like Holland's "tags," that is, on perceptions of difference, and that difference is related to order. When we build up a system based on schemata that take note of difference, this system is based on a representation of a higher logical type, a higher level of abstraction, than that of the "objects" which "have" the difference: "– difference is a non-substantial phenomenon not located in space and time; difference is related to negentropy and entropy rather than energy."[153] There is a hint here that the structure of complex adaptive systems may not exist in the time-space world we posit in our reality-binding cultural paradigm, but, in fact, are something like Kantian categories of thought or Jungian archetypes.

Bateson believed that any system which exhibited the structure of mind would have the potentialities of autonomy, death, exploration, and preference. He thought consciousness must appear as an emergent phenomenon somewhere along the line of development, as a product. One might ask whether mind, as he is defining it, may not be exactly synonymous with biological life. He summed up his thinking as follows:

> Autonomy – literally *control of the self*, from the Greek *autos* (self) and *nomos* (law) – is provided by the recursive structure of the system. Whether or not a

---

[150] Martin, Ben, "The schema," in: Cowan, G.A., Pines, D., Meltzer, D., eds., *Complexity Metaphors, Models, and Reality*, p. 276.
[151] Ibid., p. 276.
[152] Bateson, G., *Mind and Nature*, p. 136.
[153] Ibid., p 136.

simple machine with a governor can control or be controlled by itself may be disputed, but imagine more loops of information and effect added on top of the simple circuit. What will be the content of the signal material carried by these loops? The answer, of course, is that these loops will carry messages *about* the behavior of the whole system. In a sense, the original simple circuit already contained such information ("It's going too fast"; "It's going too slow"), but the next level will carry such information as "the correction of 'it's going too fast' is not fast enough," or "the correction of 'it's going too fast' is excessive." That is, the messages become messages about the previous lower level. From this to autonomy is a very short step.[154]

In a recent account of cognitive psychology known as "biogenic structuralism," Laughlin et al., the authors of *Brain, Symbol, and Experience*, connect consciousness with the somatic modeling capacities of the brain. From what is now known about brain structure and function, it seems the mid-brain creates schemata of the sensed world, and the neocortex moves up a level of modeling to make schemata about coping with the sensorial schemata:

> On the sensorial side the impetus will be toward the portrayal of a topographically veridical but fundamentally abstract model of reality; on the prefrontal side the impetus will be toward generating a feedforward anticipation or, orientation toward, and organization of cognitive processes about sensorial objects and events. The sensorial processes constitute the world; the prefrontal processes constitute the subject rising to anticipate, meet, and cope with the world-object in intentional focus within its sensorial context.[155]

It must be the case that consciousness develops in connection with prefrontal modeling schemata which have the computational power to model the modeler. However, this modeling is a process that can never include more than a fraction of the internal environment which has many separate and fragmented pathways of organization. Sensory input must rise above a certain threshold for us to be conscious of it, and these thresholds are controlled by the midbrain. We are never aware that they are operating. An unconscious process has channeled our modeling abilities by forming creodes. These creodes are connected with neural pathways in the cortex. By their nature, prefrontal neural pathways inhibit some information in order to focus and integrate. The creodes represent all that information which is frozen out. If they were not there, the information system could suffer a complexity catastrophe and be pushed into chaos. Perhaps the creodes maintain the information processing at a subcritical level. That means that our conscious modeling systems are like small spotlights that illuminate one

---

[154] Ibid., p. 136.
[155] Laughlin, C.D., et al., *Brain, Symbol, and Experience*, p. 119.

area while throwing the rest into shadow. They can integrate more and more schemata at the conscious level only at the cost of abstraction and inhibition.

What, then, happens to all the information frozen out of the conscious schemata? Biogenic structuralists postulate a second psychic, but unconscious, integrative modeling system, a second psychic complex adaptive system operating simultaneously with consciousness within the human being. This unconscious system must be responsible for the formation of the creodes on which consciousness rests. When we sleep, conscious modeling and integrating processes close down, and are replaced by unconscious integrating processes controlled by the limbic system. We experience this second system in our dreams which are inferred to be the experiential referent of brain activity, just as consciousness is.

That the organizing and integrating work connected with dreaming is crucially important can be inferred from the amount of time all young mammals spend in associated REM (rapid eye movement) sleep. Newborn infants spend fifty to sixty percent of their sleep time in REM sleep. It drops to about forty percent by the fifth month, and by two years, holds steady at the adult level of about thirty percent.[156] If adults are deprived of REM sleep, they begin to exhibit psychotic symptoms within a few days. This suggests that the integrating activity is needed to prevent information from overriding creodes. Given an opportunity to sleep, sleep-deprived subjects will do so until they make up the lost time in REM sleep. Normally, the whole process is cyclic and under the control of the autonomic nervous system. It seems to go on all the time, but when we are awake, the prefrontal cortex inhibits awareness of the process along with much else. This organizing activity goes on autonomously. We do not direct it, but live in it unconsciously.

It seems that the human organism is under the control of three separate but interconnected CAS, which have evolved over millions of years, linked with what has been called the triune brain.[157] Each CAS is made up of many other CAS as building blocks. The oldest portion of the brain, which humans share with all vertebrate animal life, is the spinal cord and the brain stem. This structure controls breathing and blood circulation and has been called the "reptilian" brain. We can exert very little conscious control over this system, and it seems to be in charge of maintaining basic homeostasis. The second CAS, the paleomammalian brain, is made up of the limbic system and the pituitary gland, which controls the endocrine system. This CAS regulates hunger, sleep, emotion, pain avoidance, and bodily orientation. It has been called the "hot brain."[158] It operates independently of conscious control, but we can sometimes put "brakes" on it through conscious effort. We can affect

---

[156] Ibid., p. 284.
[157] See for example, Stevens, A., *Archetypes*.
[158] Ibid., p. 265.

it only in the negative: we can't will ourselves to be hungry, thirsty, fearful, enthusiastic, in love, or alert rather than sleepy, but we can prevent ourselves from acting on any of these feelings to varying degrees. The neomammalian brain, or neocortex, is the locus of control of sophisticated abstract cognitive integrating models. This has been called the "cold brain" because of its largely inhibitory character. The cold brain seems to be in charge of a cool appraisal of moment-to-moment adaptation, whereas the hot brain seems to integrate the whole.

When we consider the triune brain in terms of complexity theory, some unique features emerge that are inconsistent with previous psychological schemata. First of all, CAS, as evolving computational systems, are capable of learning and recalibrating through feedback. They all have what Bateson saw as the capacity of mind, that is, they have an intelligence and integrating capacity of their own. This self-organizing factor has operated for billions of years before the emergence of either the cold brain or consciousness. In the past, the hot brain was seem as "impulsive, incautious, and wanton."[159] Therefore, it was identified with Freud's id and the "pleasure principle." Ego consciousness, depending on the cold brain inhibitory function in the neocortex, was seen as the locus of evaluation and integration. What was in the id was inferior to what was in the ego. In fairy tales, interpretations from this Freudian perspective, the hot brain was often connected with giants, who are portrayed as stupid and are often outwitted by heros and heroines, who are connected with consciousness.

In complexity theory, however, the hot brain is "intelligent" like all CAS. It is not at all inferior, but, in fact, has its own functional integration, which could be equal to, or even superior to, that of the cold brain. It actually is the schemata of the hot brain out of which the cold brain has evolved. This is far more consistent with Jung's concept of unconscious processes. Jung was deeply impressed with the autonomous and creative quality of the unconscious, which he thought must be connected with the sympathetic nervous system.

> If the facts do not deceive us, the unconscious processes are far from being unintelligent. The character of automatism and mechanism is lacking to them, even to a striking degree. They are not in the least inferior to the conscious processes in subtlety; on the contrary, they often far surpass our conscious insights.[160]

It seems that the medical model, which has been the basis for understanding the psyche in much of Europe and the United States for the last several centuries, was based on Newtonian physics relating to equilibrium systems.

---

[159] Ibid., p. 265.
[160] Jung, C.G., *Structure and Dynamics of the Psyche*, Vol. 8, p. 178.

The body was compared to a machine in equilibrium physics in which whatever moved did so automatically as a result of causal reflexes. Order and energy could not be created, only traded or lost. The human body was modeled as a linear computer program. Only the human mind was held to have free will and autonomy, operating in another realm than the body. Now that we have a model of complex adaptive systems as the origin of life, we can rethink these schemata. All CAS, modeled as parallel-processing systems, have a kind of unpredictable "free will" and autonomy. They create and build up order and energy within their structures. This new model in complexity theory is much more consistent with Jungian psychology.

If the entire human nervous system controlling the body is modeled as a CAS, it is a coevolutionary system. We saw in the last section that coevolutionary systems tend to move to subcritical computation levels. This means that the system strives toward integration so that some parts of the system can be held constant, while others are freed up toward greater modeling and exploration activity. The separation of the functions of the reptilian brain from the rest of the human brain are one evidence of such a coevolutionary tendency. The human split-brain is another. The split-brain has been modeled as two different kinds of organizing system. The left brain can be thought of as high-grid and high-group, with many specialized creodes organizing channels of function. The right brain with its integrative networks would be more like high-group, low-grid structures. Perhaps, the right brain – with its close connection to the limbic system – has the capacity to be much closer to subcriticality and the edge of chaos. If so, the unconscious might have the ability to go through phase transitions that are completely unknown to the conscious ego linked with left brain structure.

The right brain has an elaborately connected neural structure with long neuronal pathways linking large sections of the limbic system and neocortex. This system coordinates emotion, attachment (high group), love, territoriality, image formation, mythological thinking, sleep, and dreaming, all without our conscious control. It is busy, ancient, and creative, and it is the origin of the neocortex and ego consciousness. In Jungian psychology, the unconscious integrating function connected with these structures is called the "Self." In Jungian interpretations, the Self is thought to be represented in myth, dreams, and fairy tales by the child, often a child god or "divine child," while the conscious ego is portrayed as the adult. The integrating function of the Self is outside of consciousness, a "counterpole of the world." That is, "Self" and "world" are both limit concepts, indicating functional unities which can be named but never fully known consciously, because they transcend consciousness. Ego consciousness is produced, Jung thought, by separating from this integrating function, which nevertheless produces it. "Identity does not make consciousness possible; it is only separation, detachment, and agonizing confrontation through opposition that produce consciousness and insight." Thus, the ego is to the Self, as the adult is to the child. Adult consciousness has separated out from childhood integration and is unconscious of the continuing "child"-integrating activities going on in the background of conscious life. Adult consciousness believes itself to be superior to the child. In mythology, the opposite story is often told.

> Myth however emphasizes that it is not so, but that the "child" is endowed with superior powers and despite all dangers, will unexpectedly pull through. The "child" is born out of the womb of the unconscious, begotten out of the depths of human nature, or rather out of living Nature herself. It is a personification of vital forces quite outside the limited range of our conscious mind; of ways and possibilities which our one-sided mind knows nothing; a wholeness which embraces the very depths of Nature. It represents the strongest, the most ineluctable urge in every being, namely the urge to realize itself. It is, as it were, an incarnation of *the inability to do otherwise*, equipped with all the powers of nature and instinct, whereas the conscious mind is always getting caught up in its supposed ability to do otherwise. The urge and compulsion to self-realization is a law of nature and thus of invincible power, even though its effect, at the start, is insignificant and improbable. Its power is revealed in the miraculous deeds of the child hero. ... [161]

If all CAS work on the principle of using other CAS as building blocks, then any biological organism alive today has the somatic structure of a three-billion-year-old CAS. Here is an "Old One," with a cognitive apparatus like a rhizome, out of which can be drawn a huge variety of images based on its long experience. As conscious beings, we are part of a much newer inhibitory system. We are only beginning to have the capacity to imagine living tissue as a coherent learning environment. We do not yet fully understand what "it knows." If the unconscious is nearer to the edge of chaos in its connectivity than the structured ego, it may have "melting phases" that can reach down into the most primitive and archaic organizing systems of biological life. For the most part, Western culture has ignored dreams as a source of information about the inner or outer world. Depth psychology has attempted to model the adult human as two great psychic/somatic organizing systems: the unconscious one with many interconnected subsystems we share with all biological organisms, and the conscious ego-organizing system with abstract language capabilities that only humans seem to have developed.

Jung's work anticipated the development of complexity theory (and even awaited it), and a great many fruitful parallels can be drawn between Jungian ideas and complexity theory. When Jung postulated that there are two

---

[161] Jung, C.G., *The Archetypes and the Collective Unconscious*, Vol. 9.1, p. 170.

organizing systems at work in the human psyche, he realized that this idea deeply contradicted the dominant scientific paradigm. He wrote in 1946,

> [A] second psychic system coexisting with consciousness – no matter what qualities we suspect it of possessing – is of absolutely revolutionary significance in that it could radically alter our view of the world.[162]

Because the human soma is conservatively constrained by our genetic inheritance, the unconscious CAS has a layer that is as similar in different human beings as our physical structure. Just as we all have heads and hearts, parts of our neural structure are hardwired. This means that the unconscious CAS of every person is much more similar than the conscious system. Jung labeled this common feature of the psyche the "collective unconscious":

> The collective unconscious is in no sense an obscure corner of the mind, but the mighty deposit of ancestral experience accumulated over millions of years, the echo of prehistoric happenings to which each century adds an infinitesimally small amount of variation and differentiation. Because the collective unconscious is, in the last analysis, a deposit of world-process embedded in the structure of the brain and in the sympathetic nervous system, it constitutes in its totality a sort of timeless and eternal world image which counterbalances our conscious, momentary picture of the world. It means nothing less than another world, a mirror world, if you will. But unlike a mirror image, the unconscious image possesses an energy peculiar to itself, independent of consciousness. By virtue of this energy, it can produce powerful effects which do not appear on the surface, but influence us all the more powerfully from within.[163]

Jung realized that his idea of a second organizing system, although revolutionary in the environment of the materialist / positivist paradigm of the science of his time, had been shared by many other thinkers in the past. It was anticipated in Chinese philosophy several thousand years ago and in various alchemical writings, which is perhaps why Jung was so excited to find them.

Jung discovered that over five hundred years ago, Paracelsus had also postulated two psychic organizing systems. According to Paracelsus, both animals and humans have an "inborn spirit" – "the first and best treasure which the monarchy of nature hides within itself."[164] According to Paracelsus, humans have an outer and inner knowledge. The outer corresponds to mind, rationality, and logic. The inner

> is eternally transfigured and true, and if in the mortal body he appeareth not perfect, yet he appeareth perfect after the separation of the same. That which

[162] Jung, C.G., *Structure and Dynamics of the Psyche*, p. 178.
[163] Ibid., Vol. 8, p. 376.
[164] Ibid., Vol. 8, p. 194.

we now tell of is called *lumen naturae* and is eternal. – But if we are to describe the origin of the inner man or body, mark that all inner bodies be but one body and one single thing in all men, albeit divided in accordance with the well disposed numbers of the body, each one different.[165]

The idea of *correspondentia*, or a "sympathy of all things" was basic to Western Classical and Medieval thought. Hippocrates, for example, wrote:

There is one common flow, one common breathing, all things are in sympathy. The whole organism and each one of its parts are working in conjunction for the same purpose ... The great principle extends to the extremest part, and from the extremest part it returns to the great principle, to the one nature, and not-being.[166]

The three-thousand-year-old Chinese philosophy of Taoism seems also to have worked out similar ideas. Alan Watts wrote of Taoism in his 1957 book, *The Way of Zen*:

Thus, to begin to understand what Taoism is about, we must at least be prepared to admit the possibility of some view of the world other than the conventional, some knowledge other than the contents of our surface con- sciousness, which can apprehend reality only in the form of one abstraction (or thought, the Chinese nien) at a time. There is no real difficulty in this, for we already admit that we "know" how to move our hands, or how to breathe, even though we can hardly begin to explain how we do it in words. We know how to do it because we just do it! Taoism is an extension of this kind of knowledge. ... [167]

Watts claimed that the Westerners of his generation could not understand Taoism because they were trapped in a conventional (i.e. at that time, Newtonian) way of thinking. Ching, the essential dynamic of the inner and outer world central to Taoism, is that world-shaping, pattern-forming energy that is comparable to the concept of self-organization in complexity theory. The Tao is a non-Western god image that is "the intelligence which shapes the world with a skill beyond our understanding."[168]
According to Watts,

The important difference between the Tao and the usual idea of God is that whereas God produces the world by making (wei), the Tao produces by "not- making" (wu-wei) – which is approximately what we mean by "growing." ... A universe which grows utterly excludes the possibility of knowing how it grows in the clumsy terms of thought and language, so that no Taoist would dream of asking whether the Tao knows it produced the universe. For it operates

---

[165] Ibid., Vol. 8, p. 194.
[166] Ibid., Vol. 8, p. 490.
[167] Watts, A.W., *The Way of Zen*, p. 17.
[168] Ibid., p. 17.

according to spontaneity, not according to plan. ... But spontaneity is not by any means a blind disorderly urge, a mere power of caprice. A philosophy restricted to the conventions of ordinary language has no way of conceiving an intelligence which does not work according to plan, according to a (one-at-a-time) order of thought. Yet the concrete evidence of such an intelligence is right to hand in our own bodies. For the Tao does not "know" how it produces the universe just as we do not know how we construct our brains.[169]

The Tao is thus a holistic, systemic phenomenon. According to Chuang-tzu, a contemporary of Plato, "Tao is obscured when you fix your eye on little segments of existence only." Chuang-tzu also understood that schemata are based on perceptions of difference in layers of logical types. "Limitations are not originally grounded in the meaning of life. Originally, words (schemata?) had no fixed meanings. Differences only arose through looking at things subjectively. ... When affirmation and negation came into being, the Tao faded. After the Tao faded, then came one-sided attachments."[170] According to Jung, it is typical of Taoism to think in terms of the whole rather than the part. He wondered, in the 1950's, whether this Chinese philosophy did not imply a critique of the entire Western scientific method.

With its concentration on parts rather than emergent wholes, Western scientific thought has been using a different paradigm of order than Taoism for centuries. In the new paradigm of complexity theory, local rules or "distributed intelligence" create unanticipated patterns without overall planning. It is hard for us to think this way, according to philosopher Daniel Dennett, because we are used to social models of central planning:

"Global" direction from on high puts in motion a hierarchical cascade of "local" projects. This is such a common feature of large-scale human projects that we have a hard time imagining alternatives. ... Since we don't recognize the principle Kauffman discerns as one that is familiar from human engineering, we are not apt to see it as a principle of engineering at all, but I suggest that it is. Reformulated slightly, we could put it as follows. Until you manage to evolve communicating organisms that can form large engineering organizations, you are bound by the following Preliminary Design Principle: all global order must be generated by local rules. So all the early products of design, up to the creation of something with some of the organizational talents of *Homo sapiens*, must obey whatever constraints follow from the "management decision" that all order must be accomplished by local rules."[171]

Interestingly enough, the oldest diagram of the dynamic phases of ching, said to have been made by Fu Hsi 5,000 years ago, actually somewhat matches the phases noted in previous diagrams of CAS as shown in Figure

[169] Ibid., p. 17.
[170] Jung, C.G., *Structure and Dynamics of the Psyche*, Vol. 8, p. 489.
[171] Dennett, D., *Darwin's Dangerous Idea*, p. 224.

8.1. At the −+ phase where Fate holds us bound, he has thunder and lightning, Jen and Li. Here, the rain, which will release stored energy, is still trapped in the form of a potential. In the phase where the high-group, high-grid system locks in, ++, he has the lake and the creative (yang), Dui and Kian. The rain has been released and is held by the organizing pattern of the lake shore and valley. In the phase where the system has many adjustable interconnections, +−, he has wind and water, Sun and Kan. The wind and water are constantly on the move, causing ever-new evolving variations of pattern while maintaining a recognizable order. At the phase change between +− and −−, he has the mountain, Gen. The mountain is the place where we become absolutely still, meditative, and open to new inspiration. Here is the place where uniting symbols form and enlightenment is reached. In the −− sector, where things can fall apart or regroup, he has the receptive (yin) Kun, representing that without order. The dynamics of the interconnections of these trigrams are the basis of all life organization in ancient Chinese philosophy and are modeled in the I Ching. It is as if the Tao, as the whole system of order, can go through characteristic, archetypal stages of change (ching) based on the level of order and connectedness intuitively sensed in various natural phenomena.

Figure 8.1 – Tao

If complexity theory has found a schemata that can model the fundamental self-ordering principles of both psychic and somatic life, these phases are archetypal, underlying structures of all somatic and psychic phenomena which are the objects of thought. The objects of thought are constituted unconsciously in our perceptual and cognitive integration of the environment. The unconscious ordering must be occurring through an archetypal grammar that leaves its imprint on experience.

Jung, influenced by Kantian philosophy, wanted to ground psychology in a phenomenological reflection that focused on the lived experience of subjectivity. He was very clear that he was not reifying archetypal images in the "outer" world, which we never encounter apart from our images of it. In using the concept of archetypes, he was talking about an order that appeared within our images of the world.

> We live immediately only in the world of images. If we take this standpoint seriously, peculiar results follow. We find that the validity of psychic facts cannot be subjected either to epistemological criticism or to scientific verification. We can only put the question: Is a conscious content present or not? If it is present, then it is valid in itself.[172]

Archetypal phenomena can be observed "subjectively" or personally by individuals in their own experience and modeled "objectively" in our schemata. In saying this, I am using the word, "objective," in the same sense as Rorty (above). "Objectively" means within the language of discourse conventional in Western scientific thought. Complexity theory is one way to do this modeling.

Jung always insisted that many of the personal, subjective phenomena he noticed were archetypal patterns that seemed to exist in some way in every psyche as a kind of "psychoid" substrate. He borrowed the term, "psychoid," from psychiatrist Eugen Bleuler, who used *die Psychoide* to refer to the functioning of sub-cortical processes in the brain. Bleuler had written:

> The *Psychoide* is the sum of all purposive, mnemonic, and life preserving functions of the body and central nervous system, with the exception of those cortical functions which we have always been accustomed to regard as psychic ... The body-psyche of the individual and the phylo-psyche together form a unity, which for the purposes of our present study, can most usefully be designated by the name *Psychoide*. Common to both *Psychoide* and psyche are ... conation and the utilization of previous experiences ... in order to reach the goal. This would include memory (engraphy and ecphoria) and association, hence something analogous to thinking.[173]

Jung noticed that there was a kind of mixing of subjective and objective, brain and psyche in Bleuler's category that he thought might be proper for anatomy, but should be differentiated in psychology. Thus, when Jung uses the word psychoid, he is aiming at a layer of personal experience midway between the experienced life process of a living body and conscious experience. He is not denying a link to the brain, but he rightly sees that we *infer* the link and wants to approach the psyche within the science of psychology on an experiential basis. The psychoid unconscious seems to bridge the gap between our lived experience of the body and our lived experience of consciousness. It leaks at one end into conscious experience in a psychic way as dreams, moods, fantasies, and images; and it leaks at the other end into autonomic body functions in a psychoid layer. That is why worry or stress

---

[172] Jung, C.G., *Structure and Dynamics of the Psyche*, Vol. 8, p. 328.
[173] Ibid., Vol. 8, p. 176.

can cause illness like ulcers, skin rashes, heart conditions, or even paralysis, which can clear up miraculously when the psychic analogue of the source is named, symbolized, or removed. Jung then used the word, "psyche," to refer to all conscious, unconscious, and "quasi-psychic" or psychoid layers of experience.

> The uniqueness of the psyche can never enter wholly into reality, it can only be realized approximately, though it still remains the absolute basis of all consciousness. The deeper "layers" of the psyche lose their individual unique-ness as they retreat farther and farther into darkness. "Lower down," that is to say as they approach the autonomous functional systems, they become increasingly collective until they are universalized and extinguished in the body's materiality, i.e., in chemical substances. The body's carbon is merely carbon. Hence, at bottom, the psyche is simple "world."[174]

If the psychoid layer in the psyche is close to "world" or "body," one wonders if the ordering imposed on the psyche would not follow the basic patterns of complex adaptive systems in coevolution. Thus, there might be a tendency to create frozen ++ islands with lakes of +− connectivity in the context of an integrating function that linked and constantly reordered the whole. Perhaps we could then plot Jung's basic archetypes of the collective unconscious, which he claimed existed in all psyches, on the diagram we have been using for CAS. Figure 8.2 shows what this would look like.

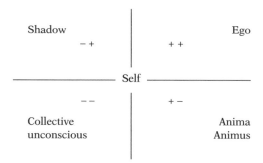

Figure 8.2 – Psychic self-organization

It seems clear that the ego is the part of the psyche with the highest grid and group in the sense that it forms a coherent, organized center, with an orientation in time, space, and logic. It is connected with the binding, repressive, inhibiting networks in the left neocortex. When this is damaged, in the case of brain injuries, very little ego structure or language use remains. The shadow or personal unconscious in Jungian psychology is what is

---

[174] Jung, C.G., *Archetypes and the Collective Unconscious*, Vol. 9.1, p. 173.

rejected from the conscious self-image as dissonant or irrelevant at any given present. When stored memories are retrieved from this reservoir, they come bound in space and time like ego contents. I can remember my first year of college in a certain city, the toy I was given on my fourth birthday, and so on. So we could think of the shadow as high-grid but low-group. Its contents are bound in time and space, but not aggregated with ego contents most of the time. The anima/animus is an irrational factor in Jung's view that pulls us out into connections with other people, the world, and the future. (A discussion here of the differences between the male and female psyche, the anima and animus, would take us too far afield, so I will consider them together in this context). The anima/animus then could be thought of as high-group, low-grid, because it searches for new forms of connectivity outside of conventional (++) relationships. Behind it, Jung said, lay "the archetype of meaning," which I would associate with a self-organizing factor at the edge of chaos. Here, where frozen islands melt and liquids merge into each other, new connections and symbols can form. The trickster, or Mercurius, as an archetype, is quite well modeled by this transforming process, which may be connected with liminality. Finally, at the – – pole, we move into the realm of turbulent formations like clouds, which form and reform in shifting patterns of weather. The collective unconscious also seems to be well-modeled by this image, as it is always going through transformations. In the human psyche, the Self is the factor that integrates these different possibilities, compensating any tendency toward one-sidedness to maintain wholeness and balance. The level of reality it operates from is psychoid or archetypal. It is connected with evolution as a self-organizing system maintaining the integrity of each organism until it suffers the complexity catastrophe of death.

Jung deduced that the orientation of space, time, and logic, which is so central to our conscious viewpoint, was relative to ego organization. Whatever crosses over into the realm of ego organization from other layers of the psyche, crosses into the realm of causality in time and space. Human beings cannot think or use a consistent language grammar in any other way, though each culture encodes these features in its own particular paradigm. These organizing features of ego consciousness are relative, constituting the ego and the ego world, but little else. Time, space, and logic would then be intrinsically emergent phenomena that feed back into the structure of thought. If this is the case, the archetypes or organizing patterns themselves can be thought of in a relatively more fluid realm where time, space, and causality can "bend," as in Einstein's physics. Such an environment would make synchronicities, or meaningful coincidences, more likely. Einstein and Jung developed their theories of relativity simultaneously during the 1920's in Zürich, where they both worked. Wolfgang Pauli, who collaborated with Jung on the theory of synchronicity, was working on quantum physics in

Zürich, and was in Jungian analysis at the same time. This "meaningful coincidence" could itself make us ask whether some archetypal "cloud formation" concerning relativity was taking place between the two World Wars in the only "neutral" country in Europe.

Jung noted that there are states of the psyche where synchronicities happen frequently, and there are also people who seem to be able to tap into these states with more ease than others. They seem to be able to go into a kind of trance state, or *abaissement du niveau mental*, which allows them to shift just below ego consciousness into a realm of relativity and creativity where meaningful knowing becomes a kind of clairvoyance. Anyone who has had the experience of synchronistic phenomena personally normally finds it most impressive; but there may be people who learn to move at will from normal ego states to heightened states of synchronicity. All divinitory techniques like the I Ching and the Tarot are based on this capacity. We could imagine that, for these people, the patterns of "the same" and "different" normally imposed on the world by the ego structure, become more fluid. So the ego maintains a critical state of order, while a second psychic organizing system, the unconscious, moves into a subcritical state. Synchronicities increase when the areas of "the same" begin to expand, yielding more connectivity. The occurrences of synchronicity, from the point of view of the ego, follow the patterns noted for other phenomena in critical states: many small synchronicities and occasional massive ones. If a massive "avalanche" or "flood" of synchronicities occurs, it might temporarily overcome the organized structure of the ego, causing trance or possession states, or even psychosis. If the ego structure became permanently susceptible to a type of involuntary override, we might call such a state schizophrenia. If the psyche learned to balance on an edge between ego-consciousness and synchronicity, the individual might be recognized in his or her society as an artist, healer, mystic, poet, shaman, psychic, or spirit-guide.

Jung was interested in the work of J. B. Rhine on parapsychology at Duke University. Rhine had shown that certain individuals do indeed have the capacity to "guess" what is on hidden cards far beyond the probability of random hits. Jung suggested that this possibility exists because at the unconscious psychoid level, there is a greater possibility of "acausal orderedness," or synchronicity. Note here that causal orderedness can be modeled by a linear computer program. Each step leads to the next step inevitably. A parallel-processing computer program of the type which models self-organized systems can exactly illustrate acausal orderedness. Thus, Jungian archetypes can be thought of as a reflection of the structure of complex adaptive systems on a psychic level. Jung himself, writing half a century before the discovery of parallel-processing systems, realized he was looking at something structural in all biological organisms: "On the organic level, it might be possible to regard biological morphogenesis in the light of the synchronistic factor. Professor A. M. Dalq (of Brussels), understands form, despite its tie with matter, as a 'continuity that is supraordinate to the living organism.'"[175]

Jung and Pauli, discussing the problem of synchronicity, came up with the idea that it must be part of an underlying ordering structure of the universe as we know it, operating at an archetypal level. They attempted to chart how it might be working and came up with a diagram. In Figure 8.3, their diagram is reoriented and + and – symbols have been added to illustrate its consistency with the other models used in the exposition of CAS.

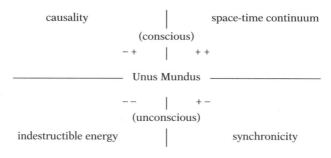

Figure 8.3 – Unus Mundus

The idea underlying their diagram was that both fixed space-time and relative space-time could be understood through a third archetypal ordering factor, the *Unus Mundus*, which, in one state, expressed itself as causality, and in another state, expressed itself as synchronicity. As the ordering principle crossed over from the unconscious to the conscious "quadrants," it went through a transforming phase change. As we have seen, the idea of phase changes is central to complexity theory. Jung expressed these insights as follows:

> A causalistic explanation of synchronicity seems out of the question for the reasons given above. It consists essentially of chance equivalences. Their *tertium comparationis* rests on the psychoid factors I call archetypes. These are *indefinite*, that is to say, they can be known and determined only approximately. Although associated with causal processes, or "carried" by them, they continually go beyond their frame of reference, an infringement to which I would give the name "transgressivity," because the archetypes are not found exclusively in the psychic sphere, but can occur just as much in circumstances that are not psychic (equivalence of an outward physical process with a

[175] Jung, C.G., *Structure and Dynamics of the Psyche*, Vol. 8, p. 512.

psychic one). Archetypal equivalences are *contingent* to causal determination, that is to say, there exists between them and the causal processes no relations that conform to law. They seem therefore to represent a special instance of randomness or chance, or of that "random state" which "runs through time in a way that fully conforms to law," as Andreas Speiser says. It is an initial state that is "not governed by mechanistic law," but is the precondition of law, the chance substrate on which law is based. If we consider synchronicity or the archetypes as the contingent, then the latter takes on the specific aspect of a modality that has the functional significance of a world-constituting factor.[176]

In this idea of "world-constituting factor," Jung is reaching for an idea like that of self-organization in nature. Writing before the widespread dissemination of the computer or computer program, Jung nevertheless had the idea that what he was looking at in the "psychoid" was related to number as an organizing structure of the natural world that would manifest itself locally in many different areas of experience. Just as the discovery of complex adaptive systems has come largely through work in mathematics and computer modeling, Jung saw that there must be a connection between synchronicity and properties of number:

> The sequence of natural numbers turns out to be unexpectedly more than a mere stringing together of identical units: it contains the whole field of mathematics and everything yet to be discovered in this field. Number, therefore, is in one sense an unpredictable entity. Although I would not care to undertake to say anything illuminating about the inner relation between two such apparently incommensurable things as number and synchronicity, I cannot refrain from pointing out that not only were they always brought into connection with one another, but both possess numinosity and mystery as their common characteristics. ... Number helps more than anything else to bring order into the chaos of appearances. It is the predestined instrument for creating order, or for apprehending an already existing, but still unknown, regular arrangement or "orderedness." It may well be the most primitive element of order in the human mind. ... Hence it is not such an audacious conclusion after all if we define number psychologically as an *archetype of order* which has become conscious.[177]

The experience of synchronicity has not been studied extensively in the West. In Jung's view, Western culture has been suffering for hundreds of years from a one-sidedness of schemata reflected in positivistic and materialistic scientific assumptions. One-sidedness is connected with a loss of symbol and ritual and a dissociation of mind and body, conscious and unconscious in modern society. One could say world-historical forces have pushed urban dwellers so far into the INDIVIDUALIST low-grid, low-group

---

[176] Ibid., Vol. 8, p. 515.
[177] Ibid., Vol. 8, p. 456.

sector that the Self in many individuals is crying out for a restoration of balance, order, and community. Jung saw his own work, and that of many other scientists, as struggling toward a unified idea of nature in this framework. It seems likely he would have been most interested in complexity theory.

> "Seen in this light, analytical psychology is a reaction against the exaggerated rationalization of consciousness which, seeking to control nature, isolates itself from her and so robs man of his own natural history. He finds himself transplanted into a limited present, consisting of the short span between birth and death. The limitation creates a feeling that he is a haphazard creature without meaning, and it is this feeling that prevents him from living his life with the intensity it demands if it is to be enjoyed to the full. Life becomes stale and is no longer the exponent of the full man. That is why so much unlived life falls into the unconscious. People live as though walking in shoes too small for them.[178]

In such a society, there is an enormously high level of spiritual suffering. It fills the consulting rooms of psychologists with people searching for meaning. Many symbols of integration or reintegration occur spontaneously both privately and publicly in a kind of interpsychic millennialism. In the negative, collective, and destructive form, this occurs as national agendas for unity and domination – the kinds of psychic infection that cause wars. At the same time, healing possibilities for reintegration also develop. In 1950, the Catholic Church, responding to the pressure of thousands of people all over the world, declared the Assumption of Mary to heaven. With this symbol, Jung thought, the West was beginning to bridge the gap between an exalted spiritual and conscious "male" world and a degraded material and unconscious "female" world. Matter was being spiritualized, and spirit materialized:

> The "psychization" of matter puts the absolute immateriality of the spirit in question, since this would then have to be accorded a kind of substantiality. The dogma of the Assumption, proclaimed in an age suffering from the greatest political schism history has ever known, is a compensating symptom that reflects the strivings of science for a uniform world picture.[179]

In complex self-organizing systems, we see a principle at work that could incorporate both grid and group, soma and psyche, time and synchronicity. Self-organization seems to require both a principle of transformation and a principle of cohesion, a many and a one. Every self-organizing life form is an ongoing integration of building blocks that are themselves integrations of other building blocks, and so on. Maybe this is why the alchemists spoke of

[178] Ibid., Vol. 8, p. 380.
[179] Jung, *Archetypes and the Collective Unconscious*, Vol. 9.1, p. 109.

scintillae – many sparks of light in matter, and why many Gods and giants in world mythology have multiple eyes. Paracelsus referred to the "interior firmament." These multiple luminosities are always in the process of reorganization and reintegration on a higher level. There is a tension between tendencies of dissociation and disintegration and the contrary tendency of further integration. The human personality is, according to Jung, capable of an indefinite expansion. "Gleaming islands, indeed, whole continents can still add themselves to our modern consciousness – a phenomenon that has become the daily experience of the psychotherapist."[180]

Computer scientists do not yet have any idea how to reproduce the magnitude of information processing circuits that would be required to imitate human consciousness. It has been calculated that a computation system based on human neuronal connections could have 10^{14} basic operations per second. Physicist Roger Penrose has suggested that current artificial intelligence programs, which are getting close to this capacity, are outstripped by the actual modeling capacities of a nematode worm.[181] Penrose wonders whether our consciousness might be based in the microtubule structures of our cells. If our psychic experience were connected with the computational structure made possible by cytoskeletal links, we would have the possibility for 10^{24} basic operations per second. This would be an information processing system so vast that it cannot be achieved artificially in the foreseeable future. Evidence that awareness is related to cytoskeletal structure rather than the nervous system comes from anesthesiology. Paramecia and amoebae, which do not have nervous systems, are immobilized by anesthetics just as humans are. Based on a schema of some sort of quantum coherence phenomena in the microtubule structure of living beings, there would be "knowing" in every cell of our bodies. This would be the basis for an "Old One" which has been in the process of learning for billions of years. Animals, the human body, and consciousness would be her offspring, and she would be like the Great Goddess of ancient myth who created the world through her dance.

Just as in complexity theory, Jung thought he saw the same basic dynamics at work in the whole range of human, social, and biological life. Exploring these depths was for him the deepest meaning to which we could aspire individually. In adding our part to the ongoing integrating agenda of biological life, we could help to dream on the mysterious unity that works within us. By doing this, we join forces with whatever source organizes the world, the unus mundus. This creates the possibility of a reimagined godhead, an Old One living in our soma and psyche who goes with us in the task of integrating and recreating the world at every moment. Such a living god, ever

---

[180] Jung, *Structure and Dynamics of the Psyche*, Vol. 8, p. 189.
[181] Penrose, R. *Shadows of the Mind*, p. 361.

cycling through dynamic changes of form in us and the world, leaves open the possibility that something unexpected and healing may emerge in our nature at the edge of chaos.

Our human work of integration, which Jung called individuation, occurs within a larger context in which all of nature is integrating for coevolution. Yet, human self-organization takes place in many small acts of synthesis in daily life, where the individual comes into contact with the social and physical environment. What, exactly, needs to happen next for each individual organism is always a matter of individual context and development. Analyst Aniela Jaffé wrote of the process of individuation:

> Individuation pursues its course in meaningful ways only in our everyday existence. Acceptance of life as it is, of its banality, its extraordinariness, respect for body and its demands, are just as much a prerequisite for individuation as a relationship to one's fellow men. The more insistent the spiritual quality of the self becomes, the more our consciousness is expanded through the integration of psychic contents, the deeper we must strike our roots in reality, in our own earth, the body, and the more responsibly we must be bound to the environment, because the "worldly" side of the archetype and its instinctual qualities must be realized too. Individuation can thus go in two typical but opposite directions. If the spiritual aspect of wholeness is unconscious and therefore undifferentiated, the goal is to expand consciousness through deeper insight into the laws that hold the psyche together. It is a question of sacrificing the primitive unreflecting man in ourselves. If on the other hand, our consciousness has become alienated from the instincts, then the worldly aspect of wholeness has been constellated, and it is a matter of accepting reality and working on it, of re-establishing a connection with nature and our fellows. In the case of modern man this often requires the sacrifice of one-sided intellectualism. Both directions correspond to archetypal situations at all levels of culture, for which reason they appear as constantly recurring variants in the symbolism of myths and fairy tales. Sometimes it is the task of the hero to conquer an animal or dragon (instinct) in order to gain the treasure (the Self). And sometimes it is the task to protect and nourish the beast at the risk of his own life, whereupon it will help him in his quest for the treasure.[182]

In our ongoing reflection on complexity theory and postmodern psychology, we will have to look at small failures and successes of integration in daily life to make sense of mental illness and its healing. We need to figure out what is frozen and what is melted in biological organisms, in order to decide where the problem lies. How can we know whether an individual needs to conquer a dragon, or nourish and protect a beast?

---

[182] Jaffé, A., *The Myth of Meaning*, pp. 82-83.

9. Default Hierarchies and Divine Child

It has always been difficult to determine where nature begins and where it ends. Especially when one recognizes oneself as being part of it. Everything is natural. Spirit, soul, energy.[183]   – Trinh T. Minh-ha

Since 1991, biologist Thomas S. Ray has published a number of papers on a computer program called "Tierra" which he created to illustrate how complex adaptive systems could evolve into the rich variety of coevolving life forms we observe in the world today. He sums up this work in an abstract of a recent paper as follows:

> The process of evolution is an important integrative theme for the sciences of complexity, because it is the generative force behind most complex systems. The surface of the Earth is covered with phenomenally complex living structures such as the human brain and the tropical rainforest, which emerged from simple molecules through evolution. While the results of evolution by natural selection are abundantly visible, the process is difficult to observe in nature because it is slow compared to the human life span. One method of observing the actual generation of complexity through evolution is to inoculate an artificial system with natural evolution. This can most easily be done in computers, where the process can be accelerated to megahertz speeds. The fundamental elements of evolution are self-replication with heritable variation. This can be implemented in a computer by writing self-replicating machine language programs and running them on a computer that makes mistakes. The mistakes can take the form of bit-flip mutations and small errors in calculations or the transfer of information. This experiment results in rapid diversification of digital organisms. From a rudimentary ancestral self-replicating "creature," entire ecological communities emerge spontaneously. Natural evolution in this artificial system illustrates well established principles of evolutionary theory, and allows an experimental approach to the

---

[183] Trinh T. Minh-ha, "Nature's r," in: Robertson, G. et. al., *Future Natural*, p. 92.

study of evolution, as well as observations of macroevolutionary processes as they occur.[184]

Programs like Tierra have allowed complexity scientists to begin to outline some general tendencies of complex adaptive systems. How coevolution emerges is a crucial question. Stuart Kauffman outlines five steps. First, each "creature" models the environment at some optimal intermediate level of complexity. That is, the creature works out a way of behaving that is like a hypothesis that can be corrected. The hypothesis tries to "predict" the environment, but not perfectly or absolutely, which would be overly complex, and, at the same time, with enough factors to catch some significant aspects. Second, models will frequently fail to predict correctly. So it would make sense for the creature to carry, or be able to make, multiple models of reality of different complexity so that when one fails, a nearby optimal model can be tried out. These models could be organized, according to John Holland, by "default hierarchies," ranging from simplest to most complex.[185] Third, each creature is in an environment with other creatures who are constantly altering their models. Every time they do, the environment changes. When creatures then alter their own models in response, the environment changes again. Therefore, fourth, we could characterize these interactive environments according to whether creatures were changing their models very slowly or very rapidly. Rapidly changing environments would be chaotic, with little predictability. These regimes have been called the Rat Race or Red Queen environments. Slowly changing regions would be orderly so that "rational expectations" would be confirmed. These could lead to evolutionarily stable strategies or ESS. At the edge of chaos, models would be subcritically poised so that a small change in one could lead to an communication of changes in others. At a just subcritical level, there would be enough islands of stability to preserve what had already been learned, surrounded by seas of evolving states that would allow maximum change and flexibility. Fifth, the dynamic would lead toward coevolution and the optimum subcritical state at the edge of chaos.

Kauffman reasons it out this way:

An internal dynamics of persistent optimal model building by the agents should drive the set of agents to the edge of chaos. If the dynamics are in the ordered regime, thus very stable and consistent, then each agent has a lot of reliable data about the other agent's behavior. Given more reliable data, each agent naturally attempts to improve its capacity to predict more precisely the other agent's behavior by constructing a more complex model of the other's

---

[184] Ray, T.S., "Evolution and complexity," in: Cowan, G., Pines, D., Meltzer, D., *Complexity: Metaphors, Models, Reality*, p. 161.
[185] Waldrop, *Complexity*, p. 192.

action. The more complex model is necessarily more sensitive to small alterations in the other's behavior, hence is more easily disconfirmed. Thus, adopting more complex models to predict more precisely tends to drive the mutually coevolving systems from the ordered regime toward the chaotic regime. Conversely, in the chaotic regime, each agent has very limited reliable data about the other's behavior. In part, this reflects the fact, that in the chaotic regime, each agent changes its own model of the other agent, hence its own decision rules governing its own behavior. To optimize the capacity to predict the behavior of the other agent, given the small amount of reliable data, each agent is driven to build a less complex model of the other's action. These less complex models predict less detail, hence are less sensitive to the behaviors of the other, hence less readily disconfirmed, and therefore less often changed. This drives the system from the chaotic regime to the ordered regime. The coevolutionary metadynamics should converge at the phase transition between order and chaos. Here no internal model of the other agents would be valid indefinitely. The system would be poised at a self-organized critical state. Avalanches of changes in models of other agents would be triggered by small events arising from the endogenous dynamics of the agents, or exogenous shocks.[186]

This theory has been applied fruitfully to economic markets. In very unstable investment environments, where currency rates are changing rapidly and the stock market is wildly fluctuating, many small investors will leave the market and look for a safe, reliable niche. They might buy guaranteed bonds or put their money in a retirement account in a savings bank, for example. If banks start crashing the way they did during the Great Depression of 1929, they may even leave the market altogether and put their money in a shoe box in the closet or under a floorboard. This kind of chaotic environment leads to a strategy of protective retreat and simplification, individual hoarding of resources, and a search for a secure haven isolated from the outer chaos.

When there is a slow growth rate, interest rates are low, and the economy is relatively stable, the opposite strategy makes sense. It is safe to leave money in the bank, but the investor gets hardly any interest on the account. In fact, if there is inflation, one is actually losing money. Here it makes sense to begin looking around for more diversified investments that are less safe, for some percentage of savings. One could try a lot of different strategies, like playing the lottery, buying property, or joining mutual funds. This environment would lead to a protected area surrounded by an edge of highly exploratory behavior. In the stable, protected area, mimicry would be a successful strategy. Even if you didn't know much about the banking system

---

[186] Kauffman, S. A., *Origins*, p. 402.

yourself, if you did what your neighbors did most of the time, it would probably pay off.

In Thomas Ray's Tierra computer program, evolving creatures began to exhibit strategies that are somewhat comparable to this behavior. On one side, under the pressure of intense competition for "energy resources" in the program, "creatures" became smaller and more compact. Then they need to copy fewer instructions to reproduce. They have thus simplified their models. Some even learned to "lie." Creatures in the program received energy resources based on their size. One creature calculated the size of its offspring as "36 instructions" but requested a "space" of "72 instructions"! This would allow its offspring to be reproduced twice as rapidly as those of other creatures, which had not learned such a strategy.

Once the self-replicating programs had filled the memory of the program, there was a great deal of information available in the environment, and it became more predictable. A class of "parasites" developed that dropped memory from their instructions and simply mimicked others. They increased in number because they needed fewer instructions to replicate. Soon, each slowly evolving host was surrounded by a cloud of rapidly evolving parasites creating exploratory random searches. This would tack the system toward chaos which would cause a tendency toward simplification, in theory. In fact, with time, the hosts learned how to make themselves immune from the parasites. They learned how to exploit the parasites by "deceiving" them into replicating the genome of the host, thus bringing them under control. This was so deleterious to the parasites that they were driven to extinction as independent creatures. Then the complex hosts found themselves in a relatively stable environment where all the creatures were closely related. Cooperation began to develop so that groups of creatures in aggregation replicated together. They produced a coevolutionary environment at the edge of chaos. This cooperation, however, could be violated. "Cheaters" could enter the community and "trick" the other creatures into replicating their genome. With this "deception," the move back toward chaos and simplification would begin again.

It is astounding that these dynamics emerge from the properties of numerical connection in a parallel-processing computer program. Of course, the Tierra program is tuned to model biological life. Kauffman has experimented with Boolean networks that sometimes end in chaos or fall into point attractors. It is only a certain range of these systems that wind up in coevolution. In addition, Ray has anthropomorphized the results. Yet, if all living beings are complex adaptive systems, biological life in action might be exhibiting parallel dynamics which we recognize and have names for. We could chart the general tacking dynamics exhibited by Tierra and other systems as shown in Table 9.1.

Environments:	ORDERED	EDGE OF CHAOS	CHAOS
Experienced as:	frozen	coevolution (ESS)	melting (Red Queen)
Resulting models:	more complex	coordinated	more simple

Table 9.1 – Environments and Models

In 1969, anthropologist Roger Wescott, in a book entitled, *The Divine Animal*,[187] suggested what he thought were two widespread fundamental strategies underlying the dynamics of all biological and cultural life. He called them pedomorphy and gerontomorphy. He noted that some animals look like the young of other animals when they are adults, for example, worms, snakes, and grubs. These he called pedomorphic. Other fauna look skeletal or old the day they are born: turtles, insects, and shellfish. These are gerontomorphic. We humans are more or less in the middle. We lack fur, scales, horns, or tusks and are rather vulnerable to attack, but, on the other hand, we have a lot more structure than snakes or frogs. Children are clearly pedomorphic, and adults are gerontomorphic. Wescott thought that the ultimate pedomorph would be an egg and the ultimate gerontomorph would be a skeleton. Westcott listed the characteristics of pedomorphy and geron-tomorphy as outlined in Table 9.2.

In general, "pedomorphs tend to be soft in body and variable in behavior, while gerontomorphs tend to be stiff in body and rigid in behavior."[188] Westcott thought that if we looked at all species in evolutionary biology, every animal phyla was predominantly gerontomorphic, though there would always be some taxa within each phyla that were predominantly pedomor-phic. The pedomorphic taxa might have the function of sustaining the phyla when large numbers of gerontomorphic taxa became extinct. One could look back at the fossil record and see surges of pedomorphy and gerontomorphy in different epics. During the Proterozoic era, cephalochordates gave up living in pedomorphic colonies and began to live independently. During the Cambrian period, they gave up the sessile habits of independent gerontomor-phs and moved into the ocean where they were mobile and ubiquitous, like pedomorphs. During the Devonian period, gerontomorphic fish, with armor on their heads and upper trunks, shed it. During the Pleistocene era, homi-nids lost the heavy brows, muzzles, and shoulders of the more gerontomor-phic adult apes and assumed the smooth, large-headed, and hairless look of infant apes.

---

[187] Wescott, R.W., *The Divine Animal*.
[188] Ibid., p. 92.

PEDOMORPHY	GERONTOMORPHY
1. few fossilizable parts	many fossilizable parts
2. soft	hard
3. moist	dry surfaced
4. warm	cold
5. smooth surfaced	rough-surfaced
6. symmetrical	asymmetrical
7. vulnerable to attack	heavily armored
8. lacking sex characteristics	marked sex differences
9. asexual or hermaphroditic	at least two-sexed
10. metamorphic	formed at birth
11. speciative	resistant to structural change
12. immortal	mortal
13. regenerative	non-regenerative
14. parasitic	sessile
15. congregative	isolative
16. ubiquitous	localized
17. ductile	resistant to behavioral change

Table 9.2 – Characteristics of Pedomorphy and Gerontomorphy

All phyla seem to have gone through periodic moves from gerontomorphy to pedomorphy and back over their millions of years of evolution. Westcott thought of the stage of pedomorphy as a kind of atavism in the service of rejuvenation: "In general terms, phyletic fetalization may be metaphorically described as a kind of evolutionary gamble, whereby groups of organisms deliberately (so to speak) take one developmental step backward in the hope (as it were) of being thereby enabled subsequently to take two steps forward."[189] He thought that one could match up the evolution of specialization and speciation with gerontomorphy and generalization with pedomorphy. In a changing environmental landscape, specialized creatures were those that were better adapted to past conditions and generalized creatures are those that are preadapted to future conditions.

What all this suggests is that the balance that every higher species must strike between pedomorphy and gerontomorphy is, when most fruitful, neither mediate or static. That is, optimal pedomorphy is not found by bisecting a line between it and gerontomorphy and then holding firmly to that point. Optimal pedomorphy is rather a dynamically fluctuating state, which reformulates

[189] Ibid., p. 104.

itself in accordance both with the needs of the species and with the requirements of the environment. Viewed diachronically, it is neither a straight line
nor a constant curve but an irregular zigzag, rather like that produced by a
sailboat tacking against the wind. In terms of this image, the "wind" is the
normal process of maturation and complexification which seems to predomi-
nate in every phylum. "Tacking," in these same terms, consists of periodic
rejuvenations, or selective reversals of maturation and complexification leading to partial restorations of juvenility and simplicity. This tacking as I see it,
is essentially the same process as that described by Julian Huxley when he
defined evolutionary progress as a blend of two alternating processes of
individuation (which I would call differentiation) and aggregation (which I
would call coordination). Assuming that the primordial state of life was one of
unity, this two-pronged process would tend successively to produce diversifi-
cation and reunification – first to separate life from its beginnings, and then to
return it to that which in its beginnings was most fruitful. An alternative model
for this dual process is that of the helix or ascending spiral, in which each
successive reversion occurs on a progressively higher level, so that restoration
never becomes retrogression. Putting this entire process into thermodynamic
terms (which subsume and transcend bioenergetic terms), we might say that
gerontogenesis produces fission and increases kinetic energy, while pedogen-
esis produces fusion and increases potential energy. Summarizing these various metaphors, we may say that the superior species rather resembles a
rejuvenated elder than a prematurely senescent youth. For the rejuvenate elder
retains the fruits of experience but enjoys them with a freshened appetite,
while the senescent youngster has the benefit neither of experience nor of
youthful zest.[190]

Now it seems we could translate the behavior of Thomas Ray's Tierra into
these terms. The initial state produced speciation or gerontomorphy in the
sense that each creature was a competing isolate with a condensed structure.
When the memory was full and change was more constrained, that is,
moving toward a more frozen regime, the system produced parasites that
lacked information structure. They were ductile, vulnerable, metamorphic,
and much less structured than their hosts, making them much more like
pedomorphs. This stage is more complex in a very specific sense defined by
complexity theory. Complexity here is characterized by more links of connection between nodes. A free-standing adult is simpler and more specialized in
this sense than a clinging parasite. Parasites make their way by mimicking,
which requires a high level of connectivity. Isolates are more self-contained
and less connected because they have all the information they need in their
own programs. The parasites and hosts in Ray's program are actually rather
like children and adults. The adults have more structure, while the children

---

[190] Ibid., p. 117.

Environments:	ORDERED	EDGE OF CHAOS	CHAOS
Experienced as:	frozen	coevolving (ESS)	melting (Red Queen)
Resulting models:	more complex	coordinated	more simple
Westcott:	pedomorphy	balance	gerontomorphy
	rejuvenation	rejuvenated elder	senescence
Evolution:	generalization	tacking	speciation
Thomas Ray:	parasites	cooperation	hosts, cheaters
Huxley:	aggregation	individuation	
thermodynamics:	fusion		fission
	more potential energy		more kinetic energy

Table 9.3 – Environments, Models, Evolution

"play" and "imitate," Then the adult hosts impose their structure on the children, just as we do when we send our children to school. When the parasite children were dominant, the system moved toward a more chaotic regime, because the parasites must at first have been less predictable. When the hosts took them over, the system settled down to a stage where there could be coevolution. "Cultural" aggregates formed in a new "speciation." Then "cheaters" started a new move toward chaos. The system seems to be tacking back and forth just as Westcott thought it should. It seems to be self-organizing and self-balancing between chaos and order. This process apparently underlies the dynamics we have been discussing so far. Table 9.3 shows the process in condensed form.

Friedrich Dürrenmatt presents the extremes of both of these tendencies very well in Figures 9.1 and 9.2. In Figure 9.1, the horse seems to be experiencing something like the Red Queen environment, which he is trying to outrun. He has tremendous kinetic energy, and his strategy is simple: run away. The communication between the blocks and the horses is distal. They do not touch. In Figure 9.2, everything lacks energy and there is a "winter" tree whose growth is frozen. Here we find aggregation, fusion, mixing, exploring. Their sexual encounter is likely to produce many offspring, a new generation of pedomorphs. Their strategy is perhaps to feel, to be, to dream, to communicate. This communication is proximal, touching, intimate. The horse would perhaps experience the force of the blocks as a dragon which needed to be conquered, whereas the animals and humans in the other picture might feel their intimacy as a vulnerable beast that needs to be protected.

Figure 9.1 – Kinetic energy in Gerontomorphy

Figure 9.2 – Potential energy in Pedomorphy (next page)

If pedomorphy and gerontomorphy are ancient strategies in evolution, can we see them at work in the present as well? Contemporary biology has discussed one phenomenon that seems to fit well into the pattern we are discussing, and which has reached crisis proportions – the problem of world population growth. Everyone who looks into the problem of the runaway population statistics almost immediately discovers that several different reproductive strategies are operative. One strategy, which is called the *K strategy*, "includes slow development, few offspring, intensive parental care, long birth interval, large body size, and complex social behavior." The *r strategy* "is thought to favor a package of traits that includes rapid development, many offspring, minimal parental care, short birth interval, small body size, short life span, and relatively simple social behavior."[191] Many species of plants and animals exhibit both K and r strategies. There seems to be a consensus that both strategies are a response to environmental stress; but there has been a long debate over what the stress is. The K strategy is often followed where there is enough nourishment, where there are possibilities for success and self-development, or where education or organization can achieve something. The r strategy seems to be set off in environments where there is starvation, or where the social or physical environment prevents full phenotypic growth by freezing out certain populations from access to important resources. The r strategy is pedomorphic as it produces many soft, vulnerable, congregative, ductile offspring. They are likely to reproduce early, perhaps, among humans, having their first babies at thirteen or fourteen years of age as their parents did. Thus, the population will tend toward fewer rigid sexual characteristics and metamorphose rapidly. Because each child will have many siblings, there will be a dense network of information sharing. The K strategy is gerontomorphic because the adults it produces are more likely to be defended, independent, or even isolated individuals, resistant to rapid behavior change.

The r strategy is more "complex" than the K strategy because it produces social environments full of children and extended families with a very rich and complicated set of kinship connections. The K strategy produces "only" children, or very small families with less connectivity. The complex, highly connected r strategy arises in frozen environments because these environments are defeating and there is no way to change them. In the terms we discussed earlier, these strategies might arise in FATALIST (–+) environments, and when they do, it is a way of plunging the community toward subcriticality at the edge of chaos. That is, by increasing the connectivity and size of the oppressed population, it moves toward the (+–) EGALITARIAN sector. When a certain point of connectivity (or phase change) is reached, there can be riots,

---

[191] Chisolm, J.S., "Putting people in biology," in: Schwartz, T., White, G.M., Lutz, C.A., eds., *New Directions in Psychological Anthropology*, p. 131.

strikes, or movements of liberation. For example, Indian history is full of periods of ferment, when previously passive and miserable subsectors of the population became chaotic and pressed for change. Thus, the r strategy is a balancing device, an unconscious attempt to move an environment that is too high in grid, too low in group, toward an opposite sector that is high in group and low in grid. The new r population, which are likely themselves to have their babies young, will not have time to learn much information. They might, like Thomas Ray's parasites, tend to mimic others in the environment. This will provide fertile ground for popular movements. As pedomorphs, they will be vulnerable, metamorphic, congregative, ubiquitous, and ductile. We could diagram it as shown in Figure 9.3.

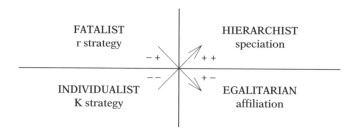

Figure 9.3 – K/r Strategies

On the other end of things, the INDIVIDUALIST sector is basically chaotic in that it changes very rapidly and new inventions and innovations constantly arise which must be adapted to. By using the K strategy, parents are acting like the hosts in Thomas Ray's computer program. They are trying to produce offspring that will get more resources by specializing, hoarding, and perhaps cheating others. That is why the chaotic sector produces individualism and individualists. If they succeed, their offspring will create HIERARCHICAL (+ +) structure. Thus, they will move society from the INDIVIDUALIST (– –) low grid, low group sector back toward the high grid, high group end of the diagram.

This analysis seems to be connected with the fact that we live in a world where fifteen percent of the world population uses eighty percent of the world resources, while eighty-five percent of the world population share the remaining twenty percent of the resources.[192] On a global scale, the world population has become trapped in a destructive autocatalytic loop. The privileged parts of the population reacting to rapid change and a sense of impending chaos, move toward hoarding, defense, and control. They create hierarchical cartels, treaty organizations, joint monetary systems, trade associations, and common markets. This freezes out ever more people from

---

[192] *World Development Report* 1994, Table 1, Table 3.

necessary resources, education, and even proper nourishment. If they then respond with more r strategy behavior, doubling the world human population every fifty years, the chaotic press for liberatory change increases and more egalitarian social movements erupt. This, then, creates more pressure for control strategies, and so on, in descending spirals of misery and hoarding. Here is a periodic attractor in global social life which is contrary to that which any feeling person would choose, if it were under any form of conscious control.

In this scenario, we may be creating something like Per Bak's supercritical wet sandpile. (See Chapter 7) In this model, a single grain of sand falling on the pile was able to set off a massive avalanche. Certain events in the sociopolitical realm seem much better modeled by this archetypal systems approach than any explanation of local causes by individual agents. For example, how else to explain that, after the death of the president of Rwanda in an airplane crash last year, half a million people were murdered within three months? People who had lived more or less peacefully all their lives with neighbors of a different tribal group got out their machetes and hacked them to death. A similar series of events were set off by the death of Tito in the former Yugoslavia. In another era, the footfall of Christopher Columbus in the Antilles in 1492 set off a surge of conquest that resulted in the killing and enslavement of thousands of people in Latin American indigenous cultures, which had maintained a stable way of life for centuries. In Europe, how was it that the a dream of Hitler for a new order resulted in a six-year war which left the landscape devastated, cities reduced to rubble, and caused the death of twenty-two million people? If human situations are able to reach critical states where catastrophes are predictable, it must be possible to make the process conscious and canalize it. If we do not do this, we could be headed for an extinction avalanche on a world scale much greater than any of those already mentioned. Perhaps the epidemic of AIDS sweeping through the world is just the tip of an iceberg.

Recent discoveries in complexity theory suggest that such patterns can be altered dramatically by changing the size of the "patches" through which subsystems are organized. That is, we can reconfigure the connectivity of any information system to include more or less channels of communication and individuals. Perhaps the current global economic organization, with transnational corporations and the world bank controlling the economies of many small and powerless national states, needs to be replaced by vibrant, more densely connected, regional economies. But that would require a leap of global consciousness we do not yet seem prepared to make. It would involve recognizing the unconscious and archetypal aspects of behaviors which are, for the most part, not acknowledged in the Western scientific paradigm or modern economic theory, which assumes rational individual actors in a neutral competitive market.

In the complexity model, affiliative strategies function as an unconscious attempt at regulating and balancing, the kind of tacking that Westcott saw in evolutionary history. When the environment gets too frozen, its residents may unconsciously begin to imagine changed models and attempt to "melt" it back toward the edge of chaos through pedomorphy. When the environment gets too chaotic, its residents may attempt to freeze it back toward order through gerontomorphy. They do this in response to "inner promptings" that produce images and symbols that energize behavior. It is as if we have a reservoir of strategies, and an inner balancing device goes down a default hierarchy of models and selects, based on life experience. This reservoir of strategies is related to what Jung called archetypes. Of course, as humans with partial voluntary control of what we do, we can refuse these promptings, interpret them symbolically and creatively, or repress them. Many cultures have noticed such tendencies and have named them in various ways in order to think about the proper relationship to them. Pedomorphy and gerontomorphy have been called *yin* and *yang*, *eros* and *logos*, the *feminine* and the *masculine*, and are named in many other local cultures in terms of binary oppositions.

We are not determined by default hierarchies, but neither are we free of them. Ego consciousness is contextualized partly by a matrix of unconscious images; we have some choice about what to do with them. On the one hand, they can be acted out in destructive ways; on the other hand, they are a source of information about the ecological health of the connectivity in our inner and outer environments. If we could read this information, we would have a thermostat constantly measuring connectivity. Psychoanalysis could be viewed as an attempt to do this reading.

These two different strategies can be seen as "coded" into the myths and cultural artifacts produced by various social groups, particularly in their representation of animals. For example, there is a Bas relief of Gilgamesh, from 800 B.C., in which Gilgamesh holds a lion he has captured around the neck with his left arm. The lion is alive, but Gilgamesh is in control. In an era which produced a hierarchical "high" civilization, we see the "beast" captured, restrained, and reduced. Here the gerontomorphic Gilgamesh brings order.

By contrast, in a several-hundred-year-old cave painting from Southern Africa, a healing ceremony is portrayed similar to those which until recently were regularly done by the Kung. The person in the center is being touched by a healer, while members of the group dance and sing outside. In response to their call, the hermaphroditic eland god Kaggen draws near to share his healing energies with the group. The rejuvenating pedomorphic ritual stresses merger, trance states, and hidden energies.

In a scene from a Greek vase, the gerontomorphic culture hero Hercules wrestles with an ancient river god serpent from a previous era. By snapping off his horn, Hercules symbolically replaces the older wisdom and powers with his own, perhaps representing the conquest of ego control over spontaneous impulse.

In a Chinese Ming Dynasty embroidery, the ancient dragon/ horse, which rose from the river of life with the signs of the Tao Te Ching on its back, evolves in the center of the universe. He represents earth, water, and the fertilizing power of rain. The pedomorphic beast has his own inner wisdom from which science, divination, and language arise.

These two strategies, then, may be seen to have a world-wide historical incidence. But how are they regulated? At the social level, the runaway pattern we discussed above does not seem to have an organizing center, the way, for example, a monarch or a council of elders functions as a center in tribal groups. Perhaps this is related to the fact that our phenotypic structure was shaped in small kinship groups over hundreds of thousands of years, and we do not yet know how to form such a center apart from the kinship and personal feeling relationships of family or clan.

There does seem to be a balancing structure in individual human beings, however, and this corrective center is what Jung called the Self. The Self is in some way duplex, like Mercurius, because it can balance in either direction. It can be father and son, mother and daughter, old and young, and therefore it has a healing capacity. The Self can be symbolized as a Divine Child, who is at once young and vulnerable and wise and old. According to Jung, "It is therefore a symbol which unites the opposites; a mediator, bringer of healing, that is, one who makes whole."[193] At a phenomenological level, the pedomorph is something like the "child archetype" and the gerontomorph, "the archetype of the wise old woman/man." In Greek mythology, the healer combines both qualities. Aesclepius, the wise old healer, is often portrayed with his daughter Hygieia, a Goddess of healing who brings with her a snake that she feeds, the beast that is nurtured. Together, they are young and old, animal and human in harmony. Aesclepius was thought to have learned healing from Chiron, the kindly Centaur who was half man, half horse. Chiron also taught him music, which was believed in Greece, as among the Kung, to have a healing effect. Music was played and sung in the Aesclepieia, the healing centers where Aesclepieian medicine was practiced. Interestingly, Chiron the healing source was wounded accidentally by the culture hero Hercules. Perhaps in a press toward ego control we lose some valuable

---

[193] Jung, C.G., *Archetypes of the Collective Unconscious*, Vol. 9.1, p. 164.

"irrational" and spontaneous element needed for healing. Aesclepius and Hygieia are associated with the serpent, and Chiron is a wounded healer. Has gerontomorphic "civilization" broken off the possibility of some kind of pedomorphic healing ritual? Jungian analyst C.A. Meier thought Chiron might represent a healing possibility of the irrational combined with the rational. "We may say then that what *works* in medicine is irrational."[194] Aesclepius is often represented with an extended family – his wife Epione, and other daughters, Panacea, Aegle, and Iaso; and typically, a group of hooded dwarves that seem to carry the meaning of irrational and fertilizing pedomorphy.

According to Meier, a festival dedicated to the Goddess of Healing was held in Greece at the end of each grape harvest, on October 11. The festival was called the Meditrinalia, and is thought to be connected with a Goddess Meditrina. This would connect it with other Mediterranean harvest festivals where Demeter and Kore were celebrated for their fertility on sacred threshing floors. In the Meditrina, the toast over the new wine was: "I, an old man, drink new wine; I heal an old sickness with a new one."[195]

The healing force within each individual is similarly young and old, rejuvenating and wise, at once. The healing Self, and the gerontomorphic and pedomorphic archetypes we have been considering, are fundamental ordering possibilities of our experience. The archetypes, Jung thought,

> cannot be reduced to experiences in the individual's past, and thus cannot be explained as something individually acquired. These fantasy images undoubtedly have their closest analogues in mythical types. We must therefore assume that they correspond to certain collective (and not personal) structural elements of the human psyche in general, and, like the morphological elements of the human body, are *inherited*."[196]

If the computer program Tierra, all of biological evolution, all complex adaptive systems, and our psyche are enacting these strategies, from whom did we inherit them? Jung quotes Gauss: "God arithmetizes."[197] We are here in the realm of what Jung called the phenomenology of spirit. According to Jung: "the hallmarks of spirit are, firstly, the principle of spontaneous movement; secondly, the spontaneous capacity to produce images independently of sense perception; and thirdly, the autonomous and sovereign manipulation of these images."[198] In living beings, spirit is related to energy, order, and number. As a force in the biological world, it is dynamic, balancing, exploratory, and evolving. It is represented in mythology everywhere as the power

---

[194] Meier, C.A., *Healing Dream and Ritual*, p. 72.
[195] Ibid., p. 25.
[196] Jung, C.G., *Archetypes of the Collective Unconscious*, Vol. 9.1, p. 155.
[197] Jung, C.G., *Structure and Dynamics of the Psyche*. Vol. 8, p. 502.
[198] Ibid., Vol. 9.1, p. 212.

of Gods and Goddesses, "the divine *nous* caught in the embrace of *physis*," like Shiva and Shakti or the infant Jesus in the arms of the Virgin Mary. We are mistaken, Jung says, if we believe that we, through conscious choice, are the cause of spirit.

> He himself did not create the spirit, rather the spirit makes him creative, always spurring him on, giving him lucky ideas, staying power, "enthusiasm" and "inspiration." So much indeed, does it permeate his whole being that he is in gravest danger of thinking that he actually created the spirit and that he "has" it. In reality, however, the primordial phenomenon of the spirit has him, and, while appearing to be the willing object of human intentions, it binds his freedom, just as the physical world does, with a thousand chains and becomes an obsessive *ideé-force*.[199]

If gerontomorphy and pedomorphy are archetypal forces tacking through time, they must have affected the construction of the human body. During some evolutionary periods, there must have been a whole series of geronto-morphic pressures and during others, pedomorphic. Those creatures with the greatest range of possibilities would have been able to survive both. Natural selection, as was suggested earlier, must have favored beings with multiple strategies. It seems to me that the "cold" brain, human conscious-ness, and ego structure are the result of gerontomorphic strategies and that the "hot" brain, the unconscious, emotional relatedness, and the possibility of dreams and fantasy represent pedomorphic strategies. Each would have evolved over millions of years under different conditions, but been retained as preadaptive possibilities for the future. The ego, with its fixed categories of time, space, and causality, is skeletal, structural, and inhibiting in its function and therefore gerontomorphic. It is armored and defensive of its categories, independent, isolated, and localizes everything in time and space. Thinking is "simpler" than feeling in the sense of complexity theory. Think-ing cuts, categorizes, and separates. Feeling joins, connects, and links.

The unconscious is, therefore, more complex and pedomorphic. It does not have the sharp either/or categories of the ego. It blurs things together, creates a union of opposites, and is more hermaphroditic, ubiquitous, and holorganic. Connected with the hot brain, it is carried by emotion, which is ductile, metamorphic, connective, warm, vulnerable, and parasitic. Deep in the heart of the unconscious rests the secret source of healing and balance Jung calls spirit. This is why the unconscious has been associated with the archetype of the divine child, who is at once both ancient and youthful, wise and spontaneous. According to Jung,

---

[199] Ibid., Vol. 9.1, p. 213.

The child motif represents the pre-conscious childhood aspect of the collective psyche. ... The child motif represents not only something that existed in the distant past but also something that exists now; that is to say, it is not just a vestige, but a system functioning in the present whose purpose is to compensate or correct, in a meaningful manner, the inevitable one-sidedness and extravagances of the conscious mind. ... Our differentiated consciousness is in continual danger of being uprooted; hence it needs compensation through the still existing state of childhood.[200]

The archetype of the divine child does not stem from our personal experience of childhood. In fact, childhood, as a biological product, originates from the evolutionary strategies of spirit. The archetypes seem to be structuring features of complex adaptive systems, as well as the human psyche. This difficult point in Jungian psychology, which differentiates it from Freudian or object relations psychologies, is, in fact, the central pivot of Jung's thought.

It may not be superfluous to point out that lay prejudice is always inclined to identify the child motif with the concrete experience "child" as though the real child were the cause and pre-condition of the existence of the child motif. In psychological reality, however, the empirical idea "child" is only the means (and not the only one) by which to express a psychic fact that cannot be formulated more exactly. Hence, by the same token, the mythological idea of the child is emphatically not a copy of the empirical child but a *symbol* clearly recognizable as such: it is a wonder-child, a divine child, begotten, born, and brought up in quite extraordinary circumstances, and not – this is the point – a human child. Its deeds are as miraculous or as monstrous as its nature and physical constitution. Only on account of these highly unempirical properties is it necessary to speak of a child motif at all. Moreover, the mythological "child" has various forms: now a god, giant, Tom Thumb, animal, etc. and this points to a causality that is anything but rational and concretely human.[201]

There seems to be some kind of energy differential between the gerontomorphic and pedomorphic strategies, well illustrated by Dürrenmatt's pictures. Huxley noted that the gerontomorphic strategy seemed to yield more available kinetic energy, like the racing horse. Pedomorphic strategies seem to be based on potential energy. The phenotype created in the K strategy uses its energy in the present whereas the phenotypes in the r strategy use their energy for the future. The ego and the left brain have a high level of attention-focusing capacity. The unconscious, dreams, and fantasies seem to be based on relaxation of attention and a lowering of mental energy, an "abaissement du niveau mental." In our bodies, reflecting these extremes, we have two

---

[200] Ibid., Vol. 9.1, p. 162.
[201] Ibid., Vol. 9.1, p. 161.

different pathways in our endocrine systems. The "ergotropic" pathways coordinate fright, fight, and flight reactions and yield a high level of vigilance; the "trophotropic" pathways coordinate relaxation, rest, and calm. The two pathways inhibit each other. We cannot relax, play, dream, or sleep when we are in danger and hypervigilant. These two systems seem to reach a characteristic homeostasis in every human being. Some of us are almost always nervous and vigilant. Others are generally calm and relaxed. These two different pathways in our bodies may be the tracks the pedomorphic and gerontomorphic archetypes have left on our body organization. According to Jung, "In the last analysis the human body, too, is built of the stuff of the world, the very stuff wherein fantasies become visible; indeed, without it they could not be experienced at all. Without this stuff they would be like a sort of abstract crystalline lattice in a solution where the crystallization process had not yet started."[202] It is this lattice that complexity theory is now modeling in its computer programs.

If gerontomorphic and pedomorphic strategies are two phase changes in complex adaptive systems, as well as two different energy formations in the human body and human psyche, how are these different energy formations experienced phenomenologically? Analyst Erich Neumann suggests in a 1956 paper that we might be dealing with energy transformations like those postulated by quantum physics. He wanted to compare the experience of the unconscious with wave phenomena and the experience of the ego with particle phenomena as forms or *Gestalten* condense out of the general wave at a specific time-space location. Yet both are, in some way we cannot explain with the either/or categories of conscious thought, the same underlying energy. When the energy is in its particle state, we perceive the world in the fixed equilibrium states of classical physics. Then we use the fixed grammatical categories of "I," "you," and "it." When the energy is in a wave state, however, many acausal connections and irregularities of time and space – that is, synchronicities – might occur. This, then, would be the basis for parapsychological phenomena, clairvoyance, precognitive dreams, oracles, and divinatory systems. We are here in the realm of transpersonal categories like Buber's "Thou," and the indescribable union which we call love. The two energy systems, like waves and particles in physics, cannot be grasped simultaneously. They inhibit each other just as the ergotrophic and trophotropic regulating systems do in our bodies. When we try to grasp a content of thought (the particle), some of the energy factor recedes. When we experience the emotional energetic connectedness of synchronistic phenomena (the wave), there is an *abaissement* of the ego threshold, and the either/or categories of the ego recede. Right at the margin between the two, symbols

---

[202] Ibid., Vol. 9.1, p. 172.

can spontaneously appear that allow some of the potential energy of the unconscious to be taken up into the ego world. If we could remain near this edge, we would have access to a deep reservoir of transformative energy with which to live our lives. According to Neumann,

> Life not only appears as free energy, but also incorporates itself into figures and forms which bind the energy in a bodily system. This happens on all planes of reality, in the inorganic realm as ordered matter, in the organic realm as organized and centered being, and in the psychic realm as directing and meaningful configuration. On every plane, the moving element appears as an unknown *numinosum*. ... The archetypes are psychic nuclear structures similar to the atom structures, or to the organic gene structures which determine the species and their behavior. Here, with the archetypes too, we are dealing with fields of energy, charges, combinations, and attractions; with changes of structure in the alchemical process; with the freeing and binding of psychic energy accompanying changes in the archetypal field; with the bombarding, for example, of the conscious system, by energy released in nuclear processes. In alchemy, and in the corresponding transformation process of individuation, however, we see that this energy takes place in forms(*Gestalten*), in "corpuscles," in incorporated energies, and that these configurations, complexes, symbols, archetypes, etc., appear as psychic molecules, or combinations of molecules, whose psychic chemistry – that is, alchemy – one must know or learn to know if one wants to understand what happens in the process.[203]

The experiences of synchronicity, clairvoyance, healing, or alchemical psychological rebirth, then, rest on potential energy, a reservoir of invested energy that reaches toward the future rather than the present. In the child motif, this process is represented as organized by the immortal, regenerative, redeeming, and healing function of the divine child archetype. Jesus, who has carried the archetype in the West for two thousand years, must have understood this when he said, "I tell you the truth, unless you change and become like little children, you will never enter the kingdom of heaven."[204]

The Bible is full of miracles and synchronistic phenomena, which the pedomorphic early Christian was to make the center of faith. "Go back and report to John what you hear and see: The blind receive sight, the lame walk, those who have leprosy are cured, the deaf hear, the dead are raised, and the good news is preached to the poor. Blessed is the man who does not fall away on account of me. ... What did you go out into the desert to see? A prophet? This is the one about whom it is written: I will send my messenger ahead of you, who will prepare your way before you." This messenger is immortal, and like the child archetype is not a vestige of the past but a living reality.

---

[203] Neumann, E., "The psyche and the transformation of the reality planes," *Spring* 1956, p. 98.
[204] Matt. 18:3.

Believers everywhere continue to have experiences of the appearance of God in visions and dreams. Jesus, the Virgin, Elijah, Legba, Tara, Khidir, Sophia, Erzulie, Yemayah, the Metatron, and many other forms of The Teacher can "prepare the way" wherever a burst of untapped psychic energy pours out of the unconscious and gives life a new and redeeming direction: "At that time you will be given what to say, for it will not be you speaking, but the Spirit of your Father speaking through you."[205]

Those trapped in frozen environments, like the poor in Jesus' era, must be far more ready to receive a pedomorphic message than those carrying out a gerontomorphic strategy of hierarchy building. Though the latter function as the wise and powerful in the social world, the child archetype holds out a promise for the future to the powerless and oppressed. "I praise you, Father, Lord of heaven and earth, because you have hidden these things from the wise and learned and revealed them to little children. ... Come to me all you who are weary and burdened, and I will give you rest. Take my yoke upon you and learn from me, for I am gentle and humble in heart, and you will find rest for your souls."[206] It seems that, wherever there is terrible oppression and hopelessness, the healing archetype of the divine child appears spontaneously.

The Tao Te Ching takes note of the ubiquitous wise child archetype as well:

Men are born soft and supple; dead they are stiff and hard. Plants are born tender and pliant; dead they are brittle and dry. Thus whoever is stiff and inflexible is a disciple of death. Whoever is soft and yielding is a disciple of life. The hard and stiff will be broken. The soft and supple will prevail. ... The soft overcomes the hard; the gentle overcomes the rigid. Everyone knows this is true, but few can put it into practice.[207]

In current biological anthropology that speaks in another language called "life history theory," archetypal strategies like the r strategy and the K strategy are believed to be "situationally determined." This theory suggests that:

we are "designed" to be sensitive to – to perceive and respond contingently to – certain aspects of our social/cultural and physical environments that have had the most consistent impact on fitness during human evolution. One goal of the life-history approach is to investigate the role of phenotypic design (e.g., alternative developmental strategies and learning biases) in the perception of these contingencies.[208]

---

[205] Matt. 11:4-10.
[206] Matt. 11:25-29.
[207] Mitchell, S., trans., *Tao Te Ching*, p. 76.
[208] Chisholm, J.S., "Putting people in biology," in: Schwartz, T., White, G.M., Lutz, C.A., eds., *New Directions in Psychological Anthropology*, p. 142.

Life-history theorists have noted that something like complexity theory's "default hierarchies" are operating behind these strategies, or alternative behavior models, "which might be thought of as a series of hierarchically arranged, conditional, if-then propositions."[209] If this is so, there are unknown standards of evaluating and behaving within the human phenotype. It has been suggested that we need to work up a "natural history" of these standards.

> This will require biological anthropologists to enlist the aid of their psychological colleagues, for a natural history of human beliefs, values, and expectations demands a sophisticated understanding of diverse cultural distinctions as a basis for generating useful typologies.[210]

If there is to be a natural history of human beliefs, it must be possible to see something like the tacking, balancing movements of pedomorphy and gerontomorphy operating in human culture. One could imagine modern social movements as being one or the other. For example, in the 1950's in the United States, gender roles were trapped in a gerontomorphic system. Roles were sharply divided, and there were unwritten rules about what men and women did and wore and said. Men could be doctors, but women had to be nurses. Women could be secretaries, but men had to be presidents (except for women's clubs). Women were supposed to be mostly pedomorphic: soft, vulnerable, smooth, warm, loving, clingy, and emotional. Men were supposed to be mostly gerontomorphic: tough, independent, unemotional, defended, firm, and reliable. The whole system was frozen. In it, there were few ways to grow or change or experiment or explore without ostracism. But frozen environments, which put a ceiling on growth and self-esteem, produce pedomorphic revolutions. In fact, the women's and the gay movement wanted both men and women to be able to be more intimate, open, free, and mobile. It wanted options for change and growth for everyone, and an end to gender-role stereotyping. Movement activists aggregated and formed groups. The dream was to be ubiquitous. Today the result of these movements in some American communities is a kind of hermaphroditic freedom. Men and women are allowed to be vulnerable or tough as necessary, dress conservatively or flamboyantly, stay home and care for babies or go out to work, cook dinners or write books.

Another example of pedomorphism that comes to mind is the Romantic Movement in Germany. In Aniela Jaffé's essay entitled, "The Romantic Period in Germany," she analyzed a fairy tale by E. T. A. Hoffman showing typical attitudes.

[209] Ibid., p. 140.
[210] Ibid., p. 142.

Anselmus renounces life and withdraws to Atlantis, to the place of the primordial images, in order to remain with Serpentina, the snake who has knowledge of eternal truths. The Romantics typically find in life itself no meaning; they strive to understand all things in transcendental terms, and hope to fulfil their longing in death ... Union is sought with the Infinite while still in the midst of life; or to merge with the cosmos, with the universe, in order to find oneself nearer to God.[211]

She quotes Novalis as saying, "Children of God are we, seeds of God are we."[212] Jaffé thought the unconscious was activated to an especially powerful degree in the Romantic period. This was related, in her view, to the rise of fascism. "The Romantics were scarcely capable of realizing that, in their disdain for the human individual and the limitation of his earthly existence, they had smoothed the way for a depersonalized mass for which nothing else remained but to seek its Führer."[213]

But pedomorphy to this extreme must have been attempting to break out of a powerfully frozen gerontomorphic nexus. Psychologist Alice Miller suggests that it was the child-rearing practices in German families that produced this reaction. She quotes, among many others, J. Sulzer's 1748 child-rearing manual, "An Essay on the Education and Instruction of Children":

It is quite natural for the child's soul to want to have a will of its own, and things that are not done correctly in the first two years will be difficult to rectify thereafter. One of the advantages of these early years is that then force and compulsion can be used. Over the years children forget everything that happened to them in early childhood. If their wills can be broken at this time, they will never remember afterwards that they had a will, and for this very reason the severity that is required will not have any serious consequences.[214]

After Miller's first book, a German reader wrote:

Do you believe that the concentration camps of the Nazi period would have been possible had not the use of physical terrorization in the form of beatings with canes, rug beaters, switches, and cat-o'-nine-tails been the rule in raising German children?[215]

Archetypal balancing attempts can also move toward gerontomorphy. Science itself is such a move. In the midst of the witch burnings, the Inquisition, fratricidal religious wars and other social upheavals of the European Middle Ages, Descartes sat quietly in his study writing, "I think, therefore I am." Modern science began as a commitment to order in a chaotic

[211] Jaffé, A., *Was C.G. Jung a Mystic?*, p. 33.
[212] Ibid., p. 35.
[213] Ibid., p. 50.
[214] Miller, A., *For Your Own Good*, p. xviii.
[215] Ibid., p. 233.

environment; but the technological revolution it produced is now deadening the world. Just as modern science saw everything in the universe as causally determined, Western countries seem bent on reducing all of the biological world to the right angles and decimal measurements of our roads, dams, fences, buildings, property boundaries, banks, and factories. Where there was once self-organized wilderness, we are building frozen grid. Trapped in a runaway autocatalytic loop, all this grid may be producing a reaction moving toward a supercritical point. In theory, this should lead to a scientific pedomorphic reaction. This could be the role of complexity sciences. They present nature not as determined, but adaptive, connected, regenerative, and metamorphic. It is probably no accident that the majority of the work done on complexity theory seems to be happening outside the rigidly specialized academic world. In the Santa Fe Institute, where many complexity theorists are working, the exploration is interdisciplinary, open, and collective. Opposites are being brought together, instead of split apart in a "hermaphroditic" redemption of nature and science.

10. Altered States at the Edge of Chaos

In order to articulate our present crisis as cross-cultural artists, we need to invent and reinvent languages constantly. These languages have to be as syncretic, diverse, and complex as the fractured realities we are trying to define. Postmodernism is a crumbled conceptual architecture, and we are tired of walking among someone else's ruins.[216]

– Guillermo Gomez-Peña

All of the strategies we discussed in the previous chapter can occur unconsciously. People may enact them without ever imagining there is anything in their behavior other than the personal choice of a mind made up. In the deterministic universe of modern (pre-complexity) science, there was no place for self-organized systems with multiple, unconscious, archetypal strategies in nested information systems. At the same time, there has always been an underground stream of scientific questioning that noted regularities for which there was no place in current theory. I would place Lao Tzu, Paracelsus, the alchemists, Jung, and many other HERMITs in this tradition.

Based on his study of perception in animal life, ethologist Konrad Lorenz thought there must be a remarkable preconscious organizing center in all animals:

I have described in detail how the process by which a *Gestalt* or form crystallizes, emerging against a background of contingent elements, may extend over very long periods, sometimes many years. – We obviously possess a mechanism that is capable of absorbing almost incredible numbers of individual "observation records," of retaining them over long periods, and on top of all that evaluating them statistically.[217]

[216] Gomez-Peña, G., *Warrior for Gringostroika*, p. 49.
[217] Lorenz, K., *Behind the Mirror*, p. 119.

He called these processes "ratiomorphous." Though they are analogous to conscious processes in form and function, he thought they were a quite separate operating system in the human being.

> The ratiomorphous function is vastly superior to the rational function so far as concerns the number of individual items of information it is able to retain, but we are not in a position to call up this information at will. ... Ratiomorphous functions are independent of abstract thought and as old as the hills...[218]

If the ratiomorphous function, which Jung called the "Self" (and others have named Creativity, Redeemer, or Tao) often energizes human behavior without our conscious involvement, how can we make the process conscious and cooperate with it or turn it off once it starts? If Kauffman is right about schemata adapting to the edge of chaos to create coordinated landscapes, the more frozen part of our psyche, the conscious ego, should be able to melt a little and the more melted part of our psyche, the unconscious, should "freeze" a little in this attempt.

Our inner world is, in fact, characterized by a constant moving back and forth between willed conscious attention and relaxed, unwilled fantasy. Our speech and other behaviors, too, seem to be based on two separate strategies. Speech can be gerontomorphic when it is formal, grammatical, distancing, abstract, or academic. Then we are paying attention to skeletal structure as in semiotics, linguistics, philosophy, poetics. Sometimes, though, speech is pedomorphic, emotional, and connective. Then we tell jokes, use slang, tell stories, recite poetry, or sing songs. We vacillate between pedomorphic and gerontomorphic moods as well. We are gerontomorphic in states of doubt, critical distancing, fragmentation, and dissociation. We are pedomorphic when we identify, fall in love, merge, become inspired, or flow.

It is when we lose the ability to move between these two poles that problems develop. Both are necessary. In music, rhythm is skeletal and gerontomorphic, while harmony and melody are pedomorphic. We cannot make music without both poles. In Victor Turner's categories, the structuring ceremonies of social interaction are gerontomorphic, and the liminal states of *communitás* are pedomorphic. Functional subcultures need access to both to adjust their behavior adaptively.

Each twenty-four hour period of our lives is divided into a pedomorphic dream phase, when fantasy creates integrative myths and fairy tales in which time and space no longer dominate, and a gerontomorphic awake phase where the world largely remains solidly and securely organized by space, time, and causality. These two systems must have ways of adjusting toward coevolution. Perhaps the occurrences of meaningful symbols and synchro-

---

[218] Ibid., p. 119.

nicities in our awake phases are the slight melting of the "frozen" ego world into more connectedness. Could we then understand dreams as an "attempt" of the ratiomorphic unconscious to share its wealth of potential energy by loading some of it into numinous fantasy images? Where these two modes join and meet as friends in myth, ritual and art, we might then create the conditions for inner coevolution, an inner strategy which allows us to live in contact with the healing energies of spirit. For most of the long history of human cultures, this joining has taken place through religious ritual.

In the cultures where schizophrenia is regularly healed, these two processes tack back and forth in liminal ceremonies, dream interpretation, myth, folklore, and indigenous psychology. Myths about spirits, ghosts, possession, and ancestor requirements are a way of making a little room in the ego world for irrational unconscious elements. They do not seem to stop these cultures from building homes, producing food, and governing society; but they provide a breathing space in daily life for the recreation of energy.

Malidoma Somé, a Western-educated Burkina Faso elder, believes modern Westerners have an image of an archetypal indigenous person within.

> This indigenous archetype within the modern soul is an archetype that is in serious need of acknowledgment within the person. A different set of priorities dwells there, a set of priorities long forgotten in higher cultures. People in touch with this archetype are in search of caring, for their spirit seeks to transcend the stress placed on the body and the mind by the rapid motion of everyday life around them. Such people would not be ashamed to express their hunger for transcendence – these are the kind of people in need of ritual.[219]

Cultures in every corner of the world have been lavish in their imaginative mythmaking while creating space for healing rituals. The ratiomorphous center of life, the immortal divine child which brings together ancient wisdom with rejuvenation, has been represented in countless beautiful animal images. The Indian story of the Buddha's conception contains such an image. Queen Maya was said to have been impregnated with the future Buddha by a radiant, immortal white elephant who walked three times around her bed in a dream.

Everywhere that religious and healing rituals are still efficacious, there has been a symbolism of the "world center," a sacred place where the ancient and the rejuvenating can come together through ritual. Mircea Eliade has documented countless examples of this center in mythologies about sacred mountains, springs, trees, ladders, cities, precincts, and temples where the heavens, the earth, and the underworld meet. The Machi who did the healing ritual for José Arnoldo in Chapter 3 enacted this myth. Here in the center,

---

[219] Somé, M.P., *Ritual: Power, Healing, Community*, p. 34.

where the world was born, one can return through proper ritual for healing and renewal.

> The summit of the cosmic mountain is not only the highest point on earth; it is also the earth's navel, the point at which creation began. There are even instances in which cosmological traditions explain the symbolism of the Center in terms which might well have been borrowed from embryology. "The Holy One created the world like an embryo. As the embryo proceeds from the navel onwards, so God began to create the world from its navel onwards, and from there it was spread out in different directions."[220]

Until recently, such myths have been interpreted in Western anthropology by a kind of "hoax theory." It was often suggested in anthropological literature that shamans or healers manipulate their childlike followers with stories and tricks of atmosphere. But what if we were to imagine that these cultures were talking about the "edge of chaos," that navel of self-organization which modern biologists have just discovered? This would be a "location" in experience where healing rituals would make space for what had not yet been said out loud in any cultural context. Set ideas could be reorganized, and new, integrative images could form in such an environment.

Space and time appear to be relative at the edge of chaos. Strangely, even in computer programs modeling the edge of chaos, there are odd phenomena of time distortion. Journalist Kevin Kelly, who has spent years discussing these programs with complexity scientists, reports,

> From his experiments in artificial life in swarm models, Chris Langton, Kauffman's Santa Fe Institute colleague, derived an abstract quality (called the lambda parameter) that predicts the likelihood that a particular set of rules for a swarm will produce a "sweet spot" of interesting behavior. Systems built upon values outside this sweet spot tend to stall in two ways. They either repeat patterns in a crystalline fashion, or else space out into white noise. Those values within the range of the lambda sweet spot generate the longest runs of interesting behavior. By tuning the lambda parameter Langton can tune a world so that evolution or learning can unroll most easily. Langton describes the threshold between a frozen repetitive state and a gaseous noise state as a "phase transition" – the same term physicists use to describe the transition from liquid to gas or liquid to solid. The most startling result, though, is Langton's contention that as the lambda parameter approaches the phase transition – the sweet spot of maximum adaptability – it slows down. That is, the system tends to *dwell* on the edge instead of zooming through it. As it nears the place it can evolve the most from, it lingers. The image Langton likes to raise is that of a system surfing on an endless perfect wave in slow motion; the more perfect the ride, the slower time goes.[221]

[220] Eliade, M., *The Myth of the Eternal Return*, p. 16.
[221] Kelly, K., *Out of Control*, p. 401.

It is exactly the characteristic of mythological world centers which can be created in ritual, according to Eliade, that they transform space and time.

> Naturally, the consecration of the center occurs in a space qualitatively different from profane space. Through the paradox of rite, every consecrated space coincides with the center of the world, just as the time of any ritual coincides with the mythical time of the "beginning." Through repetition of the cosmogenic act, concrete time, in which the construction takes place, is projected into mythical time, *in illo tempore* where the foundation of the world occurred.[222]

Under such conditions, oracles, diviners, and prophets in "altered states" have always come forth with symbolic messages that imagine reality through "melted" categories. Here is the location where the Great Goddess handed on the healing gift of second sight. To the Greeks, it was the place where the Kairos opened as a window or gate in time where creative imagination could flourish. To Taoists, it is a return to the place I knew before I was born, at the origin of all things. According to Jesus, it was the kingdom of heaven: "The kingdom of heaven is like yeast that a woman took and mixed into a large amount of flour until it worked all through the dough." As a result of his access to the kingdom while still on earth, he said, "I will open my mouth in parables, I will utter things hidden since the creation of the world." The center of his message was that this yeasty kingdom of heaven is accessible to all people: "The kingdom of heaven is like a treasure hidden in a field. When a man found it, he hid it again, and then in his joy went and sold all he had and bought that field."[223]

Anthropologist Erika Bourguignon did a worldwide survey of cultures during the 1960's to find out how widespread was the occurrence of altered states of consciousness in rituals using trance and possession states. Of 488 cultures studied, in 437 (89%) of them, such states were institutionalized. Roy D'Andrade did a worldwide sample of sixty-four cultures and found that fifty-five percent of them interpreted and used dreams in relation to supernatural powers. According to Bourguignon, "These figures are cited here to indicate that we are dealing, indeed, with phenomena of major ethnographic and theoretical significance."[224] They discovered that societies that used dreams and trance for information about the supernatural were more likely to be low grid. That is, they tended to have nonfixed settlements, only simple agriculture, no towns, small population size, close families, simple political hierarchies, and no class stratification. Apparently, high-grid requirements in a society suppress the integration of the unconscious while strengthening

---

[222] Eliade, M., *The Myth of Eternal Return*, p. 20.
[223] Matt. 13:44.
[224] Bourguignon, E., "Dreams and altered states of consciousness in anthropological research," in: Hsu, F.L.K., ed., *Psychological Anthropology*, 1972, p. 418.

the persona! Many of these low-grid cultures have, until recently, attained coevolutionary or evolutionarily stable strategies [ESS] which have sustained them in their environments for many thousands of years. During this time several dozen so-called "high civilizations" arose, built massive grid, and then crumbled into dust. Perhaps we need to begin to evaluate cultures less on the basis of how much material structure they produce and more on the basis of what kind of human environment they create. We might ask how happy are their children, how nurtured are their hungry, how comforted are their sufferers, how imaginative are their healers? In this evaluation, modern urban society will probably be nowhere near the top.

Anthropologists Mageo et al. suggest that it may be the material structure of high-grid societies that undermines the appearance of spirits carrying messages which have been suppressed.

> In various places ... people say that spirits leave places that are brightly lighted during the night. The more experience that takes place in well-lighted settings and in the built-up areas that progressively replace nearby wilderness, the less room there is for spirits. The poorly-lighted night and the socially uncolonized spaces (bush, forest, wilderness) around communities are perfect settings for uncanny experiences ... The sensations produced by these experiences are closely related to what Otto ... called "numinous feelings," feelings that are taken as a direct experiential warrant, a direct perception of the realm of the "holy." They seem to be generated in situations where it is difficult to make "those categorizations that help anchor us in 'commonsense' reality," where the familiar and dependable schemas of time, space, size, cause, and logic hold. Situations where these schemas seem not to hold are intrinsically uncanny ... Thus the transformation of numinous places into banal ones through lighting, and rebuilding – leading to the disappearance of "empty" or alien environments – may make a profound difference...[225]

It may be that extremely high-grid societies are too one-sided to allow human survival over the long run. Konrad Lorenz thought that cultures would fail when they provided over-elaborated learning environments that were deeply in conflict with human needs and tendencies.

> The regular decline of high cultures, for example, which has preoccupied so many historians from the Greeks to Spengler, may well have been the consequence of a discrepancy between the rate of development of phylogenetically controlled behavior patterns on the one hand and tradition controlled patterns on the other. Cultural development is simply too fast for human nature to keep up with and, as Klages noted, the mind can become the enemy of the soul. We urgently need to know more about these things.[226]

---

[225] Mageo, J.M.et. al., *Spirits in Culture, History, and Mind,* p. 20.
[226] Lorenz, K., *Behind the Mirror,* p. 191.

In the educated sectors of Western countries, the ego process may have fallen into a rigid development, losing contact with an unconscious ratiomorphic Self in an extreme and stressful state of vigilance. Many of us have lost access to a ritualized "world center" where deep healing and rejuvenation can occur. We do not know the way to a yeasty kingdom of heaven, and our prophets speak from television sets. We require our children to stay in school from age five to twenty-five or thirty if they get professional degrees, but rarely in this education do we make room for the integration of psyche in ritual. In many school systems in the United States, no money is made available for art, music, theater, or any other creative activity. The majority of people in the United States pay no attention at all to their dreams, and most children have thousands of dreams throughout their childhood that they never tell to anyone because no one listens or asks. The end product can be a dissociated adult who has been taught more about correct behavior, competition, and conformity than about inner wholeness.

As a result, the Western academic world has produced the credo of what Richard Shweder calls the "God is dead," or "ghost-buster" philosophy. Anthropologist David M. Schneider, quoted in Shweder, stated it forcefully in 1965: "There is no supernatural. Ghosts do not exist. Spirits do not in fact make storms, cause winds, bring illness or effect cures."[227] Here is a culture hero more determined than Hercules, so totally involved in killing the dragon that he cannot remember his ancient friendship with animals. In so extreme a position, he has cut off his own roots in the biological world.

Poet Robert Graves said we have lost our connection with poetry, which should be expressing our deepest numinous connection with spirit in nature, the ancient Goddess or Muse that animates all things. In retreat from modern civilization on the island of Mallorca, he wrote:

> This (poetry) was once a warning to man that he must keep in harmony with the family of living creatures among which he was born, by obedience to the wishes of the lady of the house; it is now a reminder that he has disregarded the warning, turned the house upside down by capricious experiments in philosophy, science, and industry, and brought ruin on himself and his family. "Nowadays" is a civilization in which the prime emblems of poetry are dishonoured. In which serpent, lion, and eagle belong to the circus tent; ox, salmon, and boar to the cannery; racehorse and greyhound to the betting ring; and the sacred grove to the sawmill.[228]

An apt image of this attitude is St. George killing the dragon. Here the victory of the conscious attitude is complete. Whatever healing capacities might have lived in the dragon are now rejected as primitive, evil, or

---

[227] Shweder, R., *Thinking Through Cultures*, p. 42.
[228] Graves, R., *The White Goddess*, p. 14.

Figure 10.1 – St. George kills the dragon

demonic. The sooner they can be killed off, the better. Figure 10.1 was taken from the boy scout certificates given to male children in Switzerland.

There has been a shift toward explanations which reduce uncanny or numinous experiences to "natural" causes in the West during the last several hundred years. According to Mageo et al.,

> When communities find themselves disenchanted, spirits depart. Possession changes its forms and may even disappear altogether. In the normative "enlightened" modern situation, even in the rare corners where the uncanny may be encountered, its *validity* as a knowledge-yielding experience is now discounted. It becomes a fascinating illusion, or a cover story for supermarket check-out magazines. Experience, doctrine, and epistemology have all shifted. As we pass beyond the modern, all this may shift again.[229]

---

[229] Mageo, J.M., et.al., *Spirits in Culture, History, and Mind*, p. 20.

In this way of thinking, there has been no room for inner systemic events related to archetypes, unconscious default hierarchies, or healing spirit. Yet, without such notions, by whatever name they are called in local cultures, we will never be able to understand the psyche of the schizophrenic or even ourselves and the cultural world we have produced. Each generation is responsible for finding its own way to symbolize and keep alive what Jung named the healing archetypes of the divine child. If we do not like the names or models other generations or other cultures have used, we have to find new ones. If we fail, and try to shut the process out through denial, we will have created a spiritual environment of cynicism and despair where no healing can occur. This will most of all wound our own psyches. Perhaps this is why physicians have one of the highest suicide rates of any profession.

We can never fully understand or finally explain the complex notion of archetypes with ego consciousness or scientific categories because they work at unconscious levels of the psyche. Complexity theorists remain quite puzzled over many aspects of the systems that they have discovered. Kauffman says they are "waiting for Carnot," (the way Beckett's characters waited for Godot), a theorist who can find a general law that will make sense of all this new material. In Beckett's play, however, it becomes clear that Godot is an image of God who will reveal meaning in an alienated world. Perhaps we are no longer in a state to accept revealed knowledge, and all we can do is name the patterns we see and try to connect them with those we have inherited in our cultural schemata. In Jung's view, our goals must be limited:

> The most we can do is to dream the myth onward and give it a modern dress. And whatever explanation or interpretation does to it, we do to our own souls as well, with corresponding results for our own well being. The archetype – let us never forget this – is a psychic organ present in all of us. A bad explanation means a correspondingly bad attitude to this organ which may thus be injured. But the ultimate sufferer is the bad interpreter himself. Hence the "explanation" should always be such that the functional significance of the archetype remains unimpaired, so that an adequate and meaningful connection between the conscious mind and the archetypes is assured. For the archetype is an element of our psychic structure and thus a vital and necessary component in our psychic economy.[230]

We need to find ways, even in our postmodern scientific environment, for what is archaic, bodily, repressed, irrational, and self-ordering in us to meet what is rational, expressive, and ego-structured. The unconscious ratiomorphic function continues to attempt its work of integration even when no one is consciously listening or watching. ("Called or uncalled, the Gods come!") When we pay it no attention, the dissociation between ego and unconscious

---

[230] Jung, C.G., *The Archetypes and the Collective Unconscious*, Vol. 9.1, p. 160.

grows ever greater, and we lose our connection a healing function that other cultures seem still able to tap into in ritual. Without this function, both society and individuals fall ill, and search unconsciously through default hierarchies for "atavism in the service of rejuvenation."

This atavism, interpreted literally and unconsciously, can lead to madness, violence, or war by new beasts "slouching toward Bethlehem."[231] Like Gina, they may dream they cause the end of the world to create new possibilities for healing. Unfortunately, it is a fragile and frightened Gina who is locked up, while many would-be world saviors are planting bombs or directing governments. To those more firmly entrenched in the canalizations of ego structure, atavism can produce a search for "imagined communities," privileged identities, or life-style fetishes appropriated from other cultures interpreted as "primitive." These can create rigid and isolated islands of homogeneity disconnected from more global flows of information.

It seems that in Western healing systems, we need a larger conscious conception of the human personality that will make room for archetypal energies and irrational unconscious symbols of compensation. We need to recognize that the defended individualistic ego, which is the norm in urban society, is not universal, but one way, among many others, for a culture to construct personality. In addition, in every culture, when the stress on an individual becomes unendurable for whatever reason, the personality is capable of moving down an unconscious default hierarchy of strategies in order to cope. Pressed to its limits, the unconscious ratiomorphic function will resort to that most complex of all organic strategies, the dream of a renewed and re-imagined world at the edge of chaos. With such a conception of human possibilities, without "shoes which are too tight for us," perhaps we can consciously re-imagine rituals to create periodic transformation and healing. These rituals must allow for the reintegration of what has been repressed and the inclusion of creative spirit, rather than a restoration of social persona. We need to be able to transform those aspects of our world that have grown brittle and regressive. In mythologies everywhere, one only becomes fully human through the ability to create and participate in rituals of transformation. Without them, the psyche fragments and dissociates, and we become "strangers in a strange land," in the very Eden where we were born.

---

[231] Yeats, W.B., "The Second Coming," in: *Collected Poems*, p. 184.

11. Complex Psyche

Have we ever seriously asked what psychosocial processes look like from the point of view of the dominated instead of from that of the dominator? Have we thought of looking at educational psychology from where the illiterate stands, or industrial psychology from the place of the unemployed, or clinical psychology from the standpoint of the marginalized? What would mental health look like from the place of a tenant farmer on a hacienda, or personal maturity from someone who lives in the town dump, or motivation from a woman who sells goods in the market? Note that we say "from" the illiterate and the unemployed, "from" the tenant farmer and the woman in the market, not "for" them. This is not a matter of thinking for them or bringing our ideas or solving their problems for them; it has to do with thinking and theorizing with them and from them. ... To take on a new perspective obviously does not mean throwing out all of our knowledge; what it supposes rather, is that we will relativize that knowledge and critically revise it from the perspective of the popular majorities. Only then will the theories and models show their validity or deficiency, their utility or lack thereof, their universality or provincialism. Only then will the techniques we have learned display their liberating potential or their seeds of subjugation.[232]

– Ignacio Martín-Baró

The local cause theory of mental illness is far too simple for the complex process that occurs in people like Gina and Edward. It seems that several very different phenomena have been lumped together under the headings of schizophrenia and psychosis. In the treatment teams in mental hospitals, separated from the patients by glass walls, too much emotional and social context was pushed away or disregarded. The building blocks of our healing schemata – milieu therapy, neuroleptics, chronic member of the mental health system – are too simplistic to heal these illnesses.

Modern psychiatric conceptions of schizophrenia are currently becoming noticeably more complex. In a recent book entitled, *Schizophrenia Genesis:*

[232] Martín-Baró, Ignacio, *Writings for a Liberation Psychology*, p. 28

The Origins of Madness, psychiatrist Irving I. Gottesman has reviewed years of research. He has noted that there appears to be some inherited familial vulnerability to schizophrenia, but none of the research has shown that it is "caused" by genes. The inherited vulnerability, Gottesman suggests, can be affected by many different types of "toxic environments."

> From the research available so far, … the clusters of significant environmental contributors to schizophrenia liability can be conceptualized as (1) insults to the brain, (2) demoralizing or threatening physical environments, (3) emotionally intrusive experiences, (4) emotionally demanding experiences, (5) affective and emotional understimulation ("institutionalism"), and (6) disruptions to attention and information processing.[233]

This new complex multifactoral model has been pictured in the literature in a number of ways. Gottesman points out that it was only in 1986 that medical geneticists gave up a search for simple Mendelian models in insulin-dependent diabetes. As with the newer understanding of diabetes, many researchers now believe we will have to relinquish the idea of a local cause in schizophrenia. Dr. K.H. Nuechterlein has imagined the chain of events leading to schizophrenia as shown in Figure 11.1.

Unfortunately, when models become extremely complex, they lose predictive quality and, in individual cases, amount to a description of a life history. In 1990, the Swiss psychiatrist, Manfred Bleuler, summed up the situation as follows:

> Manifold and numerous peculiarities of somatic, physiological, and psychological nature have been discovered as the cause of vulnerability regarding schizophrenic psychosis. Some of them are inherited, others are acquired, and in many heredity and experience participate in the origin. The "discovery" consists in demonstrating that the peculiarity in question was much more common in schizophrenics before the onset of psychosis than in the general population. However, we should remain conscious of one fact, which it would be pleasant to forget, the fact that none of the peculiarities considered today as dispositions are present in all schizophrenics either before or after the outbreak of the psychosis. And on the other hand they can also be found in some normal people or in many patients other than schizophrenics. This means: we have not discovered any specific disposition for schizophrenic psychosis.[234]

In fact, Bleuler wondered if the universal worldwide incidence of schizophrenia might point to something inherent in the human personality. "This

---

[233] Gottesman, I.I., *Schizophrenia Genesis,* p. 165.
[234] Bleuler, M., "What is schizophrenia?," 1990 Speech presented at University of Massachusetts Medical School Conference, Worcester, MA.

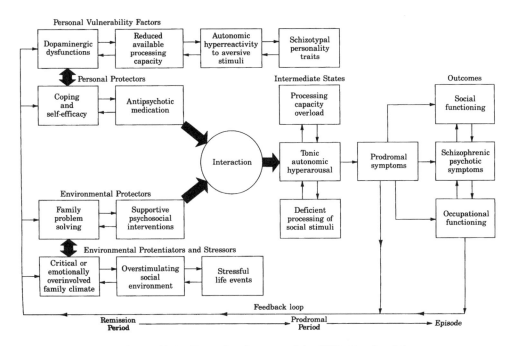

Figure 11.1 – Tentative framework by K.H. Nuechterlein

might be a hint that essential backgrounds of schizophrenic psychoses lie mainly in human nature rather than in particular trouble."[235]

Perhaps the real problem is the whole conception of mental illness and human personality as "caused," in the sense of a linear computer program where specific inputs cause definite results. Today, we can begin to conceptualize personality through the new schemata of parallel processing in complexity theory. How could we imagine a many-layered psyche with unconscious default hierarchies of models? An earlier chapter suggested that the Jungian categories of ego, shadow, Self, anima/s, and collective unconscious could be understood in terms of connectivity in grid and group. Because each culture will construct its connectivity through ritual and custom in a slightly different way, we could picture a large variety of functional combinations of these factors that would yield evolutionarily stable strategies (ESS) for individuals. By an individual ESS, I mean a coherent, comfortable, and stable personality structure that is flexible enough to adjust to changing environments without losing its coherence. One possible diagram of this is given in Figure 11.2.

[235] Ibid.

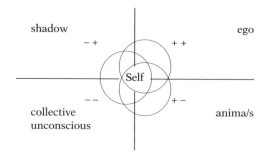

Figure 11.2 – Stable strategies

The inner circles represent the infinitely many ways it would be possible to put these elements together in any given culture. But what would happen if the personality were placed under so much stress by some element in the inner or outer environment that it was energized toward a phase change in the archetypal default hierarchy? We could imagine a ring of adjustments around the ESS which, while not ideal, would allow either continued functioning or else a clear sign of distress. These will be designated as crisis strategies. The adjustments would not always be conscious or uniform, but would be varying responses to particular environments. Different cultures would understand and name them in unique ways, but the existence of default hierarchies of strategies is probably universal in biological life. We could sort them through complexity theory by imagining these adjustments as a second ring around the first ESS circle, which is labeled according to Western diagnostic categories in Figure 11.3.

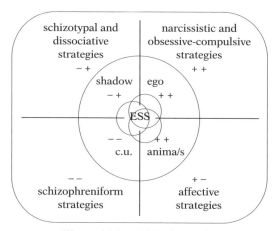

Figure 11.3 – Crisis Strategies

Above the line is high grid, and below, low grid. In general, the strategies above the line allow more easily for continued ego functioning at some level within Western society and do not appear in mental hospitals. It is those extreme cases in the low-grid quarters that end up in mental hospitals. In the ++ HIERARCHICAL quarter of crisis strategies, the normal ordering function of the ego becomes rigid and intensified. Any failure of order is attacked as polluting. This is an attempt to hold onto slipping structure, an extreme gerontomorphic strategy. I have met many people from Latin American indigenous organizations who view people from the United States and Western Europe in general as sliding in this direction. That is, they see our "normal ego" as rigid, selfish, and neurotic. Many of the Japanese psychiatric colleagues at the Jung Institute in Switzerland, as well, share this view of the normal Western ego structure, which seems to them so different from their own. Erich Neumann calls this survival strategy the "negative ego," and attributes it to an extremely patriarchal cultural canon.

> The inhibitions imposed by every cultural canon or influence upon the individuality and polyvalence of the child normally make themselves felt in the course of the primal relationship and in the first years of the child's development. But it is a question of the utmost importance whether the child is drawn smoothly and easily into the cultural canon, so that it need take no notice of the process of inhibition, or whether it is forced into the canon with a brutality which may penetrate the child's consciousness.[236]

In this case, much in the child is cut off. The "negative ego" then,

> is the expression of a later disturbance in which a consolidated ego and a systematized conscious centered around this ego become reactively rigid, defend themselves on all fronts, and barricade themselves against the world and the Self. This tendency of the negativized ego to shut itself off, intensifies the child's situation of forsakeness and feeling of insecurity, and this is the beginning of a vicious circle in which ego-rigidity, aggression, and negativism alternate with feelings of forsakenness, inferiority and unlovedness, each set of feelings intensifying the other. This is one of the main causes of sado-masochistic reactions and of the pathological narcissistic ego-rigidity that often accompanies them.[237]

A personality pushed into a crisis strategy in the ++ quadrant is therefore brittle and impersonal. It would seem that alexithymia, that painful emptiness of a personality alienated from its own feeling experience, belongs among these disorders. Many clients seen in outpatient practice suffer from resultant feelings of despair, and separation from a center of meaningful relatedness. Much emotional life has never been experienced, so that it is not

[236] Neumann, E., *The Child*, p. 66.
[237] Ibid., p. 78.

repressed, but actually absent because it has never been constellated. The most authentic experience of such clients is often simply emptiness and it is this emptiness that must first be arrived at and experienced in analysis as the only real feeling, before anything new can grow. If this cannot take place, the personality obsessively carries out rituals of structure, which preserve grid at the cost of aliveness and relatedness.

In the –+ FATALIST high grid quarter, the personality splits and dissociates in the face of crushing and painful intrusion from the outside. In this way, a core of authentic aliveness is preserved hidden within, while the outer world continues to be met by what Winnicott has called the "false self." Erich Neumann calls this strategy the *Not-Ich* or "distress-ego."

> Where the primal relationship is disturbed, the distress-ego is prematurely thrown back on itself; it is awakened too soon, and *driven* to independence by the situation of anxiety, hunger, and distress. ... It is attended by hunger, pain, emptiness, cold, helplessness, utter loneliness, loss of all security and shelteredness; it is a headlong fall into the forsakenness and fear of the bottomless void. ... If this constellation sets in too early, it leads to egoless apathy and decline.[238]

In this –+ quadrant, much personal energy is used to dissociate from painful and potentially overwhelming negative feeling states. Here, the negative feelings have been constellated and experienced, and the issues are separation, projection, and avoidance in borderline swings of affiliation and annihilation. It is amazing how often even very intelligent people can manage not to see their own grief, sadness, or pain by somatizing it as physical symptoms – an ulcer, heart condition, or migraine. Inner defense systems can be phenomenal in this sector, causing an extreme guardedness and vigilance that means almost never expressing true feelings to another. At an extreme, there is a terrifying premonition that the defense system will fail, leading to delusions of reference or paranoid fantasies. This can be a personality armed and "on the run," avoiding encounter, intimacy, or even contact.

The distress-ego and the negative-ego, then, are painful but successful attempts to cling to grid in the absence of comforting social support. Although personalities lived in this mode yield great suffering and many neurotic and psychosomatic symptoms, somehow the individual maintains a place in society. Freudian and Adlerian psychology were born in a high-grid environment, where Austrian men, women, and children molded by stern patriarchal expectations exhibited every variety of psychosomatic and dissociative symptom in their attempts to conform. Working in a dermatological clinic, Freud was impressed by the connection between these physical symptoms and the social "superego" pressures that produced them. Thinking

---

[238] Ibid., p. 74.

through a causal model, he showed that making a place in the ego world for stress and the "forbidden" could relieve symptoms. In conscious thought expressed in speech, and in relationship with a "healing authority," a broader HIERARCHY that included some repressed feelings freed the personality. Adler, more influenced by extroverted political involvement in contemporary social movements, noticed the "arrangements" by which people maintained a core feeling of inferiority while attempting to express superiority and competence.

Jung, on the other hand, developed his theories in the low-grid world of mental patients. Here, the attempt to cling to the grid of local culture has failed, and the individual has insufficient structure to adjust to social and economic conditions. Without the high-grid creode pattern normal to other members of society, the low-grid mental patient is more open to characteristic archetypal influences. It was through observing such pre-ego processes that Jung came up with the idea of the collective unconscious and its archetypal patterns.

At the low-grid, highly connected +– sector of my diagram, we see mental patients with affective disorders. Here, enough coherence may still exist to maintain some structure. In fact, the manic patient often buttonholes everyone in sight in a panicked attempt to connect. When a brittle structure impedes real relationship and prevents inner growth, unconscious needs for connectivity can pour over ego grid. According to Neumann,

> since this rigidity of the ego disturbs and often impedes the progressive development of the personality, the excluded contents and drives of the unconscious accumulate and finally break through the barrier, erupting into consciousness and flooding it. Then the oscillating twofold orientation of the integral personality and the integral ego is replaced by an alteration of rigidity and chaos, typical of certain psychic disorders.[239]

In affective disorders, the patient begins to fall out of the HIERARCHICAL connections typical of the dominant society in search of other forms of connectivity. This is first experienced as loneliness and a lowering of the energy needed to carry out the daily round of activities that no longer fulfill the heart. Sometimes this leads to a quest that results in new work and relationships that enlarge the conscious world; but when the social world is too rigid to allow exploration and healing ritual, the slightly depressed searcher can fall into a painful vegetative state of hopelessness, a major depression. Some patients then move farther down the default hierarchy and attempt to fend off the psychic pain by a passionate manic denial that defends against knowing. Here, they may experience themselves as world saviors full of psychic energy, new plans, and special powers. When this

[239] Ibid., p. 79.

tactic inevitably fails as problems develop and energy runs out, they fall again into excruciating depression and self-recrimination. This condition, then, sometimes leads to desperate suicidal, or even homicidal, thoughts and acts.

Finally, in the −− low-grid, low-group sector, schizophrenic patients have lost energy to integrate meaningful connectivity. Like Gina, they live in small villages away from urban centers with little traffic or growth. Here, they are at last safe from intrusion, manipulation, sadism, interference, and often, sexual abuse. They can vegetate, listen to inner voices, and feel little pain. In terms of complexity theory, this is the simplest strategy of the ego, a giving up or "playing possum" in the face of an overwhelming situation. Near the ancient forest of the collective unconscious, they witness numinous events that they can report on without wonder or affect. Because they lack the creodes of the ++ sector to stabilize their ego personalities, the ratiomorphic function can quietly rise to a state of subcriticality near the edge of chaos in a last-ditch attempt at a "jump-start." A stressful outer event that no one else would have noticed can plunge them over the edge in an "extinction event" of fantasy, which floods the personality with archaic content outside of space and time. This is the origin of Gina's inability to remember her life story clearly. Her problem A represents the loss of affect, a giving up of the attempt to deal with an environment over which one can have no control. It is probably a strategy that was unconsciously developing unnoticed for years. Problem B, the flood of archaic material in psychosis, could be considered as an unconscious move down a default hierarchy.

In our diagram of default hierarchies in the human personality, then, we need to include another circle, a more extreme move that comes into play when crisis strategies no longer serve. This is a move toward the edge of chaos. It is a tactic that we are set up to resist both in cultural tradition and inner creode structure. Moving toward this circle provokes first a tremendous last-ditch contraction of "kinetic energy" in maintaining current structure. In the contraction stage, the high-grid crisis strategy personalities can become delusional, hearing voices that give them commands or imagining they are the center of attention of strangers in delusions of reference; and low-grid schizophrenic and manic-depressive patients can lose touch with reality. Panic, anxiety, or acute depression can develop if the patient has a schema of "incurable disease" and anticipates complete social rejection. The danger of suicide is very high at such a moment, where the situation allows it.

If the condition is met with a different healing system, however, in which the illness is contextualized in a holding religious myth, the contraction can relax into an ecstasy of renewed meaning. Under ideal conditions, it brings one into contact with a kind of healing bath, recognized in many cultures as a "center," where, under the guidance of a traditional healer, one can restructure the personality and begin to speak with an authentic inner voice. If proper rituals and context are encountered in time, the personality can return from this "inner shock treatment" transformed, or at least not damaged. In rare cases, within great religious traditions, it can be negotiated alone through a "holding" myth. One thinks here of St. John of the Cross, Nicolas von Flüe, Rumi, Milarepa, Rabbi Akiba, the Buddha, Hildegard of Bingham, or St. Theresa of Avila undergoing profound periods of lonely suffering, which have yielded some of the world's great spiritual literature.

In some cultures, the healing potentialities of this renewing center in the heart of the personality are held to be so important that promising adepts in each new generation are put through years of training to master and guide it. The *tulkus* of Tibetan Buddhism, including the Dalai Lama, are held to be continuous reincarnations of inner healing spiritual powers. In Kung culture, one-half of the men and one-third of the women go through years of training by relatives to develop healing abilities.

In environments where there are few such healers, myths, or rituals in the environment, or if the sufferer is particularly vulnerable or afflicted, the state may lose all ordering energy and become habitual and chaotic. This is an "end state" which could be reached by many different pathways of development.[240] The patient can then fall to the hopeless and incurable next circle of numb demoralization we know as chronic schizophrenia. When the personality falls back into a womblike dream state, no further hurt can be experienced from the environment. All kinetic energy is lost, and whatever potential energy remains is invested in fantasy. Gina's picture of the "host," buried in nature and waiting to redeem her, expressed this state well. Here the core of the personality can hibernate through the winter of an unfortunate destiny. Perhaps this way a seed is stored for some future life, where conditions allow the meek in spirit to inherit the earth.

The diagram of default hierarchies can now be enlarged to include further circles in Figure 11.4.

---

[240] Andreasen, N.C., Carpenter, W.T., "Diagnosis and classification of schizophrenia," *Schizophrenia Bulletin*, 1993, 19 (2).

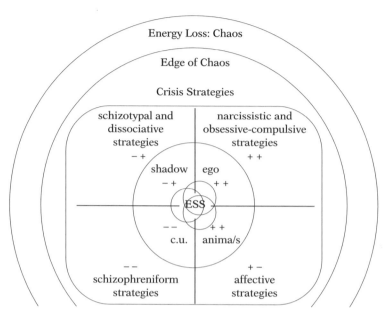

Figure 11.4 – Default Hierarchies

There is undoubtedly a modality of experience within every human personality modeled by the concept of the "edge of chaos." This modality, as well as the crisis strategies discussed above, are fundamental human possibilities inherited as default hierarchies in the basic self-organization of life. They arise as unconscious possibilities for adaptation guided by the ratiomorphous function, but they can be made conscious and altered. Each of these alternatives will be encountered in most cultures, but they will be understood in many different ways. If the sufferer of a crisis strategy is isolated, feared, and rejected, demoralization will surely occur. If, however, these strategies are recognized as the "speech" of the psyche and responded to with kindness, love, creativity, and rituals of inclusive connectivity, the sufferer may be brought back into the human fold. This "miracle" can then renew the faith and integrity of the entire community: "I tell you the truth, he is happier about that one sheep than about the ninety-nine that did not wander off. In the same way, your Father in heaven is not willing that any of these little ones should be lost."[241]

After such a journey in some cultures, there is then the recognition of a "wounded healer," saint, guru, poet, or Bodhisattva who can assist others in

---

[241] Matt. 17:12.

the passage to the "farther shore" at the edge of chaos. In many cases, what began as a negative experience can be seen as a powerful transformative potentiality deep in the center of the human psyche. It can then be sought in a controlled way for its own sake. Rumi, awakened by his contact with The Friend, wrote over 10,000 verses to share his experience. One reads:

> The breeze at dawn has secrets to tell you,
> Don't go back to sleep.
> You must ask for what you really want.
> Don't go back to sleep
> People are going back and forth across the doorsill
> Don't go back to sleep.
> The door is round and open.
> Don't go back to sleep.[242]

A vast amount of literature could be brought in at this point to support these suggestions, which really amount to an outline for future research. It seems that there is a "threshold" in the human psyche, well protected by the high grid of ego structure, that may be crossed under certain circumstances. This threshold is an "inner" or phenomenological experience that complexity theory models as the edge of chaos. It is "real" and "objective" in the same way as other more commonly experienced emotional states, like hunger or fear. This threshold experience has been reported by psychotics, mystics, healers, shamans, ethnologists, philosophers, and even some psychiatrists and cognitive psychologists, all over the world. Yet, we have lacked the courage to integrate it in scientific or medical theory in the West. It is as if we suffer an unconscious defensive contraction in our intellectual schemata at the edge of chaos as well.

The idea of such a threshold has been passed down in many Western and Eastern religions, less in their written literature on the whole, than in a secret oral tradition passed from master to student. As Gershom Scholem began his study of this oral tradition in the mystical Jewish literature of the Kabbalah, he feared he would suffer "professional death":

> To be sure, the key to the understanding of these things seemed to have been lost if one is to judge according to the obtuse standard of Enlightenment which Jewish scholars had to offer. ... And perhaps it wasn't so much the key that was missing, but courage: courage to venture out into an abyss, which one day could end up in us ourselves, courage also to penetrate through the symbolic plain and through the wall of history. For the mountain, the corpus of facts, needs no key at all; only the misty wall of history, which hangs around it, must be penetrated.[243]

---

[242] Rumi, *Open Secret*, Moyne, J., Barks, C., trans., Quatrain 91.
[243] Biale, D., *Gershom Scholem*, p. 32.

The way toward the threshold has been held in all traditions to be at once difficult, painful, and rewarding. In the traditions of Jewish *merkaba* mysticism, only four rabbis are believed to have made the final "ascent" to the "throne." The first died of a heart attack; the second became mentally disturbed; the third became a heretic; and the fourth was Rabbi Akiba, one of the wisest and most prominent Jewish writers in history.

Many people have suggested a link between mystical experience and schizophrenia, but usually the connection is drawn in the opposite way than the one that is made here. Often, schizophrenia is held to be a known and reified disease and then suggestions are made that various mystics "had" the disease. St. Theresa, Nicolas von Flüe, and Jung have all been called psychotic or schizophrenic by various writers. Here the argument is the opposite: that the threshold at the edge of chaos is a "normal" possibility, and that people all over the world have discovered it and institutionalized it in various ways. There is much evidence that we are talking about many paths up the same mountain, with the breathtaking view at the top being evaluated very differently.

In a 1981 paper entitled, "Mystical Experience and Schizophrenia," psychiatrist Peter Buckley suggested:

> The subjective experience of some psychotic episodes at their onset and of the acute mystical experience appear from these accounts to share some characteristics. The appearance of a powerful sense of noesis, heightening of perception, feelings of communication with the "divine," and exultation may be common to both. ... This raises the possibility that what is shared by some acute psychotic states and classical mystical experience is simply an ecstatic affective change which imbues perception with an increased intensity.[244]

Buckley refers to the work of A. J. Deikman in the early 1960's with normal subjects using meditative techniques.

> He conducted an experimental study of contemplative meditation and was able to invoke a number of phenomena in some of his subjects, including heightened sensory vividness, time distortion, a feeling of merging with the object that was being concentrated on, and fusing and alteration of normal perceptual modes. ... The ease with which he could invoke these phenomena in his subjects suggested to Deikman that a capacity exists, under conditions of minimal stress, for an alteration in the perception of the world and the self that is far greater than is customarily assumed to be the case for normal people. ... This is consistent with the hypothesis that a breakdown in the "stimulus barrier" is responsible for some of the subjective phenomena experienced in psychosis.[245]

---

[244] Buckley, P., "Mystical experience and schizophrenia," *Schizophrenia Bulletin* 1981, 7(3): 520.
[245] Ibid., p. 520.

Buckley quotes a number of accounts to support his thesis, and, in fact, medical and anthropological literature are full of related accounts. The following are several from non-psychotic religious experiences. Each of these people went on after these experiences to become healers, writers, or leaders of transformative vision:

From the founder of Alcoholics Anonymous:

Suddenly the room lit up with a great white light. I was caught up into an ecstasy where there are no words to describe. It seemed to me in the mind's eye, that I was on a mountain and that a wind, not of air, but of spirit was blowing.[246]

From St.Theresa:

It was our Lord's will that I should see an angel in this wise. He was not large, but small in stature, and most beautiful – his face burning, as if he were one of the highest angels, who seem to be all on fire. I saw in his hand a long spear of gold, and at the iron's point there seemed to be a little fire. He appeared to me to be thrusting it at times into my heart, and to pierce my very entrails; when he draws it out, he seemed to draw them out also and to leave me all on fire with a great love of God.[247]

From anthropologist Maya Deren, experiencing a Voodoun ritual:

"The white darkness moves up the veins of my leg like a swift tide rising, rising; is a great force which I cannot sustain or contain, which, surely, will burst my skin. It is too much, too much, too bright, too white for me; this is its darkness."[248]

From the Brazilian Macumba priestess Maria-José:

Macumba is the central axis, the center around which human activity is arranged. ... Everything can serve prophecy. You only have to pay attention. The world is full of signs. When you learn to look at things the right way, you will understand what I'm trying to say. The shape of the clouds, the way birds fly, the sounds of nature, an unexpected meeting. ... all these transmit a message that expresses the will of the Gods. The universe is a whole that fits together logically and that maintains itself and develops in a meaningful way.[249]

From Ojibwa medicine woman Catherine Ogee Wyan Akweet Okwa:

Seven days after my fasting period, as I lay in the wigwam I suddenly saw a round object come down from heaven, something like a round stone. When it

---

[246] Ibid., p. 519.
[247] Ibid., p. 519.
[248] Ibid., p. 519.
[249] Kalweit, H., *Shamans, Healers, Medicine Men*, p. 223.

got close to me I saw that it had little hands and feet like a human body. It spoke to me: "I give you the gift of seeing into the future; you must use it for yourself and the Indians, your kin, and fellow tribespeople!" Then he left, and as he flew away, he acquired wings and assumed the appearance of a red-headed woodpecker.[250]

Such states of timeless, synchronistic, and meaningful wonder are also experienced by psychotics:

1. Every single thing "means" something. This kind of symbolic thinking is exhausting. ... I have a sense that everything is more vivid and important; the incoming stimuli are almost more than I can bear. There is a connection to everything that happens – no coincidences.[251]

2. I became interested in a wide assortment of people, events, places, ideas which normally would make no impression on me. Not knowing that I was ill, I made no attempt to understand what was happening, but felt there was some overwhelming significance in all this.[252]

3. [Written in the third person]: Ordinarily unimportant information from external reality took on new dimensions for him. For example, colors power-fully influenced him. At any given moment wherever David went, colors were used to express judgement about his spirituality.[253]

We seem to be dealing here with a threshold state on one side of which is the ego world of space-time regularity, and on the other side of which is synchronicity. Marie-Louise von Franz saw it this way:

In the deepest levels of the objective psyche there is probably an acausal orderedness with a numerical structure that is equally valid both for the psyche and for matter. There, in the lattice patterns of the numerical field, psyche and matter, we may conjecture, are continuously mirroring each other, whereas in synchronistic events we become aware of this mirror-relation only exceptionally and then as specific happenings pregnant with meaning. Syn-chronistic events are therefore characterized by the intrusion into our "nor-mal" state of consciousness of a second psychic state, which usually remains below the threshold.[254]

Many observers have noted that schizophrenics seem to have special parapsychological powers of observation and insight. Erich Neumann was working on this subject at the time of his death. He wrote:

---

[250] Ibid., p. 40.
[251] Anscombe, R., "The disorder of consciousness in schizophrenia," *Schizophrenia Bulletin*, 1987, 13(2): 249.
[252] Ibid., p. 249.
[253] Ibid., p. 249.
[254] von Franz, M.-L., *Projection and Recollection in Jungian Psychology*, p. 195.

If, as now seems probable, certain forms of schizophrenia signify a regression to the phase of primal relationship, we can readily understand why, in states of inner agitation, schizophrenics should participate in the inner conflicts of those around them, why, as has been widely reported, they show an extraordinary awareness of the therapist's unconscious, and why they are often more capable than normal persons of understanding their fellow invalids' unconscious and its symbolism. This is merely to mention in passing isolated occurrence of authentic parapsychological phenomena in schizophrenia.[255]

This threshold state may be the fundamental dimension of religious experience. Almost one hundred years ago, William James made a passionate defense of the reality of such a dimension, bringing together a vast wealth of material to support it, in his work, *Varieties of Religious Experience.*[256] He argued that there exists, beside the ego realm of daily life, another region of experience that could be called "mystical states of consciousness," that were the "root and center" of all religious experience. These states, he thought, have four basic qualities wherever they are encountered. First, they are indescribable in normal language, going far beyond the fixed regularities of the scientific world. "In this peculiarity mystical states are more like states of feeling than like states of intellect. No one can make clear to another who has never had a certain feeling, in what the quality or worth of it consists." Second, mystical states give access to knowledge. "They are states of insight into depths of truth unplumbed by the discursive intellect. They are illuminations, revelations, full of significance and importance, all inarticulate though they remain; and as a rule they carry with them a curious sense of authority for aftertime." Third, these states are transient, occurring only for short periods, though these periods may be experienced as an eternity of continuous development. Fourth, these states are experienced as a going beyond personal will or individual ego. This, in James' view, connected them with trance states, clairvoyance, and prophesy. "The conscious person is continuous with a wider self through which saving experiences come, a positive content of religious experience which, it seems to me, is literally and objectively true."[257] He thought this "region" was interpreted in various religions by many "over-beliefs" which went far beyond observable facts in their myth-making. Beneath these myths, however, he thought there was much solid evidence for a threshold beyond which there are distinctive healing energies to be encountered.

The further limits of our being plunge, it seems to me, into an altogether other dimension of existence from the sensible and merely "understandable" world. Name it the mystical region, or the supernatural region, whichever you

[255] Neumann, E., *The Child*, p. 23.
[256] James, W., *The Varieties of Religious Experience*.
[257] Ibid., p. 398.

choose. So far as our ideal impulses originate in this region (and most of them do originate in it, for we find them possessing us in a way for which we cannot articulately account), we belong to it in a more intimate sense than that in which we belong to the visible world, for we belong in the most intimate sense wherever our ideals belong. Yet the unseen region in question is not merely ideal, for it produces effects in this world. When we commune with it, work is actually done upon our finite personality, for we are turned into new men, and consequences in the way of conduct follow in the natural world upon our regenerative change. But that which produces effects within another reality must be termed a reality itself, so I feel as if we had no philosophical excuse for calling the unseen or mystical world unreal.[258]

James thought that the scientific world of his era was "sectarian" and "narrow" in refusing to accept much evidence in regard to this threshold. He denied that religion was just a sentimental and compensatory covering-up of the hard facts of material reality. To postulate such a religious reality, he thought, was to suggest *new facts*.

The world interpreted religiously is not the materialistic world over again with an altered expression; it must have over and above the altered expression, *a natural constitution* different at some point from that which a materialistic world would have. It must be such that different events can be expected in it, different conduct must be required.[259]

Where the encounter with such a world is successful, it produces an influx of healing energies and a positive "faith state" that allows daily life to be dealt with better. A person who had a relationship to this region, James thought, could keep himself "sane and true."

The whole drift of my education goes to persuade me that the world of our present consciousness is only one out of many worlds of consciousness that exist, and that those other worlds must contain experiences which have a meaning for our life also; and that though in the main their experiences and those of this world keep discrete, yet the two become continuous at certain points, and higher energies filter in.[260]

In many preindustrial societies throughout the world, such states are recognized and institutionalized because of their healing capacities. Anthropologist Richard Katz reported on his research into healing trance states among the Kung in his book, *Boiling Energy*.[261] Kung healers experience the crossing of a threshold which they call *kia*, through dance, concentration, and song.

---

[258] Ibid., p. 399.
[259] Ibid., p. 401.
[260] Ibid., p. 401
[261] Katz, R., *Boiling Energy*.

The Kung say that kia comes from activation of an energy that they call num. Num was originally given to the Kung by the Gods. Though experiencing kia is a necessary prerequisite to healing, it is painful and feared. The cause of kia – the activated num – is said to boil fiercely within the person. Some at the dance avoid kia; others experience kia but fail to develop it so that it can be applied to healing. Even among the healers, not all heal at every dance.

Those who have learned to heal are said to "possess" num. They are called *num kausi*, "masters of owners of num." Num resides in the pit of the stomach and the base of the spine. As healers continue their energetic dancing, becoming warm and sweating profusely, the num in them heats up and becomes a vapor. It rises up the spine to a point approximately at the base of the skull, at which time kia results. ...

Num is an energy held in awe and considered very powerful and mysterious. This same energy is what the healer "puts into" people in attempting to cure them. For once heated up, num can both induce kia and combat illness.[262]

Until recently, Kung healers were highly respected in southern Africa, and many individuals from other tribal groups visited them for healing. They are also widely believed to have clairvoyant abilities, and there are numerous stories of their divinatory feats by travelers. In 1979, a photographer and writer published a photo essay on the Kung entitled, "The Bushmen." They began their search for groups living in the traditional way by driving into the desert in a jeep. For weeks, they were unsuccessful, since most Kung today have been brought into the margins of their former territories to live in permanent settlements. Finally, they met an old hunter who could still do divination in the traditional way. They saw him take out five eland hide disks with marks on them and throw them out the way the I Ching or Tarot is thrown. After studying them, he announced he would not hunt that day, as there was no game.

We had been told about these divining tablets, which may be made of hide, wood, or bone, by a retired white hunter at a fishing camp on the Okavango River. He had respect for the Bushman's understanding of the wilderness and was in the habit of asking his Bushman tracker to "throw his bones" on the eve of a hunt. He believed implicitly in their efficacy and told us of an incident to justify his faith.

"My client had a permit to shoot one jumbo," he said. The night before the hunt my tracker threw his bones and told me that he could see two elephants. "No," I told him, "There must be only one elephant." But he insisted not only that there would be two, but that the chief game ranger, who was the scourge of poachers, would be there too. "This time you've slipped up very badly," I told him, because I was practically certain the chief game ranger was still away on long leave. Early the next morning we picked up the tracks of a big bull and a

[262] Ibid., p. 41.

cow. When we came to where only a thicket separated us form them, I sent my client on alone with the tracker, telling him that on no account was he to shoot more than the one and that it had to be the bull. I waited in my truck and some time later I heard two shots. At the same moment I saw the chief ranger's Land Rover coming up behind me in my rear-view mirror. As he reached me, the Bushman ran up and said the client had wounded the bull with his first shot and killed the cow with his second. The ranger dashed off into the bush with his rifle, and in a few minutes, there was another shot. The ranger got the bull. There were two elephants. The bones are never wrong.[263]

The authors of the book then asked the old Bushman to throw the bones for them to help in a search for a traditional tribal group to photograph. After looking at them, he said, "I see earth in three mounds taller than many trees."[264] Two days later, while driving through an apparently uninhabited northern desert, the authors saw three mountains far to the west. They drove toward them, and at the foot of these mountains, found the encampment they were looking for.

One can imagine that, in the difficult and dangerous conditions of the Kalahari desert, where the Bushmen have lived for many thousands of years, such skills would have made the difference between survival and starvation. Laurens van der Post tells of hunting with a group of Bushmen who killed an eland many miles away from their camp.[265] When he drove them back at nightfall, they found the camp already carrying out the rituals done when an eland is killed. Somehow they already *knew*. Here there must be a complex and connected knowing by "feeling" rather than the causal categories of mind. We know that animals "feel" much more than we do because they have far more acute senses of smell, hearing, and sight. Perhaps there are people who carry exceptional abilities to feel connectivity. The environment of evolutionary adaptiveness (EEA) of all human beings is now thought to be in Africa in this kind of cultural world, where hominids evolved over millions of years. That a certain percentage of the human population could inherit such possibilities would actually be extremely useful for the survival of the group in times of extreme stress. Could this be the reason why the condition diagnosed in Western medicine as schizophrenia is found in the same one percent incidence everywhere in the world?

As a matter of fact, Richard Katz attempted to test the Bushman healers he worked with in researching his book, to see if they had any special abilities. He gave the best healers, as well as a control group, Thematic Apperception Tests (TAT) as well as "Draw-a Person" tests. He found that, in three areas, experienced healers manifested different attributes from other

---

[263] Wannenbaugh, A., *The Bushmen*, p. 10.
[264] Ibid., p. 10.
[265] van der Post, L., *The Lost World of the Kalahari*.

members of their group. First, they were more expressive or passionate. "They are said to be *xga ku tsui*; that is, their 'heart rises' more ... This trait is in harmony with *kia* and its profound emotional quality."[266] Second, the healers had a distinct body image. "Their body self-image, for example, is determined more by their own inner states than by external anatomical criteria. Healing is an extremely physical experience, expressing itself in, and through, the body. Yet, in describing themselves and their bodies during *kia*, healers emphasize the central importance of fluid psychological processes and transitions that break out of the body's ordinary anatomical boundaries."[267] Third, healers have a much richer fantasy life. "*Kia* demands from the healer an openness to the unfamiliar and a primarily intuitive and emotional response, rather than a rational or logical one."[268]

Katz asked different members of the Kung group he was working with to make self portraits. He published several examples. Drawings by adults who had never experienced *kia* showed clear and connected body outlines. Drawings done by experienced healers were noticeably discontinuous. Here, the healers experienced their body images as violating the ordinary rules of anatomy; their body images were more fluid and permeable than those of others.[269] In Figure 11.5, below, drawings a, c, and e were done by healers.

The traits exhibited by the Kung healers represent in a striking way a capacity for "melting" out of ego structure, connected with a capacity to approach a phenomenological "edge of chaos." These traits also existed in Edward Coe and Gina Bertoli, as well as in many other schizophrenic patients at the mental hospital. Edward's loving care of birds and Gina's poignant concern for the children of the world seem to be evidence of deeply emotional and sensitive natures. Both seem to have, as well, a distinct, fluid body image. Remember Gina's "red feeling," the "green man" living in her stomach, the "crow" with her mother's voice who follows her. Edward is apparently imagining himself as a loon, with a loon voice and body. Clearly, both have an extremely rich fantasy life. Although these natural personality characteristics result in various deficits in dealing with the busy, efficient, high-grid urban world, some cultures have insisted that they could also make a positive contribution to the group in terms of creativity and healing abilities.

Manfred Bleuler, summing up a century of work with schizophrenics by himself and his father Eugen Bleuler, said this about their creativity:

An impressive experience for all of us is discovering in every schizophrenic patient we have the chance to know well a lively and colorful inner life. Rather

[266] Katz, R., *Boiling Energy*, p. 235.
[267] Ibid., p. 235.
[268] Ibid., p. 236.
[269] Ibid., p. 237.

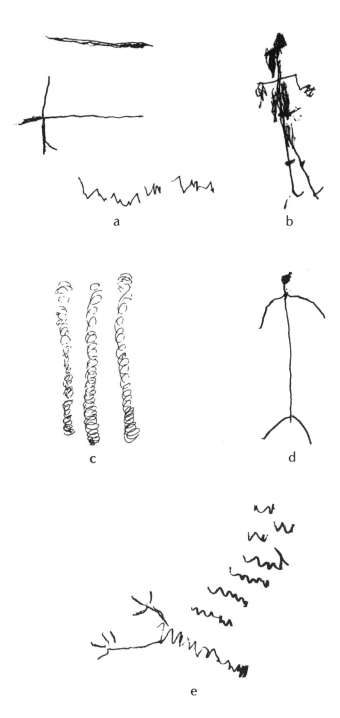

Figure 11.5 – Kung stick figures

new is the discovery that even manifold artistic abilities persist or in fact may become evident in schizophrenics. (This has been described by many authors and in a particularly impressive way by Navratil.) The course of schizophrenic psychosis never goes in the direction of increasing impoverishment of inner life, never towards a "dementia" of the type of dementia in cases of diffuse brain damage. The inner life can be hidden by lack of any expression, in mutism, but it is not lost.[270]

What if we lived in a society where the "eruption" of fantasy images like those in schizophrenia was considered not pathological, but a special openness to a living Source deep within the world, a Voice of Spirit or ancestors or gods which, if related to in the right way, could bring important values into the community? Anthropologist Renaldo Maduro has reported on such a community in western India. There, a group of 155 Brahmin folk painters and healers, a community within a community made up of 110 men and 45 women, maintain a pilgrimage center named Nathdwara. The artists work around a sacred temple complex associated with a "statue of a seven-year-old Divine Child form of Lord Krishna on earth, believed by Pushtimarga followers to be 'living.' "[271] Those destined to join the cult are recognized as having special potentialities in earliest childhood, and are placed under the guidance of a healer. This was explained by one member of the group as follows:

> The creative painter must also have guidance from a guru. He cannot do it alone. He must be persistent and take great care in his work. It is not a question of the young brahmacharya painter being religious at the time. This occurs when he is ripe, after being a householder. I will tell you about that, too. But I want to say that the brahmacharya painter can begin to learn – if his guru is spiritually advanced – how to paint sacred subjects like Shri Nathji. He begins to learn how to concentrate with all his mind and heart on the Gods within – on Him – the feeling of Shri Nathji must be manifested in the artist. Those who will become creative later know of these experiences, even from childhood.[272]

When these special children have grown to adulthood, and completed the tasks associated with marriage and family, they enter a stage of heightened spirituality where they maintain a constant contact with a fertilizing creative source, which they experience as being near the heart region. This is "an inner reservoir of creative power" that allows them to paint with great freedom and spirituality. The source, known as *maya rupa* is believed to have both creative and destructive potentialities, which is why access to it must be learned under the guidance of an experienced healer. There could be no

[270] Bleuler, "What Is Schizophrenia?"
[271] Maduro, R., "Artistic creativity and aging in India," *International Journal of Aging and Human Development*, 1974, 5(4):304.
[272] Ibid., p. 306.

better description of what a phenomenological access to the edge of chaos would feel like, than these reports of older painters:

> The imagination is located here. All originality (maulikta) and imagination (kalpna shakti) come from the forms thrown out by maya. It is all inside each of us. We can call forth every kind of image and imagination deep from this maya rupa deep inside. Each man has it all inside him, if he only tries to see it and use it, and if it is the pleasure of God to allow him this maturity.[273]

> Creativity? Oh – it's all *maya rupa* – everything. This *maya* which I have inside me is thrown out in my art. This is a sacred truth and something that grows with age. All imagination and the things of worldly appearance and form exist there first. They are not real when they come outside. These appearances in art are confused thinking, fantasies, and like the dream world. All outside forms are determined by this very same *maya* force. They are all from maya – from the inside – the whole world is, furthermore, nothing more than God's own *maya* creation. It is the dream of Brahman, and we painters contain a part of that force in us too because we are all part of Brahman (i.e., the One Universal Soul of Light, of which everything else in the world is thought to be a shadow).[274]

Medrano gave the most creative artists and the least creative artists (by their own accounts)[275] in this community a battery of psychological tests. The most creative were distinguished by four characteristics. First, they had an extremely rich fantasy life. Second, they had a great tolerance for ambiguity. Third, they had "a noteworthy capacity to form very complex symbolic identifications, fusions, displacements and condensations in striving toward wholeness and balance."[276] Fourth, the creative painters had "more fluid and permeable inner ego boundaries with a strong ego core requiring less unconscious defensive maneuvers. ... The older painter who has maintained his creativity is marked by greater intra-psychic freedom than those who have not accepted the challenge of individuation in mid-life, and it is here that the Jungian 'ego-self axis' formulation assumes importance."[277]

Medrano summed these results up in terms of a threshold of "ego permeability." "Permeability and impermeability are considered summary concepts that express an overall degree of ego openness or closedness. These two qualities are found in everybody and vary situationally, yet one tends to dominate and characterize the way in which a personality organizes the sum total of its experience. Thus degrees of permeability-impermeability exist along a polar continuum. ... "[278] Could we consider this continuum as related

---

[273] Ibid., p. 315.
[274] Ibid., p. 315.
[275] Ibid., p. 323.
[276] Ibid., p. 320.
[277] Ibid., p. 320.

to the gerontomorphic and pedomorphic structures discussed in a previous chapter? Gerontomorphic structures are impermeable and pedomorphic permeable. According to Medrano, in each person there is a boundary threshold toward the outer as well as the inner world, and each of these can be permeable or impermeable, which means that the inner and outer boundaries can be congruent or incongruent. The most creative painters had very permeable inner and outer boundaries. That would mean that creative symbolization could be "read" in both outer and inner experience. This would lead to the extremely high level of sensitivity to synchronicities that we saw in the first-hand accounts of psychotics and religious mystics. These painters are living peacefully and ecstatically with such permeable boundaries, because they live in a culture where their experience is contextualized as sacred and meaningful. What would happen to them if they were placed within the totally impermeable boundaries of ward R, stigmatized, ignored, isolated, and denied art materials?

Several researchers have attempted to investigate whether ordinary people in the West can experience the threshold we are discussing. Sometimes people fall into it spontaneously. Neurologist Richard Cytowic has been studying people who regularly experience synesthesia. Perfectly normal in every other way, their senses melt into each other regularly. Cytowic has found a social worker in Florida who, when she hears music, sees gold balls and vertical lines floating in front of her. A computer programmer in Arkansas sees the road turn bright orange in front of him whenever the Emergency Broadcast System test tone comes on his car radio. Many synesthetes don't tell anyone about their condition because they are afraid people will think they are weird. Soviet psychologist A.R. Luria reported on one such case in which a man was continually distracted by a jumble of intense visions:

> I walked over to the ice cream vendor and asked her what flavor she had. "Tutti frutti" she said, but she answered in such a tone that a whole pile of coals, of black cinders, came bursting out of her mouth, and I couldn't bring myself to buy any ice cream after she had answered that way.[279]

Cytowic discovered that, during the experience of synesthesia, the cortex nearly shuts down, and people have the type of cortical blood flow associated with severe strokes, when brain tissue is dead. Synesthetes seem to be able to place the cortex "on a back burner" and let the limbic system take over for a few seconds without causing any permanent damage. They seem to maintain a permeable threshold boundary between the limbic system and the cortex.

---

[278] Ibid., p. 323.
[279] Lemley, B., "The people who hear green," *The Washington Post Magazine*, 1986, Words by Wire.

Could this be what is happening to Gina when she has the "red feeling" or feels "a green man"?

Anthropologist Felicitas Goodman has discovered that she can train people to experience altered states of consciousness through trance.[280] Using drumming, traditional meditation postures, and concentration techniques, dozens of volunteers have experienced the crossing of a threshold leading to ecstatic mystical states. Goodman has concluded that this is a fundamental human capacity. She and neurophysiologist Johann Kluger set up experiments at the University of Munich to test what is happening in the brains of people experiencing altered states of consciousness:

> The instruments registered dramatic changes. In the blood serum, the compounds indicating stress, namely adrenalin, noradrenalin, and cortisal, dropped and at the same time, there was evidence that the brain started synthesizing beta-endorphin, the miracle pain killer of the body, which is also responsible for the intense joy felt after a trance. The EEG exhibited not the famous alpha waves, so well known from meditation, but a steady stream of the even slower theta waves, in the range of 6-7 cps, usually seen only in bursts shortly before a subject goes to sleep, or in deep Zen meditation. Most puzzling, blood pressure dropped, and simultaneously, the pulse started racing like a runner's during a hundred-meter dash. Under ordinary conditions, I was told, physicians see this kind of paradoxical behavior of the body only under extreme conditions, such as when a patient bleeds to death or is about to die.[281]

If major alterations in brain physiology can be intentionally produced by ordinary people, we should question how useful it is to base our understanding of the changes undergone in psychosis on an examination of postmortem brain tissue. It is clear that our psychological and life experiences continually affect our brain structure. We know now that a huge array of dense synaptic connections are developed in the prefrontal neurons at about ten weeks after birth. These remain stable for about two or three years and then fall gradually to an adult level, which is reached by age sixteen. At the same time, the capacity of the cortex to metabolize glucose gradually develops from age two to a peak around age eight to ten, and then declines to adult rates by age sixteen or eighteen. The cultural and family environment during this time effects a kind of pruning and shaping through its treatment of the child. In many small acts of love and understanding or, unfortunately, sometimes of cruelty and ignorance, the creodes of a growing child are formed, or fail to form. The resulting structure can probably never be shown to have a single "local cause," because it is a systemic and ecological field

---

[280] Goodman, F., *Where the Spirits Ride the Wind*.
[281] Ibid., p. 25.

phenomenon. This includes the constitutional vulnerabilities of the child; the emotional environment of the family; and the mythological, social, and economic schemata of the surrounding culture. What kind of glial cell structure would be built up in the child painters in India, lovingly tutored by their gurus to free the spirit, and how would it be different from those of Edward Coe, who grew up without love, guidance, myth, or ritual?

A peak of development is reached in young adulthood, the period when the great majority of first incidences of schizophrenia occur. In infancy, the sensorimotor cortex is the most active part of the brain; and the frontal region, thought to be most connected with ego consciousness, is the least activated. In young adulthood, the sensorimotor cortex is the least activated. The limbic system and the frontal region are relatively highly activated.[282] Puberty apparently induces a new surge of metabolic activity. It seems that those young adults who will become schizophrenic cannot integrate the two systems and they become dissociated. It is the limbic system that is the seat of emotional response that is overactive in both synesthesia and psychosis; it is the metabolism of the limbic system that is blocked by neuroleptic medications. Interestingly, it has been discovered that 24 to 48 hours before a psychotic relapse, schizophrenics have a measurable electrodermal skin response, as if energy from the limbic system has poured over the creode barriers that should have restrained it.[283] This could be evidence of Roger Penrose's idea that the cytoskeleton in every cell is involved in psychological information processing.

Perhaps we are seeing evidence, here, of exactly the permeable boundary at the threshold between ego and creative emotional life that was noted above. In that case, there is a continuum of permeability that, on one side, is mystical, ecstatic, and healing religious experience at the edge of chaos, and, on the other side, a fragmenting and dissolving ego experience which spirals out of control. The boundary would be like a strange attractor which may or may not settle into a stable pattern. If this is so, what is "ill" and "abnormal" in the schizophrenic experience is partly environmental and cultural. If, at the exact moment one nears the threshold, one finds oneself in Zen meditation, or painting at the home of a teacher, or in a nurturing religious or mythological tradition, the moment passes and a new order is born. Out of this experience can come creativity and renewal. If it occurs in an environment without holding symbol, myth, or religion, however, which is the starting place of many mental hospital patients, a wild Red Queen run toward chaos can begin. Then, the terrified sufferer can wind down through

---

[282] See, for example, Winn, P., "Schizophrenia research moves to the prefrontal cortex." *TINS*, 1994, 17(7).

[283] Nuechterlein, K.H., "Developmental process in schizophrenic disorders: Longitudinal studies of vulnerability and stress," *Schizophrenia Bulletin*, 1992, 18(3):408.

the default hierarchy toward simplicity that ends in silence. Something inside gives up, and lies down, like Gina's "pancake tree."

Fortunately, we are never finished with development. Because our personalities are based on nested complex adaptive systems, changes in our experience, thinking, and behavior can still affect brain tissue. Manfred Bleuler speaks of the "astonishing discovery" of neural plasticity.

> That means the possibility that psychological life experience might change the cerebral structure, in particular, the communication between the neurons. One is tempted to state: somatic peculiarities frequently influence the psychic life and can frequently be dispositions for a schizophrenic psychosis – but on the other hand we must take into account that our inner life also influences the cerebral structures.[284]

Bleuler was interested at the end of his life in the new chaos theory. He thought if it was applied to schizophrenia, it might show that "the physical chaos need not last forever. The order, the coherence may suddenly be reestablished."[285]

Understanding mental illness through the model of state changes in information processing systems, opens many new possibilities for healing. The world of complex adaptive systems is always open to changes in energy in the environment; it is a world where nothing is "determined" or fixed. To be alive as an organism means to constantly take energy from outside and transform it into morphogenic development. Perhaps, with this model, we can find more creative ways to meet the demoralized spirits of the mentally ill.

[284] Bleuler, "What Is Schizophrenia?"
[285] Ibid.

12. Postmodern Healing and Creativity

We must also find, find anew, invent the words, the sentences that speak the most archaic and most contemporary relationship with the body of the mother, with our bodies, the sentences that translate the bond between her body, ours, and that of our daughters. We have to discover a language [langage] which does not replace the bodily encounter, as paternal language [langue] attempts to do, but which can go along with it, words which do not bar the corporeal, but which speak the corporeal.[286]

– Luce Irigaray

Human relationships are usually held in a state of unsteady balance in daily life as new moods, ideas, and experiences are integrated into yesterday's narratives. Disability, illness, dissociation, and death disrupt social webs radically and people in every culture struggle to give them meaning. One of the most basic functions of explanatory models in healing has been to contextualize these events in the religious and social myths of the culture involved. It is only Western scientific descriptions of mental illness, according to medical anthropologist Arthur Kleinman, that have attempted to give "objective" accounts of disease devoid of cultural meaning. "Thus, one of the most basic functions of health care seems no longer to be part of the modern profession of medicine."[287] As a result, people fall back on folk or popular explanations, or, in many cases, are panicked and disoriented by their experiences exactly because there is no explanatory model at all. It may be that the low-grid, low-group modern urban environment erodes traditional religions that were based on high-grid or high-group community life.

Western healing systems for mental illness are "ill" because they are suffering from a one-sided gerontomorphy that needs to be corrected. Behind the glass walls of our observation posts, we are concerned more with watching, recording, and diagnosing than with relating. Too much energy

---

[286] Irigaray, L.; ed. Whitford, M., *The Irigaray Reader*, p. 43
[287] Kleinman, A., Kunstadter, P., Alexander, E.R., & Gate, J.L., *Culture and Healing in Asian Societies*, p. 419.

goes into "knowing about" and too little into "being with." Though this has worked well for certain types of physical illness, the healing of much mental illness requires human relationship. Mental illness has been seen more as structural than synchronistic, more as local than environmental. Treatments tend to be distal rather than proximal, objective, rational, and distancing rather than creative. The mental hospital where I worked was crowded, impersonal, cold, and rigid. Healing centers for the mentally ill need to be small, personal, intimate, and warmly supportive. We are working against nature and spirit by restraining, restricting, isolating, and medicating. We need to find ways to work with the unconscious integrative function through nourishing and protecting a process of endogenous growth.

Psychoanalyst D.W. Winnicott believed that in order to work, we need an adequate model of the normal potentials of the personality. "What I must do is to assume the general theory of continuity, of an inborn tendency towards growth and personal evolution, and to the theory of mental illness as a holdup in development."[288] Yet, no healthy human being could thrive in the restricted environment of ward R; why should it be healing for someone who has suffered a "holdup in development?"

We are probably not going to be able to return to the settings of tribal ritual, which are in any case rapidly disappearing in contact with urban culture. These rituals were, on the whole, based on feelings of kinship connection, so that, even if some of us were willing to recreate them, probably we could not convince our more conservative relatives to do so. This means that, in each individual case, a healing context needs to be created from the materials autonomously developed by the integrative function of the individual. Healing, creativity, and individuation become one path in postmodern environments, where people have lost traditional cultural and religious myths. In classical Jungian psychology, the encouragement of creativity is the crucial ritual of healing. According to Jungian psychiatrist Heinrich Fierz, "creative work can be a release from psychosis, as well as a protection against it."[289]

What we and our clients need to heal are evolving personal and social myths that find a way to state what we "mean" in the world. The problem with Edward's loon call was not that it was a myth, but that it had become frozen in a point attractor, repeating the same gestures over and over again. Such frozen patterns were named complexes by Jung, and they are notoriously difficult to change.

Joseph Campbell suggests that we need creativity to be human: "Art is not, like science, a logic of references but a release from reference and rendition of immediate experience: a presentation of forms, images, or ideas in such a

[288] Winnicott, D.W., *Psychoanalytic Explorations*, p. 194.
[289] Fierz, H.K., *Jungian Psychiatry*, p. 375.

way that they will communicate, not primarily a thought or even a feeling, but an impact."[290] The force of such myths comes, he thought, from an innate tendency in animal life to relate to "super-normal sign stimuli." For example, Adolph Portmann has shown that the male greyling butterfly prefers to mate with the darkest available female. When presented with an artificial model darker than any female in reality, he will chose the model over a real butterfly mate. Campbell wonders whether much in culture – myth, art, costume, cosmetics, gods – is not a result of this capacity to imagine and respond to super-normal sign stimuli. These images are part of a spontaneous process of pattern formation at the edge of chaos, a source of "whirlpools" of meaning within the natural world and consciousness. We live in it, and it lives in us. These images are "that which is not yet" in the process of birth.

This "not-yet" is the "lack" or "purpose" of mental illness. It is as if there are some souls who, finding themselves in a cultural environment that does not fulfill their most profound instinct for meaning, begin to grow inward in search for a not-yet. Edward's "loon parents," who care so lovingly for their young, and Gina's "host," which can redeem and heal, certainly represent a not-yet in their lives. Even Gina's Beelzebub is a not-yet that expresses the need to find meaning for levels of "evil" such as incest, rape, and the scapegoating of the "other," which are still often disowned and denied in our culture. In ancient Israel, a goat was sent alive each year out into the desert to atone for the sins of the people. It was to find Azazel, the angel thrown out of heaven by God, representing all that is rejected and not-yet from the point of view of any given culture, and known in Greek as Beelzebub. Gina needs to figure out why she was scapegoated, and she has spent her whole adult life cast out in a desert "with Beelzebub" waiting to learn. The "pathogenic secret" of such people is, in a way, a deep spiritual hunger for the not-yet.

When people who are ill can find a way to express in creative plastic forms the first outlines of such not-yet impulses, and if they are lucky enough to be able to do so in the presence of healing witnesses who see and understand, symptoms can often rapidly disappear. I know of many healers who do this type of work in a great variety of ways. It can be based on group work, body movement, dance, visualization, creative writing, journals, meditation, art therapy, sand play, or many other outer forms. It is the shared concentration and expression that seem to be the key. The important thing in this work is never to reduce the expression of the not-yet to an "already known" formula in the ego world, whether a clinical category like narcissism, a theoretical construct like mother complex or Oedipus complex, or a pathological local cause such as early wounding. Though each of these schemata may represent "what is," in some way, the human spirit has the capacity to reach beyond

290 Campbell, J., *Primitive Mythology*, New p. 42.

any what-is toward a not-yet. This teleological reach is central to the meaning of mental illness. It is the role of a healer to support and accompany this ritual journey. Jung called this unifying process in the individual, which heals through creative images, the "transcendent function."

Psychiatrist Heinrich Fierz tells of a case in his clinic in which a middle-aged man was deeply depressed and obsessed with the idea that the steering wheels in cars needed to be placed on the right side, rather than the left side. He was sent to a Freudian psychoanalyst who, after a few sessions, sent him back to Fierz, suggesting he was too depressed to be helped by Freudian analysis. He was then sent to a Jungian analyst, who told the man the steering wheel on the right had to do with an increase of consciousness over the unconscious. When this interpretation had no effect, the analyst sent the patient back to Fierz, saying he could not be helped by Jungian analysis. Fierz then took the patient himself and spent several weeks with him, discussing the steering wheel, which, in some way, must have represented a not-yet for this man. Soon, the patient had written a long paper on why steering wheels should be placed on the right sides of cars. As he did so, his depression lifted and he was able to be leave the clinic. By meeting the patient exactly where he was, and taking his expression of the not-yet absolutely seriously, Fierz somehow facilitated the return of healing energies.[291] This kind of healing can never be reduced to formulae, because all formulae are gerontomorphic and connected with the past, while psychological healing involves connection with a divine child, which is irrational and timeless.

If we do not conceptualize human beings as having a creative core that always goes beyond every current personal and cultural expression, we miss what is central to the soul. If we do not make room in our diagnoses and medical models for spirit, exactly that which can never be fully known because it is more creative than "knowing," the most important healing function of the human personality is not recognized. Just as Indians greet each other with the word *namaste*, which recognizes the god in the other, we are confronted with a great Teacher in our therapeutic work. When our clients create, we can never really "know," but must receive the work in silence and respect, as befits any epiphany of the gods.

According to Heinrich Fierz, we must never attempt to "reduce" the creative work (and, I would add, the dreams) of our clients to known categories. What is painted or dreamed is never only "my mother" or "my father" or "me."

> Another problem emerges even more clearly with sculpture than with drawing and painting, and that is the problem of interpretation. Even with pictures, we have to be careful not to undermine the language of creative, active imagina-

---

[291] Fierz, H.K., *Jungian Psychiatry*, p. 322.

tion with the interpretive language of concepts and so rob the picture of its *direct therapeutic affect*. This holds far more with sculptures. As a rule, sculpture has to be understood as direct expression, and the only thing is the patient's commentary. Sculpture shows an inner situation translated into a solid object. *This solid object gives the patient a hold.* It can also provide orientation for the therapist in his attempt to understand. Talking about it a lot usually means talking it to death. The essential thing is to *appreciate* the "work"; and often it is not even the result that is decisive, but the process of making it.[292]

Wrapping up a long period of work with a client who had taken a profound inner journey in analysis, I asked if she could tell me something about how she experienced what had happened to her. During the course of her analysis, she had brought in many dozens of drawings, paintings, and sculptures. She suggested, in a beautiful written reflection on the process, that there was some "magic" involved: "It's in your silence. It's in your readiness to see me every day without fear of being swallowed up by me, without calculating whether it's worth it. It's in your renouncing the following of experienced paths, your willingness to try unusual or roundabout ways. It's in your insistence to find means that work for me."

Together she and I spent many long months in the desert waiting, through tears, intense inner pain, silence, and emptiness, for spirit. It was clear to me from the beginning that there was nothing I could "do," and that whatever healing there would be had to come from "not-doing" (*wu-wei*, in Taoist thought). One day, she dreamed, "A path has appeared." After a year, she was able to write: "Together we started to peel off layer after layer of shoulds and musts, of behavior patterns and beliefs that were forced on me or that I just caught without realizing, or that I developed as a protection, until I can perceive my impulses, my aliveness, my sensitivity directly and honestly and can freely decide to express them. All of a sudden I realize that I start to trust in life, start to open up, that I'm on my way back to the source, to simplicity, easiness, lightness, beauty, abundance. A way full of stones and hardship and full of magic and surprises." It seemed to her that her attitude was crucial. "I believe the key is trust. The trust that man basically is good and that he carries the source in him. That he – when met with love, acceptance, awareness, fearlessness, and complete trust – grows to become a strong loving accepting person with the natural urge toward more awareness."

This trust that a source of healing exists in every person is central to the creative rituals which constellate its activity. Malidome Somé distinguishes ritual from its anatomy, which is ceremony. Ceremony "shows what is actually taking place in the visible world, on the surface, and can therefore

[292] Ibid., p. 366.

be seen, observed, corrected."[293] We begin the process of ritual through the ceremonies of establishing the time, place, the medium, and manner in which the healer and client meet. There are thousands of local and individual variations of ceremony.

The ceremony is transformed to ritual when we leave a place open within it to be joined by a spiritual or unconscious "other," a not-yet which we do not control.

> So ritual draws from this area of human existence where the spirit plays a life-giving role. We do not make miracles, we speak the kind of language that is interpreted by the supernatural world as a call to intervene in a stabilizing way in a particular life. Consequently, our role is to be human. We take the initiative to spark the process, knowing that its success is not in our hands but in the hands of the kind of forces we invoke into our lives. So the force field we create within a ritual is something coming from the spirit, not something coming from us. We are only instruments in this kind of interaction between dimensions, between realms.[294]

Jungian psychology, as practiced by Jung, is based on a similar notion. Jung believed that it is only when we let the symbols work in a living way, as symbols – that is, as the best possible representations of something that is still unknown – that they can begin to heal painful dissociations of personality.

> If, therefore, instead of reducing the dream symbols to circumstances, things, or persons which the analyst presumes to know in advance, we regard them as real symbols pointing to something unknown, then the whole character of analytical therapy is altered. The unconscious is then no longer reduced to known conscious factors (this procedure, incidentally, does not abolish the dissociation between conscious and unconscious) but is recognized as in fact unconscious. ... In this way the unconscious can be integrated and the dissociation overcome. The reductive procedure, on the other hand, leads away from the unconscious, and merely reinforces the one-sidedness of the conscious mind.[295]

The creative work of every individual client is always unique and particular to the personal situation involved. At the same time, given the links we have drawn with complexity theory, there are also archetypal constants that regularly appear. People in various phases of development tend to draw pictures with similar design elements that can be used to assess how dangerous or benign their personal situation is. Pictures can express a constellation of suicidal thoughts, the loss of stabilizing ego grid, or the discovery of a healing center. In their creative work, clients often come into contact with, and express, these archetypal patterns. Those who are hospitalized usually

---

[293] Somé, M., *Ritual*, p. 50.
[294] Ibid., p. 50.
[295] Jung, C.G.

Figure 12.1 – Lattice tunnel

begin to express them as soon as they begin to draw. Outside the hospital, my experience is that most clients eventually do so as analysis develops.

These typical patterns in psychological drawings can be connected with those discovered in research on altered states of consciousness. Psychologist Ronald K. Siegal has reported on years of research on altered states of consciousness in both tribal cultures and Western subjects taking drugs.[296] In both situations, people see what are called entoptic phenomena, as they go into altered states of consciousness. These images are called entoptic because they are generated within the subject even in darkened rooms without outside stimuli. People entering altered states tend to go through three stages of entoptic phenomena. At first, they see grids, spirals, or other geometric patterns. In a second stage, these patterns take on important iconic spiritual meanings consistent with the cultural myths of the individual. Over seventy percent of the subjects tested saw these simple form constants as well as religious imagery. The drawing in Figure 12.1 shows a lattice tunnel form often reported by Western laboratory subjects who have experienced trance states.

[296] Siegel, R.K. "Hallucinations," *Scientific American*, 1977, 237: 132-140.

It has been suggested that, in altered states of consciousness, "the nervous system itself becomes a 'sixth sense' that produces a variety of images including entoptic phenomena."[297] In a third stage, people begin to see the entoptic phenomena form into a tunnel or center or mandala. In this stage, they tend to "lose insight into the differences between literal and analogous meanings." One researcher hallucinated a human head developing the fur of a cat, and then he became the cat's head. Another subject reported, "I thought of a fox, and instantly I was transformed into that animal. I could distinctly feel myself a fox, could see my long ears and bushy tail, and by a sort of introversion, felt that my complete anatomy was that of a fox." Here we find the permeable boundaries noted in the previous chapter in the religious painters in India.

This research has been looked at with great interest by archaeologists and anthropologists doing research on tribal groups in which individuals enter possession states, trance, or other altered states of consciousness and later produce artwork representing it. South African anthropologist David Lewis-Williams has argued that cave paintings in many places in the world can be seen as reports of trance states, following rituals in which altered states of consciousness were produced. These paintings are beginning to be compared worldwide, and connected with informant reports where cultures have still living traditions of trance state. Lewis-Williams and colleagues have done an in-depth comparison of the rock art of the San (or Kung), the rock art of the California Coso Indians, and the drawings of laboratory subjects in altered states of consciousness. Summing up this work, Lewis-Williams and Dowson write:

> We argue that the model exposes the neuropsychological order underlying the seemingly chaotic, unintegrated, superimposed, juxtaposed, fragmented, and reduplicated iconic and geometric depictions of these two arts. Far from being anarchic, San and Coso art are ordered products of identifiable stages of altered consciousness and neurologically based principles in the formation of mental imagery. The painted and engraved images are in fact, informed by the functioning of the human nervous system in altered states. Because the order that results is different from the order Westerners are predisposed to seek in artistic creations, it has escaped notice.[298]

They support their theory with the chart of entoptic designs presented here in Figure 12.2.

---

[297] Lewis-Williams, J.D., Dowson, T.A., "The signs of the times: Entoptic phenomena in upper paleolithic art," *Current Anthropology*, 1988, 29: 201-245.
[298] Ibid., p. 213.

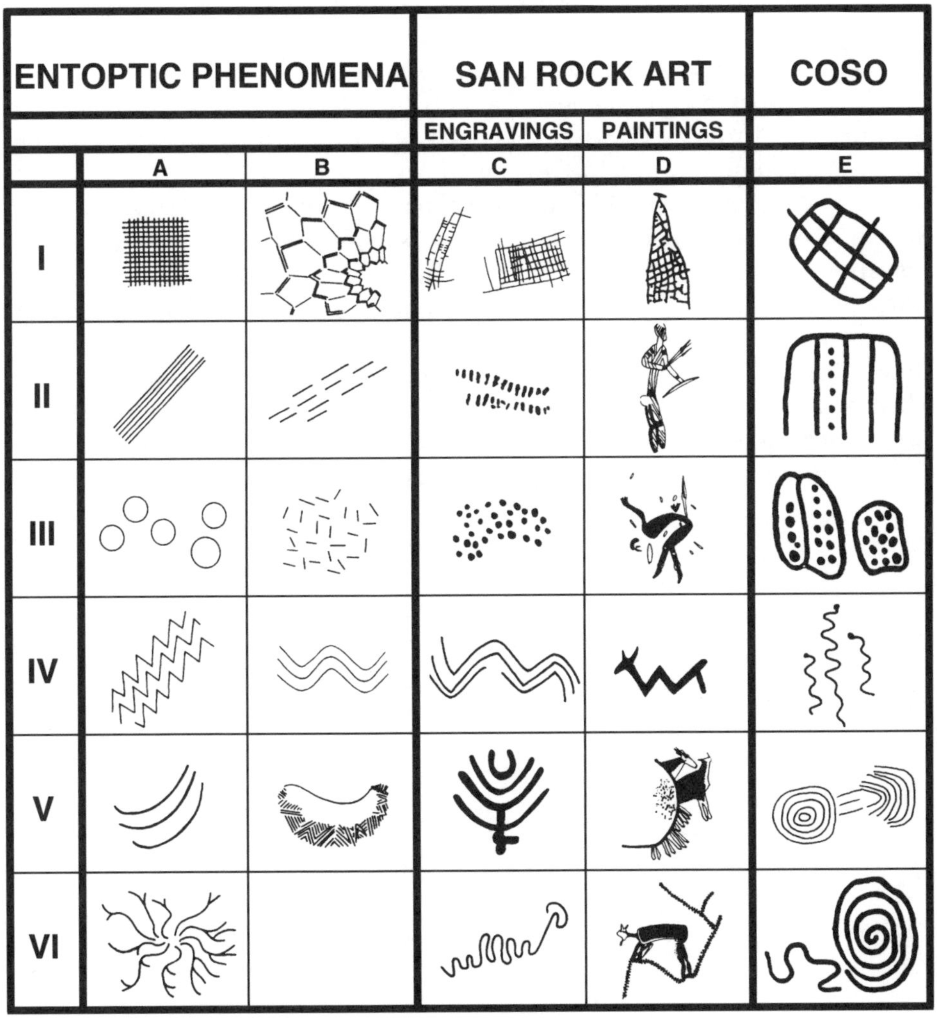

ENTOPTIC PHENOMENA		SAN ROCK ART		COSO
		ENGRAVINGS	PAINTINGS	
A	B	C	D	E
I				
II				
III				
IV				
V				
VI				

Figure 12.2 – Entoptic Designs

My clients are also drawing these same designs, and when they do, I believe it means they are beginning to come in contact with a pattern-forming function modeled by the notion of an edge of chaos. Whenever these designs begin to appear, some energy for healing and transformation seems to be drawn up from the unconscious. Their appearance is often connected with powerful dreams and new feelings. Six such designs frequently appear in analytic work with psychiatric patients. All of the pictures reproduced in Figures 12.3 through 12.8 were done by women in different wards in the hospital, aged nineteen to forty-six, who never met.

In Figure 12.3, the suicidal impulse appears as an enormous black weight at the bottom of a picture. There is an extreme dissociation between the negative life experience and the ideal that is to be somehow preserved through the suicide. The situation is dangerous when this theme is not expressed at all. When it is drawn, it can be understood as a cry for help. The first drawing in Figure 12.3 was made by a patient in the hospital during a therapy hour. I immediately reported what I had seen to the supervisor and the patient was put on twenty-four-hour observation. A cleverly planned suicide attempt was carried out the next day, and foiled by the watchful staff.

Figure 12.3a – Suicide

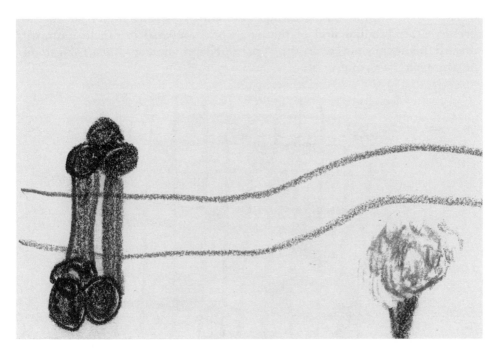

Figure 12.3b

Figure 12.3c

The clients who did the drawings in Figure 12.4 were no longer able to preserve the habitual grid of the ego world and had begun to plummet toward unknown states of feeling. A painful depression or an *abaissement du niveau mental* was in process.

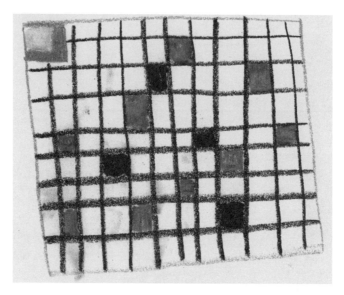

Figure 12.4a – Grid

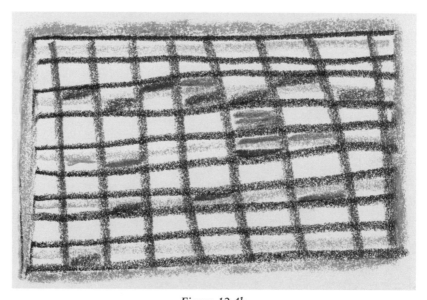

Figure 12.4b

Figure 12.4c

Figure 12.5a – Centers

In Figure 12.5, a center is found that can be experienced as potentially healing, remote and unattainable, or frighteningly powerful. When this is constellated, some transformative energy is at work. These mandalas usually radiate bright primary colors that the patients have never used before.

Figure 12.5b

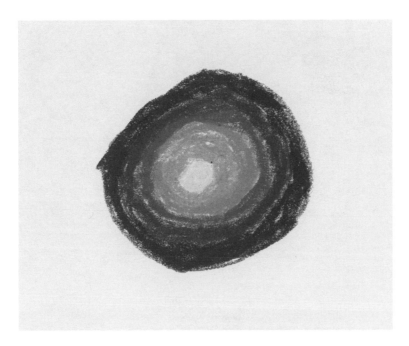

Figure 12.5c

In Figure 12.6, the client has crossed a threshold toward the edge of chaos and the picture begins to break up into greater ego permeability.

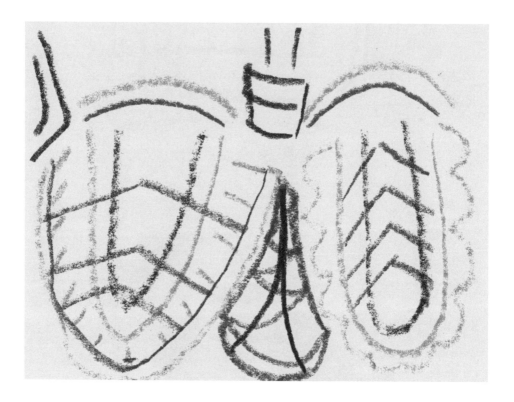

Figure 12.6 – Edge of Chaos

The clients who drew the pictures in Figure 12.7 are slipping into a chronic state of despair where "the center doesn't hold" and hope is lost.

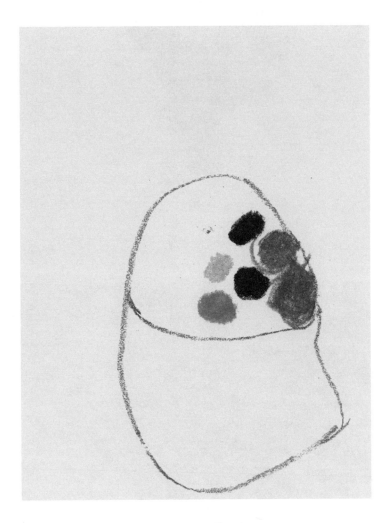

Figure 12.7a – Slipping

Figure 12.7b

Figure 12.7c

Panic precipitates a manic state. When caught and held in creative expression, a different outcome can be experienced. Here in Figure 12.8, Gina "catches" her terror and is able to return to her fragile center. Two blue birds fly into the picture on the right.

What is at work in these acts of creativity is healing spirit. The ratiomorphic function of the client has begun to "speak" at an unconscious level, drawing potential energy across a threshold into consciousness in the form of symbols. When the language of the unconscious is understood and appreciated, healing energies become available to the personality. I watch in awe as client after client discovers this "place" and uses it to find a source within the personality where there are new possibilities for life. The energy is never under conscious control, and the client is often surprised to find it is there. It can be experienced as a numinous and powerful source of meaning. Very often, though we have never mentioned religion before, the client begins spontaneously discussing it. I never raise it as an issue before they do and have not discussed these ideas about archetypal altered states, because they are not relevant to the personal journey of discovery each individual needs to suffer through. One client said, "I think I might be a religious person without a religion." Another mused, "I don't know why I am talking about this,

Figure 12.8a – Out of Control

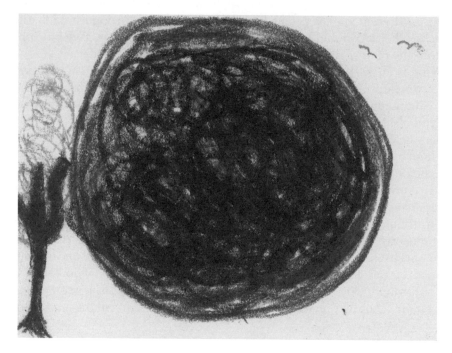

Figure 12.8b

because I have never had any religious experience." A middle-aged woman reported, "I feel flooded with grace." Another dreamed: "I have found a place where healing could occur. It is not a church, but it is, nevertheless, holy."

The experience of watching such archetypal energies constellate is always impressive. While I was at the hospital, I worked with an older woman, Myrna, who had been variously diagnosed as having paranoid schizophrenia, multiple personality disorder, and suicidal depression. In her view, she had led a life of unrelieved misery, beginning with sexual abuse and ending with hospital stays. She could only sob through most of our first hours, and I could only be with her silently as everything she said was true. In time, she began to draw, and the drawings revealed a wonderfully creative inner life. We began with her feet, which I carefully drew on a large piece of paper. She filled it in with the grid design shown in Figure 12.9, and there was no doubt she was deeply depressed.

Fortunately, she was somehow harmless enough to be housed in a rehabilitation cottage on the grounds, where patients received some attention from staff and were taken on field trips and outings. She shared a room with a roommate and was responsible for keeping it clean and helping with mealtime setup in the cottage. As a result, there was an environment where

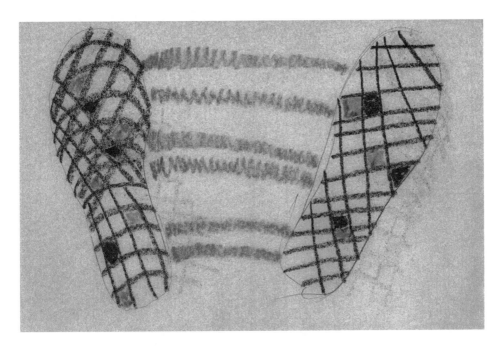

Figure 12.9 – Feet

healing could be supported. Of course, one can never say exactly what was the right combination of elements that altered the field phenomenon of her personality over the time I knew her; but it changed significantly, and I think her creative work had something to do with it. Little by little, the grid broke up in her drawings, and the black was replaced by other colors. She found a center, and the center radiated with colorful entoptic designs. She stopped crying, and began to look at me curiously and intensely during our sessions. One day, she came in and reported out of the blue: "I had a dream. I saw my own face in a mirror, and I heard a voice say: 'There is a joy in just being alive.'" This numinous dream had a transformative impact, like the wind catching a sail in a boat that has been becalmed. Afterwards, she drew a many-colored butterfly mandala, as her psyche began to cross back toward the ego world in a stage where recognizable iconic forms emerge from entoptic phenomena. The butterfly has often been associated with the soul's transformative ability. Perhaps, she inherited it from indigenous Nahuatl "ancestors," one of whom wrote a thousand years ago: "From the house of flowering butterflies was born the song: I hear it come to life, I, the singer."[299]

---

[299] Nicholson, I., trans., *A Guide to Mexican Poetry*, p. 1.

Myrna has written to me several times since we both left the hospital, and appears for the moment to be making it on her own, with the help of a local health center. She attends adult education classes and manages her life. She wrote that the first time she went shopping was "like Christmas." She thought that, "I am in a small way replacing some of the things that I have lost out of my life." Her most recent card was a picture of a young girl with her dog, sitting at a table making Christmas cookies. The dog is licking the batter spoon, and the girl her fingers, so perhaps she has finally found something that tastes good in her life.

Post-modern healing often begins with the stark realization that many people seeking psychotherapy, as well as their healers, are no longer held in any kind of meaningful myth or faith-state connected with traditional religion. Again and again, I have heard stories from clients about the failure of these traditions in their lives, even when they continue a formal relationship with some institution. At the same time, archetypal energies work in us, and without a myth through which to express them, we lose contact and begin to defend against what should be nourishing and comforting. The solution seems to consist in finding an individually creative way to come in contact with, and express, an originating source. Each expression will be unique and personal, and at the same time bring the ego into contact with a Tao or spirit experienced as numinous, powerful, and creative. Jung expressed his experience this way shortly before his death:

> Here just once, and as an exception, I will speculate transcendentally, that is I will "poetize": God has, it is true, made an inconceivably sublime and mysteriously contradictory image of himself, without the help of man, and placed it in man's unconscious as an archetype, an *arche-typos*, not in order that theologians of all times and places might come to blows, but that the unpresumptuous man might glimpse an image, in the stillness of his soul, which is related to himself, and formed of his own spiritual substance. This image contains everything which he will ever imagine concerning his gods or concerning the soul's Ground. This archetype, whose existence is confirmed not only by the history of mankind but also by practical psychological observation of individuals, satisfies me completely. It is so humanly close and yet so strange and "other"; also like all archetypes of great determining power and influence, it unconditionally demands confrontation. Therefore, the dialectical relationship to the autonomous contents of the collective unconscious forms, as we have said, an essential part of therapy.[300]

---

[300] Jung, C.G., "Reply to Buber," *Spring* 1957, p. 7.

13. Living at the Edge of Chaos

Never in the history of humankind have we had so many means of communication – television, telecommunications, telephones, fax machines, wireless radios, hot lines, and red lines – but we still remain islands. There is so little communication between members of one family, between the individuals in society, and between nations. We suffer from so many wars and conflicts. We do not know how to listen to each other. We have little ability to hold an intelligent or meaningful conversation. The universal door of communication has to be opened again. When we cannot communicate, we get sick, and as our sickness increases, we suffer and spill our suffering on other people. We purchase the services of psychotherapists to listen to our suffering, but if the psychotherapists do not practice the universal door, they will not succeed. [301] – Thich Nhat Hanh

What are the long term consequences of consciously entering into a close relationship with an experiential source, a "universal door" at the edge of chaos? What happens to people who find such a place and are able to live near it? From the point of view of complexity theory, to become conscious of an inner integrative function means that a new feedback loop has been created. All human beings constantly encounter the world through projected images which evolve as experience changes. The process of world and self-integration develops out of these projections. Often it is done unconsciously, and the images are assumed to arise from the "outer world." The projections are generally thought to be constant and independent of subjectivity. However, some cultural groups have developed disciplines which involve observing the process of projection in order to make it conscious. In this case, two self-organized systems that operate independently in many individuals, are brought together. It is possible that there are emergent experiences that result from this new level of integration and feedback. Perhaps such people activate aspects of consciousness which are not available to those who have not engaged in these disciplines. One result of this emergent level of con-

[301] Thich Nhat Hanh, *For a Future to Be Possible*, p. 48-49.

sciousness could be that synchronicities begin to ripple through experience at a much greater rate. The occurrence of a pattern of many frequent small synchronicities punctuated by a few large ones would be a marker of a system near critical state. People living in experiential worlds filled with meaningful connections, might be more relaxed and spontaneous about their participation in it.

A special emergent state of spontaneity and synchronicity has been most fully described in the literature of Buddhism and Taoism. In the words of a ninth century Zen master, Huang Po:

> The way (Tao) is spiritual truth and was originally without a name or title. It was only because people ignorantly sought for it empirically that the Buddhas appeared and taught them to eradicate this method of approach. Fearing that nobody would understand, they selected the name "way." You must not allow this name to lead you into forming a mental concept of a road. So it is said, "When the fish is caught, we pay no more attention to the trap." When body and mind achieve spontaneity, the Way is reached, and Mind is understood. A sramana (monk) is so called because he has penetrated to the original source of all things. The fruit of attaining the sramana stage is gained by putting an end to all anxiety; it does not come from book-learning.[302]

Daisetz Suzuki suggested that the awakening reached in Zen Buddhism was based on the discovery by the conscious ego of its own unconscious source.

> The awakening of a new consciousness so called, as far as the inward way of seeing into the nature of things is concerned, is no other than consciousness becoming acquainted with itself. Not that a new consciousness rises out of the Unconscious but consciousness itself turns inwardly into itself. This is the home-coming. This is the seeing of one's own "primal face" which one has even before one's birth. This is God pronouncing his name to Moses. This is the birth of Christ in each of our souls. This is Christ rising from death. "The Unconscious," which has been lying quietly in consciousness, now raises its head and announces its presence through consciousness.[303]

Westerners schooled in positivism have tremendous difficulty with these notions, because the categories of rational / irrational or logical / chaotic or conscious / unconscious are taken to be natural entities rather than conventional schemata. Usually we keep these categories strictly separated, and our thought structure is upset by the idea of an unconscious consciousness. Suzuki believed we attempt to cope with this difficulty by postulating a time sequence in which the unconscious "emerges" or "rises out" of conscious-

[302] Blofeld, J., trans., *The Zen Teaching of Huang Po*, p. 55.
[303] Suzuki, D.T., "Awakening of a new consciousness in Zen," in: Campbell, J., ed., *Man and Transformation*, p. 196.

ness. Zen Buddhism, on the other hand, understands this contradiction through the notion of synchronicity. Here, what appears is always simultaneously both conscious and unconscious.

> But Zen's way of viewing or evaluating things differs from the outward way of intellection. Zen would not object to the possibility of an "unconscious conscious" or a "conscious unconscious" – therefore, not the awakening of a new consciousness, but consciousness coming to its own unconscious.[304]

According to many reports, the meditative process undergone in Zen Buddhist training can be difficult, painful, and threatening, and normally can only be accomplished when one is accompanied by a teacher. Giving up the socially-conditioned position of ego-conscious can be an arduous journey. As Jung pointed out, "Everyone who becomes conscious of even a fraction of his unconscious gets outside his own time and social stratum into a kind of solitude ... "[305]

China scholar Erwin Rousselle had such an experience when he joined a Buddhist brotherhood in China during the 1920's. He discussed some of his training at an Eranos Conference in 1933. He said that each stage of development was assessed by his teacher who looked for "signs" that indicated progress.

> As his meditations on the circulation of light proceed, the student – from being enclosed in the circle – is befallen by a sudden "disturbance," a sense of loneliness, forsakenness, as though the whole world were sinking and he were lost. He is filled with horror, evoked by the natural man in him, who is unwilling to renounce the world. At this point, he must simply keep up his courage and persevere, for he stands face to face with the primal fundament (Urgrund) of the world and no longer with the appearance, so nothing can befall him. Through this confidence, the horror vanishes at once, giving way to a marvelous beatitude.[306]

Meditation is discontinued after the appearance of this sign. "The next 'sign' is a strange 'emptiness' accompanied by total tranquillity in the 'heart.' This is an intimation of the fundament of our own being and of the universe."[307] These signs are still only the beginning stages of a process of development which will last a lifetime. "A man must be close to forty before he is instructed in the meditation on the backward flowing movement; only at the approach of sixty does a man dedicate himself entirely to the 'tao of heaven.'"[308]

---

[304] Ibid., p. 197.
[305] Jung, C.G., *Mysterium Conjunctionis*, p. 201
[306] Rousselle, E., "Spiritual guidance in contemporary Taoism," in: *Spiritual Disciplines*, p. 94.
[307] Ibid., p. 94.
[308] Ibid., p. 95.

As Jung also suggested that the individuation process usually begins around age forty, we seem to be dealing here with a maturational window not "officially" recognized in the West. The existence of such a window has received an unexpected confirmation by contemporary neurophysiology. It has recently been discovered that myelination in the hippocampal formation of the limbic system, which was once thought to end in adolescence, increases thirty-three to fifty-five percent in the fifth and sixth decade of life.[309] Myelination in the limbic area is associated with emotional maturity, affect intensity, and meaningful symbolic connectivity.[310]

After long practice in concentration, meditation, and artistic expression, the Zen monk is said to finally reach a state of "childlikeness." Suzuki has described it dramatically:

> Man is a thinking reed but his great works are done when he is not calculating and thinking. "Childlikeness" has to be restored with long years of training in the art of self-forgetfulness. When this is attained, man thinks yet he does not think. He thinks like the showers coming down from the sky; he thinks like the waves rolling on the ocean; he thinks like the stars illuminating the nightly heavens; he thinks like the green foliage shooting forth in the relaxing spring breeze. Indeed, he is the showers, the ocean, the stars, the foliage.[311]

Frederic Spiegelberg, in *Zen, Rocks, and Waters*, suggests that it is all of Western culture that is "schizophrenic," because both our science and our religion separate the "natural" world from spirit. Spiegelberg believes a state like the one attained by Zen meditation is the optimum and healthy state of an integrated soul in an integrated world.

> To enter into Nirvana is to realize that one has always been in Nirvana from the very beginning. It *seemed* that one crossed a perilous river between this shore and the other shore, between time and eternity, but in the moment of setting foot on that other shore the river vanished. Nirvana was not attained because there was never any need to attain it. Suddenly one came to the point where one had always been. Yet the world of time was not obliterated; it was seen to be no different from the world of eternity. From this point, then, the most appropriate image of the eternal is precisely that which is most temporal, worldly, and ordinary. But somehow the image-maker, the artist, must be able to show how the most common and temporal things appear from this point of view. He must make religion vanish into reality.[312]

---

[309] Benes, F.M., Turtle, M., Khan, Y., Farol, P., "Myelination of a key relay zone in the hippocampal formation occurs in the human brain during childhood, adolescence, and adulthood," *Archives of General Psychiatry*, 1994, 51: 480.
[310] Ibid., p. 483.
[311] Spiegelberg, F., *Zen, Rocks, and Water*, p. 15.
[312] Ibid., p. 15.

From this perspective, the ideal state of the human being is as a bridge-maker between conscious and unconscious, spirit and world, heaven and earth; and the bridge is expressed through bodily activity in the real world, through creativity and healing, and through synchronicities.

> By attaining the state of consciousness symbolized by the mandala, the yogi can stand back from himself and take the position of a pure witnessing consciousness no longer confused with the pattern of thoughts and emotions, desires and fears we call the ego. But as there is no liberation in being confused with the ego, there is likewise no liberation in remaining aloof like an umpire, watching without participation. Yet, the disentanglement of pure consciousness from the ego makes it possible to participate in life in a way which was impossible so long as consciousness was rigidly locked up in an ego facing a surrounding world of objects. The individual is no longer separated; he is a wave in an ocean, a wave that is not trying to hold on to itself and yet which is at the same time an individual wave. On the one hand he is not isolated, and on the other hand he is not lost. His position is both transcendent and immanent, and his life is the *lila* or "play" of smooth and even participation in the flow of nature.[313]

As with shamans and healers in many cultures, a mysterious healing energy is held to emanate from the person who has begun to achieve a state of spontaneity. The *I Ching* speaks of healers who gain their abilities through contemplation in Hexagram 20, *Kuan*, called Contemplation or View, in the sense of a view from the top of a mountain.

> Contemplation of the divine meaning underlying the workings of the universe gives to the man who is called upon to influence others the means of producing like effects. This requires that power in inner concentration which religious contemplation develops in great men strong in faith. It enables them to apprehend the mysterious and divine laws of life, and by means of profoundest inner concentration they give expression to these laws in their own persons. Thus a hidden spiritual power emanates from them, influencing and dominating others without their being aware of how it happens.[314]

Commenting on the *I Ching* trigram *Ken* (or *Gen*), the Mountain or Keeping Still, Richard Wilhelm associates it with the new energies of early morning, "the strangest time of all." Evoking the concept of synchronicity, he suggests that,

> Keeping Still is the trigram of the northeast, where beginning and end of all creatures are completed. In China, the northeast has a mysterious significance, being at once the place of life and the place of death. ... Life is conceived as a day, a day that is gradually molded, finds its effectiveness, and that must

---

[313] Ibid., p. 21.
[314] Wilhelm, R., *I Ching*, p. 200.

vindicate itself, gather its fruits, and that eventually ends in this mysterious Keeping Still, when past and future touch one another.[315]

Wilhelm explains in his *Lectures on the I Ching* that meditation is the attempt to construct and concentrate on creative images: "The person meditating must naturally construct these images himself, because only then do they correspond to his nature and possess the power, drawn from his own soul, to hold his attention."[316] When this process is successful, the soul is able to "reach the energy sources of strength present in nature that are necessary to breathe freely in constant renewal."[317] Afterward, one lives in a relaxed state of spontaneity and creativity:

> The human being must consciously enter the stream of time, he must not stand at its banks and contemplate the past and future. For then, fear and hope unsettle the soul. Instead, the soul must concentrate its entire life in the present, the here and now, allowing to disappear what must disappear, and allowing to approach what must approach. Then the heart resembles a mirror, and, free of dust, reflects things as they come and go, always evoking the correct reaction, and never the copied imitation.[318]

Some people who go through periods of classical Jungian analysis, with an emphasis on creative work and long observation of the process of projection, approach similar states of consciousness. They seem to approach life with more spontaneity, more comfort, more energy, and more meaningful synchronicities. As a result, they are easy to be with, and other people find them understanding, accepting, and healing. Jung thought he found a discussion of this state in the alchemist Dorn's notion of the "third and highest degree of conjunction" in alchemical work: "The thought Dorn expresses by the third degree of conjunction is universal: it is the relation or identity of the personal with the superpersonal atman, and of the individual tao with the universal tao."[319]

This final state of alchemy represents a connection with a healing source that affects one's own life and that of others. "We can conclude from this that the desired realization of the whole man was conceived as a healing of organic and psychic ills, since the *caelum* was described as a universal medicine (a panacea, alexipharmic, *medicina catholica*, etc.) It was regarded also as the balsam and elixir of life, as a life-prolonging, strengthening, and rejuvenating magical potion."[320] Once found, the source was not to be wor-

---

[315] Wilhelm, R., *Lectures on the I Ching*, p. 22.
[316] Ibid., p. 155.
[317] Ibid., p. 157.
[318] Ibid., p. 156.
[319] Jung, *Mysterium Conjunctionis*, Vol. 14, p. 535.
[320] Ibid., p. 539.

shipped in a remote heaven, but to be lived with in everyday life as a *spiritus rector*[321] or guiding creative presence within psychological experience.

If an experience of the edge of chaos is a fundamental human possibility, often touched in altered states of consciousness, it should be within the experiential possibilities of Westerners as well as Easterners, urban dwellers as well as hunter-gatherers, under the right circumstances. Perhaps one of these circumstances could be the intense creative, emotional, and spiritual connectedness that can sometimes occur in the safe space of analysis. It may be the case that many people come into Jungian analysis in midlife because they are naturally developing in this direction. Jung thought there were people who had a special permeability toward the unconscious.

> I must add, however, that I have observed people and to some extent analyzed them, who seemed to possess a supranormal faculty and were able to make use of it consciously. Their apparently supranormal faculty consisted of being in, or intentionally putting themselves into, a state corresponding to an archetypal constellation – that is a state of numinous possession – in which synchronistic phenomena become possible, and even, to some degree, probable. This faculty was clearly connected to a religious attitude which led them to give suitable expression to their feeling that the ego is subordinate to the archetype.[322]

Jung apparently often encountered such states in his work:

> It is not in the least astonishing that numinous experiences should occur in the course of psychological treatment and that they may even be expected with some regularity, for they also occur very frequently in exceptional psychic states that are not treated, and may even cause them. They do not belong exclusively to the domain of psychopathology but can be observed in normal people as well. Naturally, modern ignorance of and prejudice against intimate psychic experiences dismiss them as psychic anomalies and put them in psychiatric pigeon holes without making the least attempt to understand them. But that neither gets rid of the fact of their occurrence nor explains it. Nor is it astonishing that in every attempt to gain an adequate understanding of the numinous experience, use must be made of certain parallel religious or metaphysical ideas which have not only been associated with it from ancient times but are constantly used to formulate and elucidate it.[323]

States of synchronicity may be capable of being shared. When I began to see clients in Zürich, I soon noticed an uncanny string of coincidences in my client's dreams. Week after week, four or five clients came in with almost the same dream and picture images. Even more unsettling was the fact that

[321] Ibid., p. 544.
[322] Jung, C.G., "A letter on parapsychology and synchronicity," *Spring*, 1961, p. 209.
[323] Jung, C.G., *Mysterium Conjunctionis*, Vol. 14, p. 547.

when I worked on my own paintings outside of their analytical hours, they sometimes brought in dreams and paintings with the same images I was making, without ever having seen them. One week, I was working on a painting of a woman standing on the earth with a crescent moon and a seed beneath her feet. As she held out her hands, a plant "grew" from the seed, flowered, and produced a luminous white pearl "fruit" over her head. During the week I worked on the painting, four clients dreamed of white pearls, and a fifth told me a long story about a round white object which had caused him a panic attack in the past. None had seen my painting, and none ever dreamed of white pearls before or after this week. One of the readers of this manuscript, who lived a few blocks from me in Zürich, later checked his diary and discovered he had lost his wife's pearl earrings that week and spent hours searching for them.

I decided to take notes on these coincidences, and when they had gone on for many months and I was quite sure about the phenomena, I began to interview other Zürich analysts about their experience. I discovered that only a small percentage of analysts have this experience, but when they do, it is impressive. Many had clients who were producing synchronistic images, and were experiencing frequent synchronicities in their own lives.

I taped the following account by analyst Robert Hinshaw:

> Especially when something is going on in my own life, and I seem to be having conflict in a particular area, whether it's with relationships or in connection with work or the Institute, it seems like invariably people come in one after the other with just that kind of problem at the same time. And I realize that what's constellated in me is also constellated in my clients. There have been a lot of these cases of something going on in me – often I see the starting point as being with me – but it can also be the other way around. Then I say, how come three people in a row are coming in all of a sudden with fights with their partner this week, or with disturbing dreams of being pursued by an evil force or something like that? And somehow, by working on the first one, it's almost like preparing for the second one, which is preparing for what comes in the third. There's almost a way in which they belong together and it usually has something to do with what's going on in me as well. I've given up trying to figure it out. I just sit there in wonderment and watch and feel it happen. And I completely accept it, but it's a pretty amazing thing even now, each time it happens. It isn't always there, either. There are weeks when I don't feel like something like that is going on and there are others when there are just no two ways about it.

Movement therapist and Jungian analyst Eileen Nemeth, also reported a high level of synchronicities in her work:

It's almost as if there is a level like the Tao, where we can feel connections with each other, so if someone moves, we can feel it even if we have our backs to them and they are in another part of the room. Some energy connects us at a somatic level and it's happening all the time, but we aren't conscious of it. There is almost a feeling that we're not allowed to look at that level because it's too invasive, too personal, too intimate. Someone once asked Rabbi Nachman of Bratslav why people in his day no longer had mystical experiences. He answered: "Because they don't know how to bow down low enough." For me, it's very special to sit back and just be in awe of the fact that we are all sharing this intimate body space together, which has to be respected and not abused. When we do dance improvisation in theater, you have to allow yourself to go into an unconscious state. Then you can really feel what's happening behind you, because your body becomes awake. In authentic movement training, several people move in the room with their eyes closed, so that they can't see each other, and several others sit aside to witness what is going on. Often, all of a sudden, all the dancers are looking in the same direction, or reaching with the same hand movement, or they all stand up at the same time, or they all turn the same way at once. If you witness this, your mouth drops open, and you think, "What happened there?," or, "What was that?" There are hundreds of movements, and it can't just be coincidence. It's as if the bodies in their most physiological state are dancing together. And we are all doing that all the time. We are all dancing with our eyes closed all the time. As soon as you walk into a room with another human being, you're in a bodily relationship with them. All those irrational connections are happening all the time. As therapists, our work is just to allow the material that is already there to be expressed."

Analyst Paul Brutsche, former president of the C.G. Jung Institute in Zürich, reported:

In my experience of this fascinating and deep phenomenon, there are also repetitive manifestations of the same motif. Recently, for instance, there was a day when three times in the same day there was a question in analysis of chaos and shit. The third time, we laughed together about the fact that I was speaking about this symbolism for the third time in one day. ...
There seems to be a connection between creativity and synchronistic phenomena. ... when you are very close to this creative energy – I don't think that one becomes only more sensitive – it's really constellated, too. I mean, the experience that you find interesting, or helpful quotations, or you see a book you have never seen before, but just in the moment, you are writing on it, and it happens with clients, too, in the analytical context. So there is a particular activation of this synchronistic phenomenon in times where one is deeply involved in a creative process. One could imagine that the transcendent function has something to do with this phenomenon. Doing creative work is an interchange between conscious ideas and something which is still uncon-

scious. There is a third element helping or suggesting, giving a direction which is perhaps not the one you really want to go along. ...

So you are really closer to this autonomous guiding factor, and that's probably very closely connected with the situations where you find hints or people. The transcendent function is a constellating energy. ... It's surely not a dynamic that has to do with causality. It's quite obvious. When I prepare an article or a lecture, I normally experience that I'm guided by something toward just another direction than I want. It's normally a battle or a fight, and I think it's a very common experience. In such a creative mood, one is close to a guiding principle differing from the ego, so you are probably closer to this central energy than you are in a normal state, where you are organizing your vision more according to an "I" vision. I think in order for synchronistic phenomena to occur, this energy, which is not controlled too much by the ego, has to get a chance to become very strong. In meditation or creativity, or by doing pictures, you come closer to this. ...

It's like looking into a landscape where you see things difficult to explain to people who are not in that landscape, but if you are, it's so obvious, so clear.

If there is sometimes a parallel between end states of Jungian analysis and Zen practice, it may be that in both we are dealing with an irrational factor that cannot be "known," but can be felt. The entoptic designs noted in the last chapter as markers of altered states occur frequently in Buddhist art works (including Tibetan sand paintings), the religious art of many tribal groups involved with trance and possession states, and in drawings by Jungian analysands. Jung's many published paintings are full of them. Perhaps it is the combination of creativity, concentrated attention, and accepting relatedness that aids the development of spontaneity and healing. Clearly, a person not using a great deal of energy to control and manipulate the environment or self-image is in a state of greater relaxation and ease. Such a person may more readily be able to enter into altered states of consciousness at the edge of chaos. Jungian therapist Edith Sullwold, who lectures yearly at the C.G. Jung Institute in Zürich, has stated frequently that Jungian work can be a Way, or spiritual path, if practiced in the right manner.[324]

Jung analyzed the relationship between the end-states of Buddhism and Jungian analysis in his commentary on the Chinese text, *The Secret of the Golden Flower*. He thought that both practices involved severing the state of identification or non-differentiation between self-image and world-image. If this differentiation were made through a long process of self-observation, the center of gravity of the personality would gradually shift from the ego to the Self, a functional point of integration midway between the conscious and unconscious. Jung suggested that this point was referred to by Buddhists in ancient texts as the "diamond body" or the "holy fruit."[325]

[324] Personal communication.

It was important, Jung thought, that Westerners develop toward such states in their own way, and out of their own experience rather than simply adopting Eastern meditation practices. He feared that in Europe there was a tendency toward violent repression of bodily life, an "Amfortas wound," which "hysterically exaggerates and poisons our spirituality."[326]If this is the case, meditation practice could be turned into a heroic conquest of the unconscious, rather than a coming into partnership with it. The willingness to absorb both positive and negative, heroic and shameful, spiritual and bodily, persona and shadow images into a broad understanding of the Self is what leads to wholeness.

---

[325] Jung, C.G., 1969, in: Wilhelm, R., *Secret of the Golden Flower,* London: Routledge and Kegan Paul, p. 124.
[326] Ibid., p. 126.

Conclusion

... I am participating in the creation of yet another culture, a new story to explain the world and our participation in it, a new value system with images and symbols that connect us to each other and to the planet. Soy una amasamiento, I am an act of kneading, of uniting and joining that not only has produced both a creature of darkness and a creature of light, but also a creature that questions the definitions of light and dark and gives them new meanings. We are people who leap in the dark, we are people on the knees of the gods. In our flesh, (r)evolution works out the clash of cultures. It makes us crazy constantly, but if the center holds, we've made some kind of evolutionary step forward. Nuestra alma y trabajo, the opus, the great alchemical work; spiritual mestizaje, a "morphogenesis," an inevitable unfolding. We have become the quickening serpent movement.[327]

– Gloria Anzaldúa

In the United States and Latin America these days, many groups and individuals are engaged in healing work involving multiple explorations and adaptations of old and new paths. We seem to be having an eruption of archetypal demands for expression, integration, and negotiation as the majorities in our societies become ever more fragmented and oppressed. Many of us are creating new myths and paradigms that reach for a cultural and personal not-yet. Salvadoran psychologist Ignacio Martín-Baró believes our healing work must begin with de-ideologizing our everyday experience.

> We know that knowledge is a social construction. Our countries live burdened by the lie of prevailing discourse that denies, ignores, or disguises essential aspects of reality. ... It goes along, deceptive and alienated, conforming to a fictional common sense that nurtures the structures of exploitation and conformist attitudes. To de-ideologize means to retrieve the original experience of

---

[327] Anzaldúa, Gloria, 1990 *"La conciencia de la mestiza*: Towards a New Consciousness," in: Anzaldúa, Gloria, ed., *Making Face, Making Soul* = Hacienda Caras: *creative and critical perspectives by feminists of color,* San Francisco: aunt lute foundation, p. 380.

groups and persons and return it to them as objective data. People can then use the data to formally articulate a consciousness of their own reality ... [328]

The new model of complex adaptive systems, explored on these pages, with its emphasis on constant change and renewal at the edge of chaos, presents a possibility for a relationship between the culture of science and experiences of de-ideolization, healing, individuation, and synchronicity. Connectionist ways of thinking have a capacity to link the inner workings of community and individual, soma and psyche, biological environment and spirit. They constitute an important step toward the integration of science, religious experience, social change, and psychological healing. The tendency toward constant reorganization and reintegration is part of the living process of biological evolution in this theory. Throughout our lives, we are always participating in a biological and spiritual individuation process that has taken billions of years.

Today, we know that some biological life forms evolve ever more elaborated structure partly in order that they communicate and be sensed by each other. This gives them more options to respond to change. As biologist Adolf Portmann has pointed out, it is impossible to explain the enormously rich variety of feather, fur, leaf, flower, song, and speech apart from the simultaneous development of organs of sight, smell, touch, taste, and hearing in biological organisms. Structure, communication, and perception are meant for each other in a biological world that developed and constantly evolves near a source at the edge of chaos. According to Portmann,

> The highest expression of individuals, i.e., the possibility of manifesting their internal condition, is of use in helping them to find one another. Only the most outstanding organic forms, which reach the highest measure of individuality, have been endowed with the ability to break the ban of isolation so as to possess that common life which rests on a rich inwardness and on preformed organs of mutual recognition.[329]

The most elaborate methods of communication rest, in the words of Portmann, on spontaneity. Spontaneity allows us to express the process we are participating in, as it happens.

> All higher types of animal life are distinguished ... by the possibility of spontaneous manifestations, which are always the sign of an enriched inner life.[330]

The worlds of complex adaptive systems are constantly in a spontaneous state of change and communication as new patterns develop. Emergent

---

[328] Martín-Baró, Ignacio, *Writings for a Liberation Psychology*, p. 31.
[329] Portmann, A., *Animal Forms and Patterns*, p. 196.
[330] Ibid., p. 197.

forms of information-processing allow evolution to evolve itself. Kevin Kelly suggests:

> What we witness in the fossil record of earthly life is the gradual accumulation of various types of simpler evolutions into the organic whole we now call evolution. Evolution is a conglomeration of many processes which form a society of evolutions. As evolution has evolved over time, *evolution itself has increased in diversity and complexity and evolvability.* Change changes itself.[331]

There is hope in this paradigm that we, as humans in the process of evolution, can enter life with openness, creativity, and a groundedness in the body, and still have healing possibilities before us personally and culturally. This healing work involves forming and reforming our models of the world and our praxis in ever new rituals of integration.

In a world of complex adaptive systems, integration can never be done once and for all. Because we live in an inner and outer environment that is spontaneously changing, the practical organization of it, as well as our symbols and models, need to be ever creatively renewed. We always have the possibility of restoring more optimal levels of connectivity and evolvability in our personal and cultural environments.

In environmental theory, "restoration" has been defined as a proactive process which recognizes that there are always areas of disarticulation in any communications system. By recognizing their existence, we can begin to search for them in order to begin a process of conscious reintegration. According to Canadian environmentalist Alexander Wilson:

> Restoration actively seeks out places to repair the biosphere, to recreate habitat, to breach the ruptures and disconnections that agriculture and urbanization have brought to the landscape. But unlike preservationism, it is not an elegiac exercise. Rather than eulogize what industrial society has destroyed, restoration proposes a new environmental ethic. Its projects demonstrate that humans must intervene in nature, must garden it, must participate in it.[332]

Those of us who live in rapidly changing urban environments in crisis also need to do constant restoration work in our personal and social worlds. By conceiving of ourselves in terms of hybridity, creolite, or *mestizaje* – as the inheritors of millions of years of diverse biological development and thousands of years of diverse cultural creativity –, we can draw on an immense reservoir of strategies, images, and rituals for reinterpreting and changing the structures in which we live.

Our interpretive paradigms need to be relevant to the present and adequate to the actual situation in which we find ourselves, in the world and in

---

[331] Kelly, K., *Out of Control*, p. 417.
[332] Wilson, A., *The Culture of Nature*, p. 12.

our inner lives. They cannot be perfect and eternal, because perfect and eternal schemata, especially in the realm of identity and culture, eventually become oppressive as conditions change. Every moment must have the possibility of being spontaneously felt and spoken anew, as images arise in a living way within the psyche. Sometimes this means feeling, naming, or expressing unhappiness, doubt, ambiguity, or pain. Sometimes it means challenging dominant institutions and old, established customs. It means daring to speak the truth as we see it, in our own voices, from our limited perspectives.

Every second of time is an opportunity to develop rituals of restoration and redemption for ourselves and our communities. Whatever suffering, violence, and oppression we find in the world can be remodeled if enough people can be inspired to become forces for creativity or change. The whole idea that evolution is driven by competition for survival can be modified to include an intentional self-organizing process in the heart of life connected with coevolution. Life can also be about the recreation of form and meaning, and the possibility of healing. As biological organisms, we originate in this process as well as contribute to it. To work at creating meaning and integration in our lives may be our destiny. Daring to live spontaneously at the edge of chaos may be our closest approach; and the discovery of synchronicity and spirit in our own experience may be the nearest we can come to a healing source of energy.

Bibliography

American Psychiatric Association, *Diagnostic and Statistical Manual of Mental Disorders*, Washington, DC: American Psychiatric Association, 1994.

Anderson, R., *Art in Small Scale Societies*, Englewood Cliffs, N.J.: Prentice Hall, 1979.

Andreasen, N.C., Carpenter, W.T., "Diagnosis and Classification of Schizophrenia," *Schizophrenia Bulletin*, 19 (2), 1993.

Anscombe, R., "The Disorder of Consciousness in Schizophrenia," *Schizophrenia Bulletin*, 13(2), 1987.

Anzaldúa, Gloria, "La conciencia de la mestiza: Towards a New Consciousness," in: Anzaldúa, Gloria, ed., *Making Face, Making Soul* = Hacienda Caras: *Creative and Critical Perspectives by Feminists of Color*, San Francisco: Aunt Lute Foundation, 1990.

Bach, S., *Life Paints Its Own Span*, Einsiedeln: Daimon, 1990.

Bateson, G., *Mind and Nature*, New York: Dutton, 1979.

Benes, F.M., Turtle, M., Khan, Y., Farol, P., "Myelination of a Key Relay Zone in the Hippocampal Formation Occurs in the Human Brain during Childhood, Adolescence, and Adulthood," *Archives of General Psychiatry* 51, 1994.

Berry, T., *The Dream of the Earth*, San Francisco: Sierra Club Book, 1988.

Biale, D., *Gershom Scholem*, Cambridge: Harvard University Press, 1982.

Bleuler, M., "What Is Schizophrenia?," Speech presented at University of Massachusetts Medical School Conference, Worcester, MA, 1990.

Blofeld, J., trans., *The Zen Teaching of Huang Po*, New York: Grove Press, 1958.

Bohm, D. and Peat, F.D., *Science, Order, and Creativity*, New York: Bantam Books, 1987.

Bourguignon, E., "Dreams and Altered States of Consciousness in Anthropological Research," in: Hsu, F.L.K., ed., *Psychological Anthropology*, Boston: Schenkman, 1972.

Buckley, P., "Mystical Experience and Schizophrenia," *Schizophrenia Bulletin* 7(3), 1981.

Bührmann, M.V., "Psyche and Soma: Therapeutic Considerations," in: Saayman, G., ed., *Modern South Africa in Search of a Soul*, Boston: Sigo Press, 1990.

Burt, Sir C., "Psychology and Parapsychology," in: Koestler, A., ed., *The Roots of Coincidence*, London: Hutchinson, 1972.

Buskist, W., *Psychology: Boundaries and Frontiers*, Chicago: Scott, Foresman, 1990.

Campbell, J., *Primitive Mythology*, New York: Penguin Books, 1969.

— *The Inner Reaches of Outer Space*, N.Y.: Alfred Van Der Marck Editions, 1985.

Capra, F., *The Web of Life*, N.Y.: Doubleday, 1996.

Chisholm, J.S., "Putting People in Biology," in: Schwartz, T., White, G.M., Lutz, C.A., eds., *New Directions in Psychological Anthropology*, 1992.

Costello, T.W. & Costello, J.T., *Abnormal Psychology*, New York: Harper Perennial, 1992.

Coveney, P. and Highfield, R., *Frontiers of Complexity*, New York: Fawcett Columbine, 1995.

Cowan, G.A., Pines, D., Maltzer, D., eds., *Complexity: Metaphors, Models, and Reality*, Reading, MA: Addison-Wesley, 1994.

Crutchfield, J.P., "Is Anything Ever New? Considering Emergence," in: Cowan, G.A., Pines, D., Maltzer, D., eds., *Complexity: Metaphors, Models, and Reality*, Reading, MA: Addison-Wesley, 1994.

Crutchfield, J.P., Farmer, J.D., Packard, N.H., Shaw, R.S., "Chaos." *Scientific American*, December, 1986.

Davis, P., *The Cosmic Blueprint*, New York: Simon and Schuster, 1988.

Dawkins, R. *The Extended Phenotype*, New York: Oxford University Press, 1990.

— *The Selfish Gene*, N.Y.: Oxford University Press, 1978.

Dennett, D.C., *Darwin's Dangerous Idea*, New York: Simon and Schuster, 1996.

Douglas, M., *Natural Symbols*, New York: Pantheon Books, 1970.

— *Implicit Meanings*, N.Y.: Routledge, 1991.

Eiser, J.R., *Attitudes, Chaos, and the Connectionist Mind*, Cambridge, MA: Basil Blackwell Inc., 1994.

Eliade, M., *The Myth of the Eternal Return*, tr. Willard Trask, New York: Pantheon Books, 1954.

Ellenberger, H., *The Discovery of the Unconscious*, New York: Basic Books, Inc., 1970.

Fierz, H.K., *Jungian Psychiatry*, Einsiedeln, Switzerland: Daimon Verlag, 1991.

Fordham, M., *New Developments in Analytical Psychology*, London: Routledge and Kegan Paul, 1957.

Geertz, C., *Local Knowledge*, New York: Basic Books, 1983.

— "From the Native's Point of View," in: Shweder, R.A. & Le Vine, R.A., eds., *Culture Theory*, New York: Cambridge University Press, 1984.

Gell-Mann, M., "Complex Adaptive Systems," in: Cowan, G.A., Pines, D., & Meltzer, D., eds., *Complexity Metaphors, Models, and Reality*, Reading, MA: Addison-Wesley, 1994.

— *The Quark and the Jaguar*, New York: W.H. Freeman & Son, 1994.

Gomez-Peña, G., *Warrior for Gringostroika*, Saint Paul, MN: Graywolf Press, 1993.

Good, B.J., "Culture and Psychopathology: Directions for Psychiatric Anthropology," in: Schwartz, et al., *New Directions in Psychological Anthropology*, 1992.

Goodman, F., *Where the Spirits Ride the Wind*, Bloomington, IN: Indiana University Press, 1990.

Gottesman, I.I., *Schizophrenia Genesis*, New York: W.H. Freeman and Co, 1991.

Gould, S.J., *The Flamingo's Smile*, New York: W.W. Norton and Co, 1987.

Graves, R., *The White Goddess*, New York: Farrar, Straus, Giroux, 1983.

Griffin, S., *The Eros of Everyday Life*, New York: Anchor Books (Doubleday), 1995.

Guarnaccia, P.J., Good, B.J. & Kleinman, A., "Culture and Psychopathology in Latin American Cultures," *The American Journal of Psychiatry*, 11, 1990.

Haraway, D., "The Promise of Monsters: A Regenerative Politics for Inappropriate/d Others," in: Grossberg, L., Nelson, C., Treichler, P.A., eds., 1992, *Cultural Studies*, New York: Routledge.

Hayles, K., "Towards a Conclusion," in: Cronon, W. ed., 1995, *Uncommon Ground*, New York: Norton and Co.

Hebb, D.O., The Organization of Behavior, New York: Wiley, 1949.

Holland, J., "Complexity Made Simple," The Bulletin of the Santa Fe Institute, 9(3), 1994.

Hollinger, D.A., *Post-ethnic America: Beyond Multiculturalism*, New York: Basic Books, 1995.

Irigaray, L., Ed. Whitford, M., *The Irigaray Reader*, Oxford, U.K.: Basil Blackwell, 1991.

Jablensky, A., Sartorius, N., Ernberg, G., Anker, M., Korten, A., Cooper, J.E., Day, R., & Bertelsen, A., "Schizophrenia: Manifestations, Incidence, and Course in Different Countries," *Psychological Medicine* (Monograph Suppl.) No. 20, 1992.

Jaffé, A., *The Myth of Meaning*, Zürich: Daimon Verlag, 1984.

— Was C.G. Jung a Mystic?, Einsiedeln: Daimon Verlag, 1989.

James, W., *The Varieties of Religious Experience*, New York: Collier Books, 1961.

Jung, C.G., "Reply to Buber," in: *Spring*, Dallas, Texas: Spring Publications, 1957.

— "A Letter on Parapsychology and Synchronicity," in: Spring, Dallas, Texas: Spring Publications, 1961.

— The Practice of Psychotherapy, Vol. 16 Princeton: Princeton University Press, 1966.

— in: Wilhelm, R., *Secret of the Golden Flower*, London: Routledge and Kegan Paul, 1969.

— The Archetypes and the Collective Unconscious, Vol. 9.1, Princeton: Princeton University Press, 1969.

— The Structure and Dynamics of the Psyche, Vol. 8, Princeton: Princeton University Press, 1969.

— Mysterium Conjunctionis, Vol. 14, Princeton: Princeton University Press, 1977.

Kalweit, H., *Shamans, Healers, Medicine Men*, Boston: Shambhala, 1987.

Katz, R., *Boiling Energy*, Cambridge: Harvard University Press, 1982.

Kauffman, S.A., "Self-organization, Selective Adaptation, and Its Limits," in: Depew, J. and Weber, B.H., 1985, *Evolution at a Crossroads*, Cambridge, MA: MIT Press.

— At Home in the Universe, New York: Oxford University Press, 1995.

— Origins of Order, New York: Oxford University Press, 1993.

Kelly, K., *Out of Control*, Reading, MA: Addison-Wesley, 1994.

Kirk, S.A., Kutchins, H., *The Selling of the DSM: The Rhetoric of Science in Psychology*, New York: Aldine de Gruyter, 1992.

Kleinman, A., "Neurasthenia and Depression: A Study of Socialization and Culture in China," *Culture, Medicine, and Psychiatry* 6, 1982.

— Illness Narratives, U.S.A.: Basicbooks (HarperCollins), 1988.

Kleinman, A., Kunstadter, P., Alexander, E.R., & Gate, J.L., *Culture and Healing in Asian Societies*, Cambridge, MA: Shenkman Publishing, 1978.

Kristeva, J., *Strangers to Ourselves*, tr. Leon S. Roudiez, New York: Columbia University Press, 1991.

Kuhn, Thomas S., *The Structure of Scientific Revolutions*, Chicago: The University of Chicago Press, 1962.

Laszlo, E., *Evolution*. Boston: Shambhala, 1987.

Latour, B., *The Pasteurization of France*, Cambridge, MA: Harvard University Press, 1988.

Laughlin, C.D., McManus, J., d'Aquili, E.G., *Brain, Symbol, and Experience*, Boston: Shambhala Publications, 1990.

Leff, J., Sartorius, N., Jablensky, A., Korten, A., & Ernberg, G., "The International Pilot Study of Schizophrenia: Five year Follow-up Findings," *Psychological Medicine* 22, 1992.

Lemley, B., "The People Who Hear Green," *The Washington Post Magazine*, "Words by Wire," 1986.

Levy, R.I., Mageo, J.M., and Howard, A., "Gods, Spirits, and History: A Theoretical Perspective," in Mageo, J.M. and Howard, A., *Spirits in Culture, History, and Mind*, New York: Routledge, 1996.

Lewin, R., *Complexity*, London: J.M. Dent, Ltd., 1993.

Lewis-Williams, J.D., Dowson, T.A., "The Signs of the Times: Entoptic Phenomena in Upper Paleolithic Art," *Current Anthropology* 29, 1988.

Lorde, Audre, *Sister Outsider*, Freedom, CA: The Crossing Press, 1984.

Lorenz, K., *Behind the Mirror*, New York: Harcourt, Brace, Jovanovich, 1973.

Maduro, R., "Artistic Creativity and Aging in India," *International Journal of Aging and Human Development*, 5(4), 1974.

Mageo, J.M. and Howard, A., *Spirits in Culture, History, and Mind*, New York: Routledge, 1996.

Mainzer, K., *Thinking in Complexity*, Berlin: Springer Verlag, 1996.

Martin, Ben, "The Schema," in: Cowan, G.A., Pines, D., Meltzer, D., eds., *Complexity Metaphors, Models, and Reality*, Reading, MA: Addison-Wesley, 1994.

Martín-Baró, Ignacio, *Writings for a Liberation Psychology*, ed. Adrianne Aaron and Shawn Corne, Cambridge, MA: Harvard University Press, 1994.

Maturana, H.R. and Varela, F.J., *The Tree of Life*, Boston and London: Shambhala, 1992.

Maturana, H.R., Varela, F.J. "Autopoieses and Cognition: The Realization of the Living," *Boston Studies in the Philosophy of Science*, Vol. 42, Dordrecht: D. Reidel, 1972.

Meier, C.A., *Healing Dream and Ritual*, Einsiedeln, Switzerland: Daimon Verlag, 1989.

Foucault, Michel, "Two Lectures," in Gordon, Colin, ed. *Power/Knowledge*, New York: Pantheon Books, 1980.

Miller, A., *For Your Own Good*, New York: Farrar, Straus, Giroux, 1983.

Mitchell, S., trans., *Tao Te Ching*, New York: Harper and Row, 1988.

Morphy, H., *Ancestral Connections*, Chicago: U. of Chicago Press, 1991.

Neumann, E., "The Psyche and the Transformation of the Reality Planes," in: *Spring*, Dallas, Texas: Spring Publications, 1956.

— *The Child*, Boston: Shambhala, 1973.

Ngugi, wa Thiong'o, *Moving the Center: The Struggle for Cultural Freedoms*, London: James Currey, Ltd., 1993.

Nicholson, I., trans., *A Guide to Mexican Poetry*, Mexico City: Minutiae Mexicana, 1968.

Nuechterlein, K.H., "Developmental Process in Schizophrenic Disorders: Longitudinal Studies of Vulnerability and Stress," *Schizophrenia Bulletin*, 18(3), 1992.

Oudshoorn, N., "A Natural Order of Things? Reproductive Sciences and the Politics of Othering," in: Robertson, G., Mash, M., Tickner, L., Bird, J., Curtis, B., Putnam, T., *Future Natural*, London: Routledge, 1996.

Oyarce, A.M., *Vida Entre Dos Mundos*, Temuco, Chile: Grupo de Registro y Comunicacion Audiovisual, 1988.

Penrose, R. *Shadows of the Mind*, Oxford: Oxford University Press, 1994.

Perry, J.W., *Roots of Renewal in Myth and Madness: The Meaning of Psychotic Episodes*, San Francisco: Jossey-Bass, 1976.

Plant, S., "The Virtual Complexity of Culture," in: Robertson, G. et al., *Future Natural*, London: Routledge, 1966.

Podvoll, E.M., *The Seduction of Madness*, New York: HarperCollins, 1990.

Popper, K.R., *Objective Knowledge: An Evolutionary Approach*, Oxford: Oxford University Press, 1972.

Portmann, A., *Animal Forms and Patterns*, New York: Schocken Books, 1967.

— "Color Sense and the Meaning of Color from a Biologist's Point of View," in: *Color Symbolism*, Zürich: Eranos Excerpts, Spring, 1977.

Prigogine, I., & Stengers, I., *Order Out of Chaos*, New York: Bantam Books, 1984.

Ray, T.S., "Evolution and Complexity," in: Cowan, G., Pines, D., Meltzer, D., *Complexity: Metaphors, Models, Reality*, Reading, MA: Addison-Wesley, 1994.

Redgrove, P., *The Black Goddess and the Unseen Real*, New York: Grove Press, 1987.

Robertson, G., Mash, M., Tickner, L., Bird, J., Curtis, B., Putnam, T., *Future Natural*, London: Routledge, 1966.

Rorty, R., *Philosophy and the Mirror of Nature*, Princeton: Princeton University Press, 1979.

Rousselle, E., "Spiritual Guidance in Contemporary Taoism," in: *Spiritual Disciplines*, New York: Pantheon Books, 1960.

Rumi, *Open Secret*, Moyne, J., Barks, C., trans., Putney: Threshold Books. Quatrain, 1984.

Scheflen, A.E., *Levels of Schizophrenia*, New York: Brunner/Mazel, 1981.

Scheper-Hughes, N., "Hungry Bodies, Medicine, and the State," in: Schwartz, T., White, G.M., & Lutz, C.A., eds., *New Directions in Psychological Anthropology*. Cambridge, U.K.: Cambridge University Press, 1992.

Schwartz, T., White, G.M., & Lutz, C.A., eds., *New Directions in Psychological Anthropology*, Cambridge, U.K.: Cambridge University Press, 1992.

Shiva, V., *Staying Alive*, London: Zed Books, 1989.

Shweder, R.A., *Thinking Through Cultures: Expeditions in Cultural Psychology*, Cambridge, MA: Harvard University Press, 1991.

Siegel, R.K. "Hallucinations," *Scientific American* 237, 1977.

Somé, M.P., *Ritual: Power, Healing, Community*, Portland: Swan Raven, 1993.

Spiegelberg, F., *Zen, Rocks, and Water*, New York: Pantheon Books, 1961.

Stevens, A., *Archetypes*, New York: Quill, 1982.

Suzuki, D., "Awakening of a New Consciousness in Zen," in: Campbell, J., ed. *Man and Transformation*, Princeton: Princeton University Press, 1964.

Taylor, G.R., *The Great Evolution Mystery*, New York: Harper and Row, 1983.

Thich Nhat Hanh, *For a Future to Be Possible*, Berkeley, CA: Parallax Press, 1993.

Thompson, M., Ellis, R., & Wildavsky, A., *Cultural Theory*, Boulder, CO: Westview Press, 1990.

Thompson, R.F., *Flash of the Spirit*, New York: Vintage, 1984.

Tooby, J., & Cosmides, L., "The Past Explains the Present." *Ethology and Sociobiology* 11, 1990.

Toure, Ali Farka, CD liner notes to "Talking Timbuktu," produced by Ry Cooder at World Circuit Music, Ltd., 1994.

Trinh T. Minh-ha, "Nature's r," in: Robertson, G. et. al., *Future Natural*, London: Routledge, 1966.

Turner, V., *Body, Brain, and Culture*, New York: PAJ Publications, 1987.

— *The Ritual Process*, Ithaca, NY: Cornell University Press, 1969.

van der Post, L., *The Lost World of the Kalahari*, London: Hogarth Press, 1969.

von Franz, M.-L., *Projection and Recollection in Jungian Psychology*, La Salle: Open Court, 1980.

Waldrop, M.M., *Complexity*, New York: Simon and Schuster, 1992.

Wannenbaugh, A., *The Bushmen*, New York: Mayflower Books, 1979.

Watts, A.W., *The Way of Zen*, New York: Vintage Books, 1957.

Werker, J., "Becoming a Native Listener," *American Scientist* 77, 1989.

Wescott, R.W., *The Divine Animal*, New York: Funk and Wagnalls, 1969.

Wilhelm, R., *Lectures on the I Ching*, Princeton: Princeton University Press, 1979.

— *I Ching*, Princeton: Princeton University Press, 1990.

Wilson, A., *The Culture of Nature: North American Landscape From Disney to the Exxon Valdez*, Cambridge, MA: Basil Blackwell, 1992.

Winn, P., "Schizophrenia Research Moves to the Prefrontal Cortex," *TINS* 17(7), 1994.

Winnicott, D.W., *Psychoanalytic Explorations*, Cambridge: Harvard University Press, 1989.

World Development Report, 1994, New York: Oxford University Press.

Worthman, C.M., "Cupid and Psyche," in: Schwartz, T., White, G. M., & Lutz, C.A., eds., *New Directions in Psychological Anthropology*, 1992.

Yeats, W.B., "The Second Coming," *Collected Poems of W.B. Yeats*, ed. Richard J. Finneran, New York: Collier Books, 1989.

Author Index

Subject Index

The Rock Rabbit and the Rainbow
Laurens van der Post among Friends
edited by Robert Hinshaw

Authors from around the world have combined their talents in a tribute honoring this one-of-a-kind writer, soldier and statesman, a man of his time. Contributions include: Joseph Henderson: "The Splendor of the Sun"; Alan McGlashan: "How to be Haveable"; Ian Player: "My Friend Nkunzimlanga"; Jean-Marc Pottiez: "Rainbow Rhapsody"; T.C. Robertson: "A Triad of Landscapes – a Day in the Veld with Laurens"; and numerous other essays and works by Aniela Jaffé, Jonathan Stedall, Harry Wilmer, Jo Wheelright, C.A. Meier and many others. (ca. 340 pages, illustrated)

Miguel Serrano
C.G. Jung and Hermann Hesse
A Record of Two Friendships

The author, a Chilean diplomat and writer who has travelled widely in India studying Yoga, had a close friendship with Jung and Hermann Hesse at the end of their lives. The book is the outcome of his meetings and correspondence with them. Many letters are reproduced including a document of great importance written to the author by Jung shortly before his death, explaining his ideas about the nature of the world and of his work.

Hayao Kawai
Dreams, Myths and Fairy Tales in Japan
The well-known Japanese author, university professor and Zürich-trained Jungian analyst, Hayao Kawai, presents here the long-awaited second of his works in English. Originally presented as lectures at the historic Eranos Conferences in Ascona, this book describes five Japanese fairy tales, insightfully examined from Eastern and Western vantage points by an author intimately familiar with both.
(158 pages, illustrated)

Rainer Maria Rilke
Duino Elegies
Translated by David Oswald

The *Duino Elegies* are one of the twentieth century's great works of art. In the space of ten elegies, presented here in a bilingual edition, an impassioned voice struggles to find an answer to what it means to be human in a world torn by modern consciousness.
(128 pages)

Alan McGlashan
Gravity and Levity
The Philosophy of Paradox

This book heralds a breakthrough in human imagination, not a breakthrough that may take place in the future, far or near, but one that has already occurred – only we may not have noticed it. Life, as the author shows, is open-ended and full of paradoxes. Its principles cannot be understood by logic and causal reasoning. We can only come to terms with life if we accept that there is no final answer to it and that adjusting to life's natural rhythm is the key to finding release from the horrors and problems around us. (162 pages)

Mary Lynn Kittelson
Sounding the Soul: The Art of Listening
"In this delightful, phenomenological account, Kittelson writes in lively pursuit of the language of hearing, an ode to the persistent primacy of the ear. ...
It's right here, she says, just around the corner from our noses.
Kittelson's ear awareness finds side-doors into the topic. She lets us in on a secret as intriguing as Freud's footnote about the gradually diminishing sense of smell in human beings: we have a lapsed instinct for interiority. For turning inward, for spiraling deep into the dark, for following evocative reverberations to their source."
— from the Foreword by Nor Hall, Ph.D. (300 pages)

Talking with Angels – Budaliget 1943
A document transcribed by Gitta Mallasz
Budaliget 1943: A small village on the edge of Budapest. Three young women and a man, artists and close friends are gathered together in the uneasy days before Hitler's armies would destroy the world as they knew it. Seeking spiritual knowledge, and anticipating the horrors of Nazi-occupied Hungary, they met regularly to discuss how to find their own inner paths to enlightenment.
For 17 months, with the world locked in a deadly struggle for survival, the four friends meet every week with the spiritual beings they come to call their "angels"; Gitta Mallasz takes notes, the protocols which form this book, along with her commentary. The angels' message of personal responsibility is as meaningful and as urgent today as it was for its initial recipients half a century ago. (474 pages, third edition)
I am deeply touched by the dialogues with the angels.
Yehudi Menuhin
I could read it over and over again and never get tired of it.
Thank you, thank you, thank you for sharing this book with me.
Elisabeth Kübler-Ross

George Czuczka
Imprints of the Future
Politics and Individuation in Our Time
C.G. Jung's unique Swiss vantage point, in the midst of two world wars, enabled him to observe the catastrophic and cataclysmic events in the surrounding world and led him to conclude that modern man stands at the threshold of a new spiritual epoch. There is a "longing for rest in an age of unrest," he wrote, "a longing for security in an age of insecurity". We are still waiting at the threshold in anticipation of a new form of existence. This book by a retired U.S. Foreign Service officer demonstrates the relevance of Jungian psychology to the political process and to international relations. (112 pages)

Verena Kast
A Time to Mourn
Growing through the Grief Process
In what is often called her most important book, Verena Kast examines the role of mourning in the therapeutic process. Working as a psychotherapist, Frau Kast has often observed depressive illnesses caused by painful losses which have not been adequately mourned. Traditionally, mourning has not been a subject of psychologists' attention. Frau Kast uses dreams to illustrate the stages of mourning and shows systematically how the unconscious stimulates us to encounter our grief. (176 pages)

ENGLISH PUBLICATIONS BY **DAIMON**

Susan Bach – *Life Paints its Own Span*
E.A. Bennet – *Meetings with Jung*
George Czuczka – *Imprints of the Future*
Heinrich Karl Fierz – *Jungian Psychiatry*
von Franz / Frey-Rohn / Jaffé – *What is Death?*
Liliane Frey-Rohn – *Friedrich Nietzsche*
Yael Haft – *Hands: Archetypal Chirology*
Siegmund Hurwitz – *Lilith, the first Eve*
Aniela Jaffé – *The Myth of Meaning*
– *Was C.G. Jung a Mystic?*
– *From the Life und Work of C.G. Jung*
– *Death Dreams and Ghosts*
Verena Kast – *A Time to Mourn*
– *Sisyphus*
Hayao Kawai – *Dreams, Myths and Fairy Tales in Japan*
James Kirsch – *The Reluctant Prophet*
Mary Lynn Kittelson – *Sounding the Soul*
Rivkah Schärf Kluger– *The Gilgamesh Epic*
Paul Kugler – *Jungian Perspectives on Clinical Supervision*
Rafael López-Pedraza– *Hermes and his Children*
– *Cultural Anxiety*
Alan McGlashan – *The Savage and Beautiful Country*
– *Gravity and Levity*
Gitta Mallasz (Transcription) – *Talking with Angels*
C.A. Meier – *Healing Dream and Ritual*
– *A Testament to the Wilderness*
Laurens van der Post – *The Rock Rabbit and the Rainbow*
R.M. Rilke – *Duino Elegies*
Miguel Serrano – *C.G. Jung and Hermann Hesse*
Susan Tiberghien – *Looking for Gold*
Ann Ulanov – *The Wizards' Gate*

Jungian Congress Papers:

Jerusalem 1983 – *Symbolic and Clinical Approaches*
Berlin 1986 – *Archetype of Shadow in a Split World*
Paris 1989 – *Dynamics in Relationship*
Chicago 1992 – *The Transcendent Function*
Zürich 1995 – *Open Questions in Analytical Psychology*

Available from your bookstore or from our distributors:

In the United States:

Continuum
P.O. Box 7017
La Vergne, TN 37086
Phone: 800-937 5557
Fax: 615-793 3915

Chiron Publications
400 Linden Avenue
Wilmette, IL 60091
Phone: 800-397 8109
Fax: 847-256 2202

In Great Britain:

Airlift Book Company
8 The Arena
Enfield, Middlesex EN3 7NJ
Phone: (0181) 804 0400
Fax: (0181) 804 0044

Worldwide:
Daimon Verlag   Hauptstrasse 85   CH-8840 Einsiedeln   Switzerland
Phone: (41)(55) 412 2266   Fax: (41)(55) 412 2231
e-mail: Daimon@compuserve.com   Write for our complete catalog!